A CASE-BASED APPROACH TO ARGUMENTATIVE WRITING

A Case-Based Approach to Argumentative Writing

Sonja Launspach
Idaho State University

Laura Aull
University of Michigan

New York Oxford
OXFORD UNIVERSITY PRESS

Oxford University Press is a department of the University of Oxford.
It furthers the University's objective of excellence in research, scholarship,
and education by publishing worldwide. Oxford is a registered trade mark of
Oxford University Press in the UK and certain other countries.

Published in the United States of America by Oxford University Press
198 Madison Avenue, New York, NY 10016, United States of America.

For titles covered by Section 112 of the US Higher Education
Opportunity Act, please visit www.oup.com/us/he for the latest
information about pricing and alternate formats.

CIP data is on file at the Library of Congress
978-0-19-021121-9

Printing number: 9 8 7 6 5 4 3 2 1
Printed by Sheridan Books, Inc., United States of America

BRIEF TABLE OF CONTENTS

TABLE OF CONTENTS

PREFACE

A Proven Approach, A New Textbook

A "case study" approach to learning places students in the role of decision maker as they confront complex, real-life situations in which there are no simple solutions. This approach, which dates back to its use at the Harvard Business School in 1924, is widely used today in fields from business to law to health sciences to simulate real-life scenarios and to cultivate authentic responses and problem-solving skills through learners' responses to those scenarios. Yet there is no textbook for first-year writing students that draws on this productive, student-centered approach. Even so, the goals of the case study approach resonate with values championed in 21st-century composition instruction and research, as seen in calls for student-centered instruction and authentic tasks in writing assignment research.

A Case-Based Approach to Argumentative Writing fills this gap, offering a case-based textbook for first-year writing students that challenges students to engage in the writing process as they respond to complicated real-life scenarios in ways that must take into account multiple, often competing views. This is a textbook that can be used by a diverse set of writing programs and student populations in higher education. Whether students are attending a two-year or four-year college or university, or whether they are entering their composition courses knowing their college major and career plans or not, this textbook emphasizes critical thinking, reading, and writing skills that facilitate effective problem solving and argumentation, which are important in a range of paths students pursue.

New Application for Common Goals

Writing instructors already have numerous teaching resources available to them. Janice Lauer[1] and Ann Berthoff's[2] depictions of composition as "multi-modal" and "allatonceness" are reflected in the many tools that instructors have to teach

---

1. Janice M. Lauer, "Rhetoric and Composition Studies: A Multimodal Discipline," *Defining the New Rhetorics*, eds. Theresa Enos and Stuart Brown (Newbury Park, CA: Sage, 1993), 44–54.

2. Ann Berthoff, *Forming, Thinking, Writing: The Composing Imagination* (Portsmouth, NH: Boynton/Cook, 1982).

writing. Most if not all first-year composition textbooks combine two or more pedagogical approaches (among them current-traditional, modes of discourse, expressivist, cognitive, process, post-process, social constructivist, classical rhetoric, collaborative, cultural studies, critical pedagogy, service learning, and inquiry-based learning), demonstrating that the field is open to a variety of pedagogical methods. Despite this abundance of pedagogies, however, composition textbooks still tend to exhibit a select group of features that bind them together. For example, the teaching of writing as a recursive process—one of continual drafting, rewriting, and revision—is reflected in composition textbooks of all kinds. In addition, most textbooks emphasize argument; for instance, they begin with a definition of "argument"—a term that still too often calls up images of heated fistfights rather than reasoned exchange—and they address argument types (e.g., Classical/Aristotelian, Rogerian, Toulmin). Finally, most composition textbooks emphasize rhetorical principles such as audience, purpose, and genre.

This textbook addresses these shared concepts in composition—a recursive writing process; approaches to recognizing, analyzing, and producing arguments; and rhetorical principles—while challenging students to enact them as they confront real-life case study scenarios. The instructional chapters in Part One address important writing concepts while drawing attention to how they will apply as students consider the case studies—for instance, how asking questions about a particular stakeholder's view can help students approach academic argument as critical inquiry (see Chapter 1). Then, the Part Two case studies challenge students to not only recognize such concepts and principles, but to enact them as they form reasoned responses to case studies that have multiple stakeholders and multiple answers. In their responses to case studies, these concepts become real. For instance, because students' responses must account for clear, conflicting stances in a given case study, they must not only understand but also must apply the concept of balanced academic argument, because they can neither focus solely on one view nor on their own opinions. In other words, responding to case studies means accounting for the complex reality of multiple possibilities and multiple audiences and views—from the instructor who is required to follow university plagiarism protocol to the student whose life is derailed by unknowingly plagiarizing (see Chapter 9).

Student Responses and the Value of the Case Study Textbook

Using these materials in our own courses, we have appreciated students' thoughtful responses to the case study approach. For instance, students noted: "I really enjoyed the challenge of thinking about what would be the right decision," "I really enjoyed the cases because they were actually interesting to me," and finally, "I learned that it is often critical to address the main ideas of your opposition. Even if it seems the information will hurt your argument, leaving unanswered questions for your reader is far worse."

These responses highlight that the case study approach can work within a range of priorities in a composition classroom by providing an avenue for students to apply their knowledge. In this vein, we can point out features of our textbook that set it apart from its competitors. First among these features is the case study method, which not only encourages but indeed requires students to participate actively if they are to resolve the case effectively. In years of teaching, we have found that our students respond enthusiastically to cases, which offer them a dynamic story or narrative rather than a static paper topic. An added benefit of the case method is its critical focus. Cases are, at their core, critical exercises. Drawn into the ambiguous scenarios brought up by the cases, students must acknowledge multiple points of view and counterarguments, carefully research issues related to the case, take a stand on the issues, collect valid evidence to support their stand, articulate and defend this stance to their peers, and, finally, commit their critical thought and reading to a persuasive written argument that accounts for multiple stakeholders. We also provide a fresh take on well-established concepts, such as in Chapter 8, "Analyzing Arguments," which breaks down analysis into context analysis, information analysis, and rhetorical analysis and which was met with very positive responses from reviewers.

ACKNOWLEDGMENTS

First and foremost, we would like to thank our students for providing the motivation for writing this textbook, for testing the case studies, and for showing us different ways to think about the material. We would especially like to thank Hannah Moore who helped to edit some of the case study materials. We would also like to thank Angela Petit, the original collaborator on this project. Without her hard work and early contributions, this textbook would have never gotten off the ground. Next, we would like to thank the editors and editorial assistants at Oxford University Press that we have worked with over the course of this project. They have all been very gracious and helpful as they guided us through the longer than planned process of writing this textbook. The authors and Oxford University Press would like to express their appreciation to the following reviewers for their feedback on the manuscript during various stages of development:

Melvin E. Beavers, University of Arkansas-Little Rock
Anthony D. Cavaluzzi, SUNY Adirondack
Kamilah Cummings, DePaul University
Adam Kaiserman, College of the Canyons
Rachel Luria, Florida Atlantic University
Kathleen Volk Miller, Drexel University
Daniel Stanford, Pitt Community College

INSTRUCTIONAL CHAPTERS

1 UNDERSTANDING ACADEMIC ARGUMENTS

What is an argument? What about an *academic* argument? What makes them what they are, and why are they important?

Learning objectives for this chapter

- Understand characteristics of *argument* and *academic argument*
- Explore argument as inquiry and conversation
- Identify the basic structure of an argument

Key concepts addressed in this chapter

- Argument
- Academic arguments
- Non-arguments
- Argument structure

Introduction

The idea of argument should be a familiar one. Think about the conversation you had just before class. Perhaps you were chatting with your roommate about going to the movie at the student union on Friday. Your roommate hesitates and you spend the next few minutes convincing them to go with you. These types of casual arguments happen every day.

Arguments surround us. We find them in many areas of our lives: advertisements, conversations, work, political speeches, teaching, scientific theories, and case studies. They can have profound effects on our lives, on history, and on society.

Some examples of historically important arguments include:

- Nicolaus Copernicus argued that the earth revolved around the sun.
- Charles Darwin argued for the theory of evolution.
- Susan B. Anthony argued that women should have the right to vote.

- Margaret Sanger argued that women should have access to birth control.
- Martin Luther King Jr. argued for the end of segregation and social and economic empowerment of African Americans and other minorities.
- Wangari Muta Maathai argued that protecting the environment and empowering women would improve communities and livelihoods. She founded the Green Belt Movement in Kenya.

Argument is one way to communicate ideas in a reasoned manner. But even reasoned arguments can be controversial. Many of these arguments were controversial in their time and some still are, but they all have had long-lasting effects.

Check Yourself

1. Pick one of the arguments listed above and research it. Can you identify the effect of changes it made then and now?
2. Can you think of an argument that has had an important influence in the last 10 years?
3. Can you come up with important arguments that have made a change in the way you see the world?

Not all arguments are oral or written. Some arguments can be visual. Images can be used to make implicit or explicit arguments. You usually see visual arguments in ads and news programs. Let's look at Image 1.1, a photograph of two graves in a Dutch cemetery. On one side of the wall is the grave of a woman, who was Catholic, and on the other side is the grave of her husband, who was Protestant. What argument do you think the photograph is making?

[Hint: In the 19th century, Catholics and Protestants were often in conflict with each other and did not often mix socially.]

Check Yourself

Find an iconic image. Explain the argument embedded in the picture. What story does it tell and what effect does the image have on viewers?

IMAGE 1.1 'The grave with the little hands,' 1888, Roermond, the Netherlands
Source: Frank Janssen

Learning to Argue

Argument goes hand in hand with critical thinking and problem solving, which are valued attributes in many fields and businesses. These are also key components of case studies, one reason this textbook approaches the teaching of argument using the case study method.

A case is a story that contains a conflict about an issue or an event that creates a problem that needs to be solved. Different perspectives on the central issue are represented by the different people involved in the case, who are the stakeholders. Case study scenarios ask you to think critically about the different positions of the stakeholders and then attempt to negotiate a solution(s) that will benefit as many of the stakeholders as possible. Case studies will also introduce you to specific aspects of academic arguments since arguing a case involves research and incorporating evidence. Because cases are deliberately messy and contain multiple points of view, as well as stakeholders with different and sometimes competing needs, they will challenge you to go beyond the surface of the issue in your thinking and your writing.

Academic Arguments

Academic arguments share many features with arguments in other contexts. Like most arguments, they contain a central premise or claim that is supported by reasons and evidence whose goal is often to persuade the reader. However, they differ in the standards used for what counts as evidence and the way they are connected to other arguments and other texts. Academic arguments normally reference the work of other scholars in order to connect the argument to prior knowledge on the topic. Knowledge creation through research and knowledge dissemination through teaching are two of the basic functions of a university, and these characteristics are reflected in the way written arguments are structured.

Ask Yourself

Use these questions to help you connect your paper to prior writing on your topic:

Who has said what about your topic already?
Who disagreed with them and why?
Where do you fit?

When experienced academic writers write, they situate their writing within the wider context of both the topic (for example, mental health care) and the field (psychology). As a beginning academic writer, you need to start thinking about how your writing can also begin to connect to other texts and ideas.

In addition, academic arguments are not usually focused on who wins, but rather on persuading a reader to think about the topic in a new way. Because two of the goals of academic arguments are knowledge creation and knowledge dissemination, persuasion in academic writing is more than a simple win/lose type of rhetorical situation.

Viewing argument as a way to connect to your audience instead of a competition that you must win allows you to expand your perception of argument and shape it into a powerful tool, one that lets you form a better understanding of a question, a topic, an issue, or a problem—a tool that can be used to test your understanding of the class's content.

Experienced academic writers tend to use argument to do different things such as test theories, contribute to a field's body of knowledge, argue for certain ways of thinking, and present solutions to problems. As a developing academic writer, you can use arguments in similar ways, especially as you begin to write more in your major. You may be asked by your instructors in your other classes to write arguments to demonstrate your critical thinking since writing arguments can help you better understand what you are learning. As you take more and more college courses, you'll be expected to use argument to explore issues from new perspectives, to demonstrate your knowledge of course content, and to present solutions to problems. The process of writing an argument asks you to share what you've learned.

Academic Arguments as Inquiry

Argument as inquiry asks you to take an intellectual journey of discovery where the argument becomes a method of exploration and investigation. Inquiry and investigation allow you to use argument to test your ideas against yourself and others.

Ask Yourself

Use these questions to help you explore your writing ideas:

What do you want to say now about your topic?
Why is what you've learned worth considering?
Why is your solution worth implementing?
How do your preconceived ideas or beliefs stand up to the research and reflection?
How do your ideas, beliefs, and research stand up against the ideas of others?

Argument as inquiry also encourages an in-depth examination of concepts and topics. Pragmatically, of course, topics are often assigned or arise as part of the coursework; nevertheless, even an assigned topic is an opportunity to delve more deeply into the subject matter. Argument as inquiry consists of the following.

Observing

Be open as you observe.
Take careful notes of the things or behaviors that puzzle, confuse, or interest you.
Take note of the things that challenge your beliefs, values, or preconceptions.

Asking Questions

Use questions as a way to understand or to get at different points of view.
What does it mean that . . . ? Why is it that . . . ?

Examining Alternatives

Ask "what if" questions.
Seek out alternative points of view.
Play the devil's advocate.

Evaluating, Analyzing, Reflecting

Examine critically the research you did to answer your questions.
Determine the relevance or the significance of what you have discovered.
Take the questions together with their answers and reflect on what you have learned.

Writing

Draft your text.

For instance, you might become interested in service learning because you observed your roommate has a service learning project they are really excited about. You begin to ask questions about service learning and its learning goals. You compare your roommate's enthusiasm for their class with a friend who is taking the same subject from a different professor who doesn't use service learning and decide that service learning can enrich a student's learning experience. You decide to write up your findings to share with other students in the school newspaper.

Check Yourself

Case study example: If you were investigating the campus speech code case from an argument as inquiry perspective, it might look like this:

Observations

Conflict between groups about what types of speech should be allowed in a public venue
Conflict between different viewpoints on acceptable forms of sexuality
Conflict between what the purpose of a university community is
Conflict between the rights of the individual versus the rights of the group

Questions

Is speech an action?
Where is the gap between intention and effect?
Should people be held accountable for the effect of their actions?
Was wearing the T-shirt hate speech?
Why should all points of view be treated equally?
If a speech code is put in place, which groups should be protected and why?

Alternatives

- What if the protest had led to violence?
- What if someone had gotten hurt or killed?
- What happens when ideas or groups are silenced?
- What happens when civil debate no longer occurs?
- What if religious beliefs are considered above the law?
- What would happen if the two sides learned about each other's perspectives instead of staying entrenched in their own point of view?

Evaluating, Analyzing, Reflecting

- Look for a question you are interested in answering.
- Look for a common thread among your observations, questions, and alternatives.
- Do research and seek out the answers to your questions.
- Examine critically what you find.
- Look for counterarguments.
- Outline in preparation for drafting.

Asking questions and doing research opens your thinking process on topics and issues. The process helps you to figure out what you know and how to clearly communicate what you've learned.

Academic Arguments as a Turn in the Conversation

The metaphor of conversation is often used in composition courses to describe academic writing. The metaphor highlights the fact that all writing is done in response to something—an idea, a blog post, a problem, a text message, or an assignment. We argue all the time in conversation, so thinking about writing as just another type of conversation becomes a way to make any writing, but especially academic writing, feel more familiar and less daunting. When you argue with your friends about the chances of your favorite sports team winning or whether the movie you saw last night was any good, you are using reasoning to convince an audience. Writing is just a more structured way of doing the same thing.

For example, you might argue in your physical education class about the impact of sports on college campuses or you might argue in your film class whether *The Maltese Falcon* or *Blade Runner* belongs in the film noir genre. You are still arguing about movies or sports, just in a more formal style and context.

In academic argumentative writing, you need to lay out your evidence about your topic in a way that will convince your academic audience that your ideas have merit—just like you did when you convinced your friend you were right about the movie. However, the rules for what counts as evidence in academic writing are different from conversation. So think of your paper as your turn in a conversation since it is your opportunity to respond to what you're learning and present your point of view.

Furthermore, academic writing, like conversation, is always situated in a context:

The context of the course (writing an paper for a composition course, writing a lab report for a biology course, writing a newspaper article for a journalism course)
The context of the assignment (persuasive versus descriptive, tables versus paragraphs, APA style versus MLA style)
The context of the case scenario (which stakeholder, which issue, which solution)

Because academic writing is less immediate than conversation, you will need to anticipate what a reader might ask or you will need to be more careful of tone. It also means that you need to create a background understanding of your topic for your reader. Focus on three things:

- Here's what has happened so far.
- Here's what I'm going to tell you.
- Here's how it relates to what has happened so far.

In writing, just like in conversation, connecting to your audience is important, so your first step in any writing task is to connect with them. You want them to listen to you, but, in order to do that, you must first listen to them and show that you respect their ideas because without the cooperation of your audience, your words and ideas will go nowhere.

What Isn't an Argument

Many topics, ideas, and issues can be argued, but some claims are self-evident: "child abuse is wrong," for example. Things no one would disagree with are not worth the time arguing. Any argumentative claim must pass the "so what?" test.

Other things that can't be argued are:

- Explanations or observations
- Personal taste
- Facts

Sometimes you have a perfectly arguable topic with supporting evidence, but you can't argue it because your audience refuses to cooperate and accept your evidence as valid. For example, climate change deniers who don't accept the correlation between global warming and a rise in extreme weather events like stronger hurricanes, tornados, and floods are not going to be persuaded by any evidence that goes against what they believe.

Ask Yourself

The "so what" test asks the question "so what?" about the claim of the argument in order to test it. Other questions to ask are:

Why does this matter?
What's at stake?
Why should the reader care?

Check Yourself

Apply the "so what" questions above to the following claims. Which ones would make a better argument?

First World counties should take in more refugees.
Blue is my favorite color.
Plastic polluting the ocean is killing marine life.
Cats make the best pets.

What did you conclude and why?

Basic Argument Structure

The structure of academic writing shares several characteristics:

It is evidence-based and organized around a central question.
It has a claim.
It is done in collaboration with others.
It often uses field-specific technical terms or jargon.
It is usually trying to fill a gap or contribute to the knowledge of a particular field.

You will be expected to include all of these characteristics in your academic writing. Your papers should be organized around a central claim or focus; they should provide evidence; you should use feedback from your peers and instructors to write and revise them. Even though you will not be expected to do original research, you should still use critical thinking questions to help you create

Table 1.1 The main structural elements of an argumentative paper

Introduction	
Connects to the reader States the problem the case deals with Gives some background on the issue(s) States the thesis	
Arguments in support	**Refutation or counterarguments**
Uses sources taken from your research to present your point of view on the case	Presents evidence for the other point(s) of view and their reasons for the claim(s) they are making
Provides evidence relevant to your audience in support of your claim	Demonstrates that others hold legitimate opposing and/or different points of view
Uses the reasons given in the thesis as a guideline	Shows why your audience should be persuaded by your point of view
Documents all outside sources correctly	Documents all outside sources correctly
Conclusion	
Pulls your argument together Reemphasizes your main points States implications and significance of your claim	

new habits of mind that automatically look at topics and texts from new angles. Table 1.1 lists the main structural elements of an argumentative paper.

Except for the introduction and conclusion, these elements can be arranged many different ways. In your other classes, you might find the structure of papers may differ. How papers are written depends on the field, the genre, and the purpose. Always ask your instructor if you are unsure about how an assigned paper should be organized.

Fundamentally, argument comes down to two things: thinking and acting. When you use argument as a way of critical thinking, as inquiry, you use it to gain better understanding of your topic or to form positions about an issue. Once the thinking and exploring are done, then you can move on to the action aspect. Given what you've learned through inquiry, what action(s) or position do you want to argue for? Why? What actions do you want your reader to take as a result of your argument?

CHAPTER SUMMARY

Argument is an effective way to communicate ideas, challenge preconceptions, explore problems, and persuade others. Different modes of communication (oral, written, and visual) can be used to construct the argument. An argument is always designed for a specific audience, uses a basic structure, and is situated in a particular context. "Argument as inquiry" and "argument as conversation" are two ways argument can be understood as both a tool for learning and a tool for communication. Argument has specific uses in the academic setting. Experienced academic writers use argument to present research findings, advocate for theoretical perspectives, and present solutions to problems. Developing academic writers are often asked to write arguments in order to demonstrate critical thinking skills and knowledge about a topic. Case studies are an effective way to teach argument since they present multiple viewpoints on a central problem. Using case studies can help you to develop critical thinking and analytical skills as well as sharpen problem-solving skills.

Think about how you use argument in both your everyday life and in your college classes.

2 WORKING WITH CASE STUDIES

How do writers make their arguments responsive to different scenarios and audiences? How can you adapt your own arguments to specific cases?

Learning objectives for this chapter

- Understand the goals for using case studies in a writing course
- Identify the five steps to writing about a case study
- Analyze an example case

Key concepts addressed in this chapter

- Case study

Introduction

Case studies teach you how to construct effective arguments by asking you to respond to complex, real-life scenarios. They place you, the writer, directly inside the situation, and they require you to consider it from multiple perspectives. Case studies also require that you consider the effects of your decisions on various individuals and groups in the case.

In addition, case studies are designed to guide you to more critical ways of thinking. Often, this means transitioning from memorization and linear ways of thinking (e.g., A is a problem, B is a consequence, C is a solution) to more layered and context-specific problem solving (e.g., A is a problem in X case, B is a consequence for certain people, C is a solution for some people but not others, D may be a compromise). Further, case studies ask you to apply what you already know or what you learn through research to a specific situation. Since case studies have no right or wrong answer, they ask you to move beyond regurgitating facts and general arguments. You must instead think through situations that are complex and have many possible solutions, and decide how to make a case for your solutions.

One crucial aspect of cases is the emphasis they place on your credibility as a writer. You will see that to effectively communicate your ideas and persuade your audience, you must present yourself as knowledgeable—having a credible perspective—on all the issues. An integral part of this credibility is the presentation of multiple perspectives, and an integral part of presenting multiple perspectives is the language writers use: Most academic and other formal writing tasks require diplomatic, civil language.

Thus, skilled writers are more likely, for example, to write:

(a) "The following evidence suggests that this perspective is not fully accurate because . . .," versus
(b) "This perspective is wrong because . . ."

In iteration (a), the words *evidence suggests* and *not fully accurate* allow the writer to draw attention to evidence and refute an idea with some politeness. Research shows that developing writers often instead use the more direct or attacking language in (b), but formal and academic readers tend to prefer the language in (a).

Diplomatic language may be a new focus for you, but you can gain practice as you write your responses to the case studies. Likewise, you may be most accustomed to basic paper forms such as five-paragraph essays, but you will gain practice writing in a range of ways based on the particular case study. In this way, you will practice rhetorical flexibility, adapting how you write to your purpose and audience.

In sum, case studies prepare you to think through problems critically, to respond to them with attention to multiple perspectives, and to write about them in diplomatic, organized ways. Let's establish a few learning goals you can keep in mind as you write about the case studies in the textbook.

Learning Goals for Each Case Study

- Identify the key issues.
- Interpret and articulate situations from different perspectives.
- Identify crucial decision points and possibilities for action.
- Recognize alternative actions and their possible consequences.
- Challenge your own viewpoints as well as those of others.
- Locate and evaluate effective sources.
- Generate supporting evidence for a response.
- Clarify reasoning and explain evidence.
- Use language that frames and organizes ideas, builds credibility, and shows thoughtfulness toward multiple perspectives.

How to Do a Case Study

Writing about a case is a multi-step collaborative process. First, you discuss the issues in the case with classmates, instructors, and even friends. Then, you consult the reference librarians and your instructor if you need help finding credible and relevant sources for your paper, and you read the sources thoroughly. Finally, you begin to craft your ideas into a coherent response and participate in peer editing while you draft and revise your written response.

Five Basic Steps to Writing About a Case Study

1. Read the case scenario.
2. Discuss the situation presented in the case and the resulting issues.
3. Conduct research on the case issues.
4. Analyze and engage in decision making.
5. Draft and revise your written response.

Let's look at each of these steps in detail.

Step 1: Read the Case Scenario

First, you must read the case scenario. Here is where you will want to employ your critical reading skills in preparation for the class discussion. Take notes as you read, identifying the key facts and issues in the case. What are the issues? Who are the stakeholders? What is the main problem presented? Use the journalism questions and critical reading questions from Chapter 3 to help you identify all the relevant aspects of the case before the class discussion. Your instructor might assign free writing at the beginning of class as a way for you to record your impressions and thoughts about the case before the class discussion.

Step 2: Discuss the Case Scenario

Discussing the case with your classmates and instructor allows you to see and hear different perspectives on the case, ensuring you have thought of every issue and side. This is especially important since there is no right or wrong answer to a case: There are only more or less thorough responses, and you want yours to be thorough. Discussing and debating with your peers is one way for you to collaboratively think through the issues presented in the case.

The following questions identify aspects of the case you may want to consider in a class discussion:

1. What are the main issues in the situation?
   How would you rank the issues (from most to least important)?
   What reasons can you give for your rankings?

2. Who are the stakeholders?
   What is at stake for them?
   What do they have to gain or lose?
   How does the case appear to the different stakeholders?
3. What is the main problem presented?
   How does the immediate problem or issue tie into larger social issues?
   What conflicts in values or belief systems form part of the problem?
4. What are the possible courses of action and solutions?
   How would you rank them?
   What are the advantages and disadvantages for each one?
   Is your solution a short- or long-term solution?
   What are the consequences of your solution for each of the stakeholders?

These questions represent only a small part of what you might discuss, depending on the case, what you know about the case topic, what your classmates know about the topic, and the different issues your instructor may want to cover. Throughout the discussions on the case, you can be generating your own relevant questions about the case issues.

Step 3: Research the Case Study Issues

The purpose of research is twofold: it provides **information for the open-minded writer**, and it provides **evidence for the thoughtful writer**.

The first purpose is informational. In order to make a decision that will benefit as many of the stakeholders as possible, you will need to know as much information as possible about the issues in the case. You may read through much more information than you will actually use in your paper, but this is time well spent, since the more you know, the more thoughtful you can be in your response. Keeping an open mind throughout this process will allow you to discover unexpected ideas, even ones that fully change your mind. This will help you as you represent multiple perspectives in your response to the case study. The second purpose is to provide evidence, ultimately, for the solution you propose. Good research makes the writing process easier and more thorough because it allows you to find and understand evidence, both for and against a particular solution to a case study.

As you begin your research, consider the following: What background information is necessary to understand the case? Where can I find that information, and how should I evaluate it? Because a paper is only as good as the research that supports it, you will need to evaluate the sources you find for their credibility and usefulness. Chapter 5 provides practical information on how to conduct research and find relevant sources.

As you compile and read research, take good notes. Note answers to questions such as the following: What are the main issues, and what are the main responses to them? In what ways do the readings agree? In what ways are they different? What do the readings discuss, and what do they *not* discuss?

Step 4: Analyze and Engage in Decision Making

We list analysis and decision making as Step 4 in order to highlight its importance, but they are related to all the other steps, including Step 5. Your reading, note taking, discussion, drafting of your paper, peer reviewing of your peers' papers, and revising of your paper will all be part of your analysis, reanalysis, and decision-making process. One good way to ensure you have not just read and understood but have *analyzed* the issues is to go back through your notes and determine key points. Circle each key issue, place a check by supporting evidence, and draw arrows to one or two solutions. Then you can focus on these specific ideas as a starting point as you draft your paper.

Step 5: Draft Your Paper

We all struggle with the blank piece of paper or the blank screen, but preparation and planning make writing a bit easier. If you have successfully completed Steps 1 through 4, you are ready to start. Where writers often get stuck—why they end up going off topic or stating and restating their ideas rather than explaining and supporting them—is when they haven't yet taken enough time to read, discuss, and think through issues while taking good notes. This often takes more time than we think, so give yourself enough time to go through Steps 1 through 4 thoroughly, and be ready to repeat them. Remember, writing is not a mechanical process; it is a creative and recursive one.

As you look back over your key ideas in your notes (see Step 4) and begin drafting, consider your assignment task: a paper that (a) shows knowledge of the case and multiple perspectives toward it, (b) offers a way forward with clear supporting evidence, and (c) uses language and organization that will make your response clear and credible for your given audience.

Modeling the Case Study Process: A Sample Case

This section presents a sample case as a model for working through the cases in Part Two of the textbook. As you read through the case, consider the skills you will need to work through a case study (critical reading, analysis, discussion, collaboration, research, writing) and how you can transfer these skills to the cases in Part Two.

Case Scenario: The Patriot Act

You are a lawyer at a firm that specializes in civil liberties and constitutional law. Erica Johnson, the reference librarian for the local community college, and Terrell James, the director of the library, have come to see you.

They have been visited by two FBI agents and served with a National Security Letter demanding "any and all subscriber information, billing information, internet access logs, and the circulation access logs" for the five names listed in the letter. The information is being sought to protect national security. Erica recognized the names as local students from Dr. Norris's history class. She'd been helping them to find sources for their research papers.

The FBI agents had pointed out the part of the letter that said that the recipient of the letter could not disclose to any person that the FBI had sought or obtained access to information or records. The agents had explained to them that this was a lifetime gag order and that "any persons" also included the students named in the document.

Terrell had asked to see the court order for these records, but he was told the FBI didn't need a court order. Erica told them that their request was unconstitutional. She was not going to turn over these records without a court order. The students have rights and the library was going to protect them, she said.

According to the agents, Sections 215 and 505 of the Patriot Act give them this authority:

- Section 505 of the Patriot Act authorizes the use of National Security Letters by the FBI to demand records such as medical records, book purchase records, membership lists, subscription lists, and lists of website visitors from third parties.
- The FBI does not have to demonstrate probable cause, only declare it has "reasonable grounds" to suspect that library records may be relevant to an investigation. They don't need to show that a crime has even been committed.
- FISC[1] search warrants and National Security Letters override state and local privacy laws.
- They contain a "gag order" prohibiting a library from notifying users under suspicion, the press, or anyone else that an investigation is under way.

Reluctantly, the FBI agents gave Erica and Terrell time to consult with a lawyer but told Erica and Terrell that they would return for the information.

In your office, Erica points to the National Security Letter sitting on your desk. "We want to challenge the constitutionality of this," she says. As the lawyer Erica and Terrell have consulted, what are you going to advise them to do?

Analyzing the Case

Once you have read the case scenario, you will need to identify the key elements in the case. The following is a guide you can follow to help you identify the different elements of this case on your own and during class discussions of the case. Figure 2.1 shows a sample annotation of the case scenario.

1. Foreign Intelligence Survey Court

Case Scenario: The Patriot Act

You are a lawyer at a firm that specializes in civil liberties and constitutional law. Erica Johnson, the reference librarian for the local community college, and Terrell James, the director of the library, have come to see you.

They have been visited by two FBI agents and served with a National Security Letter demanding "any and all subscriber information, billing information, internet access logs, and the circulation access logs" for the five names listed in the letter. The information is being sought to protect national security. Erica recognized the names as local students from Dr. Norris's history class. She'd been helping them to find sources for their research papers.

The FBI agents had pointed out the part of the letter that said that the recipient of the letter could not disclose to any person that the FBI had sought or obtained access to information or records. The agents had explained to them that this was a lifetime gag order and that "any persons" also included the students named in the document.

Dr. James had asked to see the court order for these records, but he was told the FBI didn't need a court order. Erica told them that their request was unconstitutional. She was not going to turn over these records without a court order. The students have rights and the library was going to protect them, she said.

According to the agents, Section 215 of the Patriot Act gives them this authority. This section states that:

- Section 505 of the Patriot Act authorizes the use of National Security Letters by the FBI to demand records such as medical records, book purchase records, membership lists, subscription lists, and lists of website visitors from third parties.
- The FBI does not have to demonstrate probable cause, only declare it has "reasonable grounds" to suspect that library records may be relevant to an investigation. They don't need to show that a crime has even been committed.
- FISC search warrants and National Security Letters override state and local privacy laws.
- They contain a "gag order" prohibiting a library from notifying users under suspicion, the press, or anyone else that an investigation is under way.

Reluctantly, the FBI agents gave Erica and Terrell time to consult with a lawyer but told Erica and Terrell that they would return for the information.

In your office, Erica points to the National Security Letter sitting on your desk. "We want to challenge the constitutionality of this," she says. As the lawyer Erica and Terrell have consulted, what are you going to advise them to do?

point of view character
Stakeholder
How big is this library?
Stakeholder
Why does the FBI want this info about these students?
what are they researching?
why is the gag order necessary?
Why don't they need a warrant?
right to privacy
background info
what constitutes reasonable grounds? Is that defined anywhere?
how could this be abused?
What about the 4th amendment? Why doesn't it protect them? It's federal.
Why the secrecy? what is the government afraid of?

FIGURE 2.1

1. Who Are the Stakeholders?

In this case, the main stakeholders are:

- The librarians
- The five students from Dr. Norris's class

- The FBI agents
- The lawyer
- The community college
- The community

Check Yourself

See if you can come up with a list of what is at stake for each stakeholder. Think about what each one has to gain or lose. Consider how much power or influence each stakeholder has in the decision-making process.

In this case, the different stakeholders stand to gain or lose different things. The librarians, for example, could lose their jobs, their professional reputations, even their freedom if they are jailed because of their actions. The students could also lose their freedom, if the FBI pursues criminal charges against them. They could also suffer other kinds of repercussions. As the lawyer, you have at stake your professional reputation, which is also linked to your economic situation. The community college could be held responsible for the actions of its employees.

Other questions you could ask:

1. What other things might be at stake for the stakeholders?
2. How does each person's perspective on the situation change what they might have at stake?
3. What will help me be thoughtful about everyone's perspective while also proposing a clear solution?

2. What Are the Issues in the Case?

In determining what some of the important issues in the case might be, you will want to brainstorm with other classmates or identify the issues during class discussions or in small groups. The following are examples of issues relevant to the case:

- Rights to privacy
- Public safety
- Constitutional rights
- Professional ethics
- Freedom versus security
- Economic consequences
- Limits of democracy
- Fear of what is unfamiliar, foreign, or unknown

Ask Yourself

Use the following questions to explore the issues:

1. How would you rank the issues (from most to least important)?
2. What reasons can you give for your rankings?
3. How are the issues interrelated?
4. What are the possible courses of action the lawyer could advise?

One of the toughest aspects of a case is deciding what you, a participant in the case, would do, especially since cases do not offer clear right or wrong answers, only more workable or less workable solutions. In the Patriot Act case, you will draft your paper from the point of view of the lawyer consulted by Erica Johnson and Terrell James and must decide among several courses of action. For example, you could advise your clients to:

- Give the FBI the information about the students
- Refuse to give the FBI the information
- Fight the secret warrant in court
- Fight the gag order in court

Ask Yourself

Use the following questions to explore the possible courses of action:

1. How would you rank each course of action?
2. What are the advantages and disadvantages for each one?
3. What are the consequences of your solution for each of the stakeholders?

Researching the Case

Once you have identified several key issues and possible courses of action, you can use these to develop areas that you may need to research in order to argue the case effectively. In light of the expectations of the assignment, you can divide the research into different areas:

1. Things I need to know more about
2. Support for my course of action
3. Support for alternative courses of action

Check Yourself

Before reading on, make your own list of research topics. Brainstorm the areas you would need to research for the case and compare your list with the following ones.

(1) Things I Need to Know More About

Under this heading, you could list the areas where you need more background information in order to make a decision and advise a possible course of action. Your peers might also suggest possible areas of research. For this case, some areas might include:

- The Patriot Act
- Civil rights
- Constitutional rights to privacy
- Library ethics and obligations to patrons
- Precedents set by earlier cases if any

(2 & 3) Support for My Ideas and Alternatives

Once you have learned more about the issues from your background reading, you can begin to look for evidence to support the different ways forward. Some resources might include:

- The American Library Association
- The LexisNexis legal database
- Political science resources

Drafting and Revising the Case

Once you have done your research and gone through your notes—completing Steps 1 through 4 outlined earlier—you are ready to begin drafting your ideas in a more formal way. Remember the elements of your assignment task: introduction to the topic and the main idea of the paper; explanation of the topic, including discussion of various (well-researched) perspectives on it; explanation of the course of action you propose, including support for it; and conclusion to the paper.

Most academic introductions include three elements: an introduction to the main topic, the "problem" or lingering issue or question, and then the thesis or response to the "problem." The body of the paper then adds all the details, offering knowledgeable explanations and support for various perspectives on the case and what to do about it, and using formal, diplomatic language so that the writer's ideas are credible and clear. As you draft and revise, remember to properly cite all of your sources both in text and on your "Works Cited" or "References" page.

CHAPTER SUMMARY

Case studies directly involve students in real-life scenarios so they can learn to take more in-depth contextual approaches to analytical thinking and problem solving. Using case studies is a multi-step process that involves a recursive reading, analyzing, discussing, and writing. One begins by critically reading and annotating the case scenario. Next the case issues are identified and explored through discussion. Students add to their knowledge of the case problem through research. Analysis and decision making are integrated into all the steps, including drafting and revising. In the case study approach, the writer's credibility—supported by reliable, solid research and diplomatic attention to multiple perspectives—is important. In the last half of the chapter, a sample case on a dilemma faced by librarians as a result of the Patriot Act provides a model for how the case study method works.

3 CRITICAL READING AND CRITICAL THINKING

What is the difference between reading and reading *critically*? How can you read in ways that will help you with your writing?

Learning objectives for this chapter

- Understand aspects of critical thinking, including questions of procedure, preference, and reason
- Understand aspects of critical reading, including strategies for understanding texts and making connections across texts and ideas
- Reading academic texts

Key concepts addressed in this chapter

- Critical thinking
- Critical reading
- Synthesis
- Concept maps

Introduction

Critical thinking and critical reading are complementary skills that allow you to engage in new kinds of thinking and meaning making. Critical reading is integral to thoughtful writing. Note that in this context, *critical* does not mean to find fault; instead, it means the ability to carefully reflect and evaluate. This chapter will introduce you to critical thinking and critical reading and will provide you with strategies for building thinking and reading skills necessary for success in college.

Critical Thinking

You've probably heard the term *critical thinking* used in a school context. But you also do critical thinking in other contexts as well. For instance, you might ask yourself: What did my friend/parent/instructor mean by that? How should I word this text message? What would be a funny way to tell this story? These types of questions are similar to the types of questions one might use in critical thinking.

So what is critical thinking, exactly? Critical thinking is purposeful, reasonable, reflective thinking that involves the ability to analyze, synthesize, and evaluate information. It is usually emphasized in specific contexts such as arguing, exploring, or solving problems. A key characteristic of critical thinking is asking searching questions—questions that go beyond the surface of facts and probe deeper to get at the connections and different levels related to an issue or situation.

Check Yourself

What helps writers to become critical thinkers?

- Questioning knowledge
- Using many forms and/or sources of evidence to inform conclusions, including sources that represent alternative perspectives
- Questioning one's own perspectives and assumptions with honesty
- Questioning others' perspectives and assumptions with honesty
- Being open-minded
- Seeking out and assessing new information

Critical thinking approaches stress an active learning experience. The goal is to move you from lower-order thinking skills—including memorizing, understanding, and limited application of knowledge—to higher-order thinking skills that promote a complex and flexible thinking process: analyzing, evaluating, and **synthesizing** (see more later in the chapter). Part of becoming a critical thinker is developing critical thinking habits—learning to value good thinking, developing intellectual standards, and being unwilling to settle for less, even when it is easier or takes less time.

Building critical thinking habits is not just an isolated one-time exercise. This section of the chapter will walk you through some of the basics of critical thinking. Since critical thinking applies to all aspects of the writing process, you will have other opportunities to learn and practice critical thinking strategies throughout the rest of the book.

Components of Critical Thinking

How does critical thinking work? One key component is asking questions. Questions are your guide to analyzing, interpreting, critiquing, evaluating, and reflecting. Three categories of questions can help guide your questions and answers: procedure, preference, and reason.

Questions of Procedure

These questions usually have facts or definitions for answers. Examples are:

- What is the botanical name for blue flax?
- What is the capital of Luxembourg?
- How many dialects are spoken in the United States?

Questions of Preference

These questions ask about a person's opinion based on personal experience. The answers to preferences questions are all subjective, such as:

- Do you like Belgian or Swiss chocolate better?
- What city in Europe is your favorite to visit?
- Do you want grilled cheese or a ham sandwich for lunch?

Questions of Reason

These questions have more than one answer that can be supported with credible reasons. They require the fair consideration of multiple and often conflicting viewpoints. Questions like these lead to critical thinking:

- What is the best way to help the homeless?
- Should the dams on the Columbia River be breached and river habitat restored?
- Are there times when books should be banned?
- What is the best way to ensure safe, respectful dialogue on college campuses?

While asking questions is central to critical thinking, equally important is listening to the answers. Respectful and careful listening is a crucial part of the process of understanding and thinking critically about your own and others' perspectives.

Critical Reading

Like writing, reading is an active process of constructing meaning. In your daily life, you are constantly reading. Between posts on social media, signs, newspapers, billboards, websites, text messages, notes, advertisements, books, and class handouts, you spend a lot of your waking moments reading.

Now that you are in college, you will encounter different kinds of texts: textbooks, lab reports, experiment results, the writings of scholars and thinkers from different fields and time periods. You probably read some of these texts in high school; however, while in high school, you may have read primarily to figure out the content of the text—the "what" of the message. In college, however, you will read for:

- the *what* (What is the text about?)
- the *why* (Why do the ideas matter?)
- the *how* (How did the writers come to their conclusions? How did they articulate their conclusions?)

Reading to decipher the *why* and *how* means looking beyond the surface of the text and deciphering authors' purposes and approaches, their assumptions and possible biases, and the reasonable inferences and connections you can make. It means building new habits of mind that enable critical engagement with the ideas in the text. While you may initially view texts as repositories of facts, your critical reading skills will help you expand your view to texts as conversations or dialogues between scholars and ideas.

Reading Strategies

Successfully comprehending a text combines three aspects: (1) what you, the reader, already know, (2) the text itself, and (3) the context. Some factors that can affect your understanding are:

- Your prior knowledge of the topic
- Your interest in the topic
- The difficulty of the text, in terms of grammar and language
- The familiarity or unfamiliarity of the writing style or genre

As you progress through the semester and continually practice and apply your critical reading strategies, you should see your comprehension of academic texts improve. In this section, we will discuss specific critical reading strategies, some of which may already be familiar to you. One element crucial to developing critical reading habits is time. You will need to set aside enough time to do your new critical reading steps. This method of reading might seem slow at first, but you will get faster at it as you practice more.

The main critical reading steps are as follows:

Ascertain your purpose.
Ask prereading questions.

Read and reread.
Annotate.
Look up vocabulary.
Make connections/summarize.
Use concept maps/summary.

As an example, we will be using Nancy Knapp's "In Defense of Harry Potter: An Apologia" for the Harry Potter case (see Case 1). This paper or another like it might be assigned for the case on censorship and the public schools.

So how do you approach critically reading this paper?

Ascertain Your Purpose

Before you begin reading, ask yourself: What is your purpose? What is the instructor's purpose? Why are you reading this text? The reason for reading a text will shape the types of questions you ask and the focus of your annotations (what you look for and take notes on as you read). For example, if you are reading to learn more about the topic of a particular case study, you will be taking notes on interesting facts and paying attention to the information that is new to you. If you are reading an article in order to learn more about a particular side of an argument, then you will be looking for the reasons and evidence the authors used to make their claims.

Let's think about what our purpose might be for reading Knapp's essay. For instance, could this article give us more information about the perspective librarians might take on censorship? Can you think of other ways that this article might help you to understand the case better? Write down your answers and remember to keep them in mind as you read it.

Check Yourself

Questions to help determine your purpose:

Am I reading for basic understanding and knowledge building?
Am I reading to understand a new concept?
Am I reading to analyze or critique something?
Am I reading to locate sources for a research paper?
Am I reading to find evidence for my argument? For counterarguments?

Prereading Strategies

Prereading steps help you put together a background for your text by exploring the context or setting in which it was written. Knowing the context will help you comprehend the ideas in the text better since you have an idea of how it fits into a bigger picture. This, in turn, will give you valuable insights into what the paper is about before you start reading.

Another aspect of prereading questions is prediction. You makes guesses about the content using prereading strategies. Then, as you read, you check to see if your predictions were right—that keeps your interest in the reading.

Before you begin reading a text, answer the following prereading questions:

1. Who is the author?
2. When was it published?
3. Where was it published?
4. What is the genre?
5. Who is the audience?
6. What can I expect from the title?
7. How does this information help me before I start reading?

Let's answer these questions for our assigned reading:

1. Nancy Knapp is a professor of educational psychology. She does research on at-risk and reluctant readers. I found this information at the end of the article. (A brief biography of the author is usually found at either the beginning or the end of a journal article.)
2. It was published in 2003. This was during the middle of the controversy over the Harry Potter books.
3. It was published in a journal called *School Libraries Worldwide*. The journal is a peer-reviewed journal published by the International Association of School Librarianship. (If you've been assigned to use scholarly sources, it's good to know if the journal is peer-reviewed.)
4. This is an academic paper.
5. Given the journal's name, we can assume that the main audience for this paper is school librarians. Other audiences might include teachers, school principals, and others interested in schools, reading, and censorship.
6. It's good to look for key words in the title that will give hints for what to expect in the paper. The obvious key words here are "Defense," "Harry Potter," and "Apologia." The first two seem self-explanatory, but what is an "apologia"? Time to check the dictionary. An apologia is "a formal written defense of a cause or one's beliefs or conduct."[1]

---

1. *Collins English Dictionary—Complete and Unabridged*, 12th ed. (HarperCollins Publishers, 2014).

7. So now we know the author is a person who studies reading and that she's talking to school librarians who are also interested in getting students to read. Since the article was published during the time there was an active controversy in the public schools over the Harry Potter books, we can assume the article is going to respond to that controversy. The title tells us which side she is on. Her use of the term *apologia* in the title also tells us that this will be a reasoned defense, so we should be looking for the reasons she uses to defend the Harry Potter books in schools and school libraries. As part of our prediction strategy, prereading sets up the scene by helping us anticipate what might be in the paper.

Reading Annotation

Now that you have some idea about what to look for in the paper, read the text all the way through once. Underline or circle any unfamiliar words, but otherwise try not to stop. The first read through is intended to give you a sense of the text as a whole. Once you've read the text all the way through, take your pencil or stylus and really dig into the text. Your most important tool at this stage is **annotation.**

You're probably used to underlining or highlighting things in the texts you read for school, but annotation takes underlining one step further: It creates a habit of interacting with the author's ideas as you read. The margin comments you write help you to remember why that section of the text interested you. Annotating texts opens the door for you to become more involved in your reading, build better comprehension skills, and maximize study efficiency. Some of these advantages include:

- Reading with a purpose
- Helping to promote active reading
- Organizing information into main points as you read
- Identifying parts of the paper you don't understand/find confusing
- Connecting ideas in the text to other things you know

There are two ways to approach annotation: **reading like a reader** (or reading for information) and **reading like a writer** (or reading for strategies and structure). You might use different-colored pens or highlighters for each one. As you annotate, try to mentally organize the information in the text—identify the key points, main ideas, evidence, and supporting details. Isolating the key points and supporting details will help you review later.

Reading and Annotating Like a Reader (Reading for Information)

When reading like a reader, write your comments and questions in the margin. Use whatever commenting functions you are comfortable with: pencil/pen, track changes in Word, or the comment function in PDFs. Try out a few and see which one works best for you. There are also many apps that can be used for annotation.

Use questions to identify the parts of the text you are having trouble understanding as well as to get deeper into the text—for example, to ask about implications, the author's assumptions, the rationale, and logic of the ideas or argument. Next, connect the ideas in the paper to other things you already know, to other elements of the case, or with ideas from other texts you have read, either for this class or from your other classes. Examples of parts of the text you might mark in the text are:

- Word/phrases that are unfamiliar to you
- The author's main/key idea
- Key support for main idea
- What type of evidence is used
- Information that doesn't agree with what you already know
- Any ideas that don't seem to fit together (e.g., because of contradictions, ambiguous references, misleading topic shifts)
- Information that seems missing or not clearly explained
- The "so what" or significance of an argument or idea

In addition, you can write comments that record your reactions to the reading. These can express a range of responses. For example:

> This point remind me of [fill in the blank].
> Really?!? Seriously?!?
> Nice example. I can really relate to it.
> Who sponsored this study?
> I don't agree.
> Never thought about it this way.
> This is confusing.
> This relates to class discussion.

You should also circle any words you don't know the meaning of—write a quick, short definition in the margin so that when you reread the text, you will have the definition right there. Use the definition to help you build a contextual understanding of the word's meaning.

Reading and Annotating Like a Writer (Reading for Strategies and Structure)

"Why should I pay attention to structure?" you might ask. "Isn't what the author is saying more important?" There are two main reasons to pay attention to a text's structure. One, a writer's ideas and a writer's rhetorical strategies are not separate from the structure of the text: The writer's strategies provide clues to the main idea. And two, you can use other writers' strategies as models for your own writing.

The good news is that the structure of academic writing is fairly consistent. Most academic writing is expository—that is, it's written to inform more than to entertain. It is normally uses a hierarchical structure, which usually consists of:

Level 1: a central controlling idea
Level 2: supported/explained by subordinate sub-points
Level 3: evidence

Many academic texts also follow an overall rhetorical structure that moves from general to specific back to general.

The central or controlling idea governs the entire text. If you can correctly identify the controlling ideas, then you will be able to see how the other pieces fit together to support the main idea. A central idea can be explicitly stated and thus easy to find (["This paper will do . .."] or it can be implicitly stated, which means you, as a reader, will have to infer it. The structure of the text helps highlight main ideas and connections.

Check Yourself

How can you be sure you have identified the main ideas?
With each text you read, write out the main/controlling idea for your reading in one sentence.

As writers, we often read to provide ourselves with models. The texts we read become resources for our own writing. When you read academic papers or journal articles, it is a good idea to train yourself to identify the different parts of the structure, especially the structure of the types of texts you are being asked to write. This knowledge of the genre's structure can help you when you begin to write your own papers.

When you annotate for structure, underline and note elements like these:

- The main idea, including where it is first noted and where it is repeated
- Where and what kind of background information is offered
- Where problems, concerns, or questions are posed
- Reader "hooks"
- Where and what kind of evidence is offered
- Transitions, or cohesive ties between sentences, paragraphs, and sections
- Where and what kind of concessions and counters are offered

- Where solutions are posed
- What kind of conclusions are offered (are they broad? narrow? somewhere in between?)

After you're done annotating, reread the text. Put it all together. Use the insights gained from annotating to help you build a picture of what the author's main ideas are and the overall purpose of the text. Also write down how the article fits into the case you are working on.

One of your tasks as a critical reader is to figure out the author's point of view. All texts are written from a particular perspective with a particular purpose in mind. No text is objective. All authors have a particular point of view that they use as a starting point for their ideas. Some of the elements that make up the author's point of view are:

- The content of the text—the message
- The language the author uses—the word choices, tone
- The author's opinions, hypotheses, and omissions
- The author's biases and assumptions

Authors make assumptions on two levels. The first level involves their assumptions about their audience and the audience's knowledge. All authors make assumptions about what their audience already knows and what they need to explain or clarify for the audience. Analyzing what your audience knows and needs is a basic step of any type of writing. The second level involves the background or underlying assumptions the author holds. Authors may or may not be aware of their underlying assumptions since assumptions are often unexamined. The author doesn't try to prove these assumptions since they are beliefs that the author takes for granted as true without questioning them. Some questions to help you identify author assumptions:

- What opinions does the author give or imply?
- What beliefs does the author follow or imply?
- Why do you think the author holds that belief or opinion?
- What reasoning has the author based their conclusions on?
- How does the author justify taking these assumptions for granted?
- Why would the author make that assumption(s)?
- What background information do you know about the author that might help you figure out their assumptions?
- Would another writer have taken a different point of view?
- What is the author's purpose?
- What facts, evidence, and beliefs about the world does the validity of the argument depend on?

Assumptions play a role in every text, but they are especially important for you to recognize in arguments. Assumptions can be explicit—the author will tell you straight out—or they can be implicit or hidden. Implicit assumptions are usually ones the author is not conscious of. You, as a critical reader, need to identify these in order to evaluate the validity of the author's argument. In arguments, identifying the underlying assumptions is crucial because false or unsound assumptions can lead to false or unsound conclusions—which puts the whole validity of the argument in question. (We will discuss analyzing arguments, including assumptions in arguments, in Chapter 8.)

Summarizing

After you're done reading and annotating, you're ready to summarize. Put the text aside—close the book, close the file, turn the article over. As part of the critical reading process, summarizing performs two important functions: (1) It helps you check your comprehension and (2) It serves as a resource for studying. First, summarizing functions as a kind of self-test. Did you understand the reading? Because summary writing asks you to restate the author's ideas in your own words, it can help you identify the parts of the text you might still be unsure of. Then, you can go back and reread that section, and look up new vocabulary in order to figure out what the author is saying. It's better to find out during the reading process that you don't understand what the author is saying on page 2 than on the day of the test or quiz! Second, summarizing is a good study tool as well as a resource for writing your research paper.

There are different ways to approach summarizing—outlines, concept maps, traditional written summaries, and lists of main points. Experiment and find the method that works best for you. For each of the following methods of summarizing, the preparation steps are the same. Begin by writing out on a note card, Evernote (or other note-taking app), or your class notebook a list of the main points, the author's claim, examples, and any other interesting points. These approaches will be discussed in more detail in this section.

Traditional Summary

Write a summary of the text without looking at it. You have probably been asked to write summaries before, so the basics of summary writing should be familiar. Be sure to write down all the citation information (title, author, journal, date) above your summary. You will need that information if you use that reading as a source in your papers.

After you have written your summary, go back to the text and check yourself. Did you include all the main ideas? Is the summary accurate? Adjust your summary as necessary, adding any parts you forgot the first time. If you find yourself skipping over parts of the text, that might be an indication you are having trouble with that part of the paper. Go back and reread the paper.

Check Yourself

Use these questions to help you evaluate your summary:

Does your summary show "the big picture"?
Does your summary indicate the relationships between the main points?
Does your summary signal that it's about someone's else's ideas (mention of author's name, use of third person)?
Is your summary written in your own words (no quotes)?

Question Summary

Another strategy for summing up the text is to use a series of questions as a guide to check your understanding. Start by writing down all the citation information (title, author, journal, date) at the top of the page. Put the text away and then answer the following questions for your reading/text:

1. Why am I reading this?
2. What was the author's main point/claim/thesis?
3. How convincing are the author's arguments/evidence?
4. What was the author's purpose in writing this article/paper?
5. What new information (about the case) did I learn from reading this article?
6. How can I use this article to help me write my paper?
7. What points might I want to cite in my paper (keep track of page numbers)?

Check Yourself

After writing out your answers, go back to the paper and check your answers. Are they accurate? Did you miss anything? If you find gaps, go back and reread the paper.

Concept Maps

Another way to help you build your comprehension and increase your active reading skills is to draw a concept map. A **concept map** is a visual representation of the relationships between key ideas and concepts in the text. It looks like a complicated flow diagram, and it can be especially helpful if you are a visual

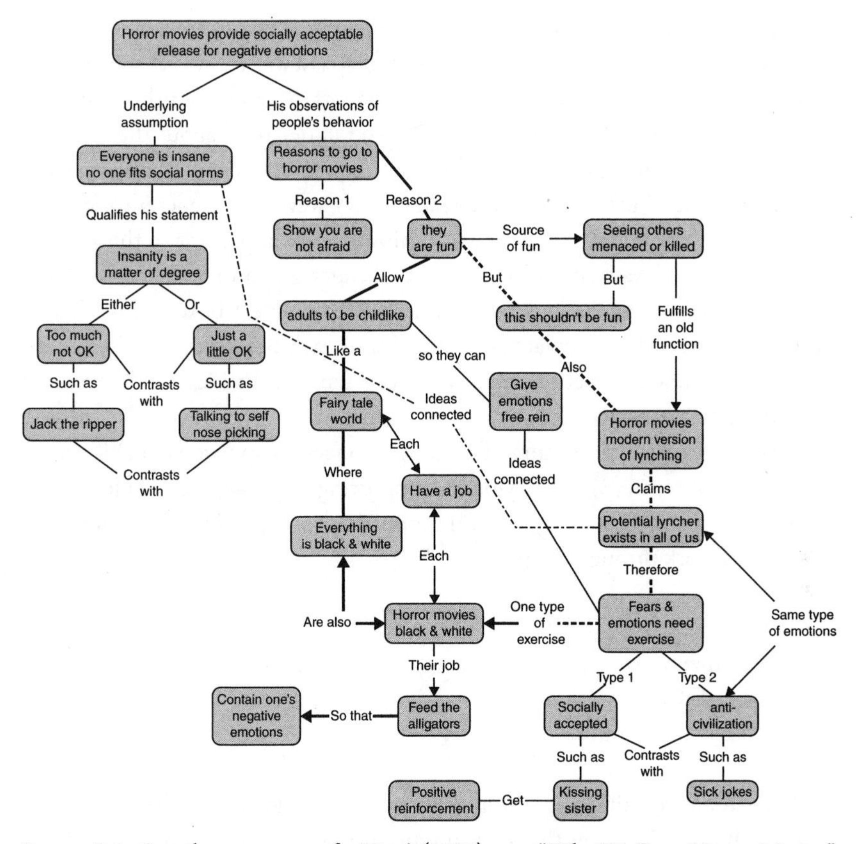

IMAGE 3.1. Sample concept map for King's (1982) essay "Why We Crave Horror Movies."

learner. Sample concepts in composition would include events, objects, claims, reasons, evidence, and counter-evidence. Concept maps help writers and readers with **synthesis**, or the higher-order thinking skills of bringing together, distinguishing, and/or connecting ideas. Image 3.1 shows a sample concept map for Stephen King's 1982 essay "Why We Crave Horror Movies."[2]

There are several advantages to concept maps:

- Define the central idea within the context of the text
- Visualize relationships between the different parts of the text
- Differentiate key or essential concepts from minor points or examples
- Help with recall of main ideas
- Show gaps in reader comprehension
- Lead to new questions about the topic

2. Stephen King, "Why We Crave Horror Movies," *Models for Writers: Short Essays for Composition*, 11th ed, eds. Alfred Rosa and Paul Eschholz (Boston: Bedford/St. Martin's 2011) 524–527.

As a critical reading tool, they can be used as an aid to create a written summary, or they can be the summary. A concept map is a way to "see" the main ideas in a text by mapping out the concepts from the text. Mapping out the main concepts gives you a chance to figure out what you understood about the text, discover what you didn't get, and reflect on and discover connections between parts of the paper you didn't see when you read it. It is a way to go deeper into the text. The map helps you focus on the relationships that are important to the author's message. In some ways, it looks similar to a spider graph or association graph, but the crucial difference is the labeled links that connect boxes. This labeling helps you to verbally articulate how the idea in each box relates to the others. Articulating these connections helps you make sense of the ideas in the text and how they relate to each other.

Overall, the basic procedure of creating a concept map involves (1) identifying the key concepts, (2) identifying the supporting concepts, and (3) identifying the relationships between the key and supporting concepts. Here are some steps to help you work through the process:

1. Brainstorm.
2. Organize.
3. Label links.
4. Check your work.

In the brainstorming stage, from memory (without looking at the essay) make a list of all the things you think are important: facts, terms, ideas. Write down everything you can think of. You may not use it all, but it's good to have a large list to work from (You can use Post-it notes, index cards, or scrap paper if you want. It will make the next step easier.) Another way to approach this step is to select terms that represent the central idea, write the term in the middle of a piece of paper, and then write down other terms and phrases from the text that relate to the main idea (like a spider graph). Don't edit or judge what you have at this stage. Just write things down.

Next, take what you have written from the brainstorming list and organize the items into groups and sub-groups of related items. Try to arrange your groups into some kind of hierarchy—for instance, put the general concepts at the top of your chart and the more specific concepts below the general ones. Some concepts may belong to more than one group, and that is perfectly normal. On a blank sheet of paper, arrange your groups in a way that represents your understandings of the interrelationships between each grouping. Place related items from sub-groups near each other. As you work, you may see relationships that you weren't initially aware of. You may need to move things around at this stage or redo your layout.

Once you have the groups arranged like you want them, the next step is to use lines and arrows to connect the items. Write a phrase or sentence beside each line/

arrow that describes the relationship between the two boxes. These labeled links show how the different parts of the map relate to each other. Some of the links might show a perspective that you hadn't thought of or seen before. Such realizations are what makes concept maps so helpful in the process of creating new knowledge and critical thinking. As a critical thinking tool, concept maps allow us to represent hierarchical structure and cross-links between concepts.

After you are satisfied with your layout, you may want to draw it/write it up neatly (especially if your instructor asks you to turn one in for a particular reading). Be creative. Use different colors, line thicknesses, fonts, etc. There are various software programs for drawing concept maps available online.

Check Yourself

Use these questions to double-check your concept map:

1. Are the concepts and relationships correct?
2. Are there any concepts missing?
3. Does the layout accurately reflect the relationships between the different concepts?
4. Do you have all the lines labeled with your links?

Creating concept maps takes practice. Don't be discouraged if it seems hard at first, or if you are not coming up with the connections quickly. As you develop your critical reading skills and build your reading comprehension over the course of the semester, critical reading and concept maps should become easier to do. You can see a sample concept map at the end of the chapter.

Making Connections

You are already making connections every day, because texts, news reports, magazine essays, and social media posts all exist in a dialogue with each other. Like these everyday texts, academic texts also exist in a dialogue with each other. Discovering connections between different texts is part of critical thinking and critical reading. It is also an essential component of research and argumentation. As you read critically, you will need to develop new habits of mind so that you can connect one idea/concept to another, creating a web of knowledge in your brain.

Seeking out and discovering relationships between ideas, between different viewpoints, between different types of knowledge, between texts, and between different fields of study is part of what distinguishes advanced thinkers. It is also part of what makes learning and writing so exciting. However, making connections is not always straightforward. In other words, you need to train yourself to look for connections. You need to situate the texts in the relevant conversation. Where do they fit in a dialogue? When were they written in relation to each other? Why were they written in response to a given topic or event? What prompted the author to write it? Which conversational turn does each text represent: the initiation? an extension? a response? a support or counter?

Connections in reading and writing can occur in several overlapping perspectives. First, look for the different levels of connections within the essay itself. Making a concept map, discussed earlier, is one way you can discover and record these connections. Second, look for connections to other texts. For example, can you link the text you are currently reading to other things you've read in the past? Can you find links, for example, between the different texts you are reading for the case study? Get into the habit of connecting what you are reading to things you already know, all the while taking care to maintain an open mind.

Here are some questions to help you get started as you make connections between ideas and texts:

- Do the different ideas or readings corroborate the same facts?
- Do any ideas or authors contradict each other?
- Which sources, if any, add new information/evidence to the same topic/issue?
- What assumptions or background information informs each text or idea? Are any of these the same or different?
- Does each idea or text address the same aspect of the issue?
- How do the different ideas or texts work together to create a more complete picture of the issue/topic?

You Try It!

1. Pick a reading from the case.
2. Find connections within the reading itself.
3. Find a connection between it and another reading for the case.
4. Find a connection to some information you already know about the topic.
5. Compare and evaluate the connections you've discovered. How do the connections you've found help you better understand the issues of the case?

Whatever your reading assignment, the information, ideas, and opinions in those readings are important resources. Combining critical reading with connection strategies will give you an advantage as you navigate your college career.

Reading Scholarly Sources

In this section, we will focus on strategies to help you critically read academic journal articles. These journal articles form the foundation of most research papers, but at first you may find them daunting and difficult to read and interpret. One reason for this is that undergraduate students like you are not the intended audience for scholarly journal articles. Other scholars are the intended audience. However, you will be expected to use scholarly sources such as academic journal articles because they contain reliable information written by experts.

Read your sources with a specific purpose in mind, such as:

- Is it relevant to my research question?
- How can this information help me write my paper?
- Does it provide me with a way to better understand the situation I am writing about?
- Does it provide me with evidence, examples, counterarguments, or background information?

There are different types of journal articles: ones that report research results, review articles, and theoretical articles. Articles that discuss the results of the author's research are the most common. Review articles review and critique a number of different articles on the same topic. Theoretical articles discuss existing theories or present new theories in a field. Keep in mind that different fields write journal articles differently and what counts for methods, data, and data presentation will also vary.

Although it might not seem like it, a journal article tells a story: the story of the research project. It tells the reader what prompted the researcher's ideas, how the research was conducted, and what the results were—in other words, *what happened*. Another part of the story is *why these things might have happened*. And a third part of the story is *why this is important to know*—the significance of the research. As a savvy reader of journal articles, you want to identify the basics (the *what*) and then pay attention to the *whys* (the explanations of the results and the significance of the results). Here are some reading tips:

- Apply same kind of prereading strategies to journal articles as you would to other types of texts.
- Read the abstract. It will help you determine if the article will be useful to you. You can't always tell by the title alone.
- Give yourself enough time to read it more than once.
- Take notes as you read.
- Focus on the information relevant to your research question. It's okay to skim over other parts.

- Focus on the main idea(s) and the explanations. Don't worry if the statistics don't make sense; just look for the author's interpretation of the statistics.
- Read only the parts that are relevant to your purpose or your paper.
- Read the conclusion/discussion section first.

Table 3.1 lists the main sections of a journal article, the main function of each section, and some things to look for as you read.

Table 3.1 Elements of a journal article

Journal section	Section description/ function	What to look for and questions to ask
Abstract	Gives a summary of the article Lists the focus of the research, the methods, results, and meaning of the results	*Overview of the article* Usually lists the main points and the conclusion
Introduction	States the problem or the topic States why the author is interested—the reason for doing the research States the focus and the purpose of the argument Depending on the field, gives some hint of the conclusion or states the thesis	*Why the author did the research* What questions the author hopes to answer
Literature review	Provides contextual background on the topic or problem Shows where the research fits into the wider picture Discusses what work has already been done on the topic Discusses the theoretical frame-work the research will use and why	*What the context of the research to the field is* Does the research build on an existing theory or body of knowledge? Does the research challenge an existing theory or body of knowledge?
Methods	States how the data were collected How large the dataset is What methods were used and why they were chosen What type of analysis will be used	*How the research was done*

Table 3.1 Elements of a journal article (*Continued*)

Journal section	Section description/ function	What to look for and questions to ask
Results	Gives the findings of the study May include tables, graphs, statistics, textual excerpts, or examples	*What the research discovered or found* What are the major findings? Was the author's hypothesis supported? Was the evidence presented effective?
Discussion Conclusion	Summarizes and interprets the results Discusses the implications and the significance of the findings, states the contributions to the field, makes recommendations about further research	*What the research means* Discussion of key issues and the meaning of the research project and its results Discusses what the author learned What new information does the study provide about the problem?
References	Lists the sources cited in the text	*What resources the author(s) used* Useful as a resource for finding sources for your project

CHAPTER SUMMARY

This chapter focused on critical thinking and critical reading, two overlapping processes that help writers carefully reflect and evaluate on their own and others' ideas. Both critical thinking and critical reading are essential, related components of good writing, and they include making connections across texts that lead to new meaning-making. These practices will help prepare you to successfully build the knowledge base you need to understand cases and issues, develop your ideas, and articulate and argue for those ideas effectively. As you read more and more for college, think about how you can use critical thinking and reading to help you learn more about the case issues and write a better paper.

4 DISCUSSING ARGUMENTS AND CASES

Have you ever thought about discussion as a skill? Or have you always thought that some people were just naturally better at talking in class?

Learning objectives for this chapter

- Understand discussion as a learnable skill
- Articulate *do's* and *don'ts* for a successful discussion
- Identify resources to use for preparing for and participating in discussions
- Recognize differences between small and large group discussions and what to do after the discussion is over

Key concepts addressed in this chapter

- Discussion
- Preparation
- Participation
- Listening
- Reflecting on discussion

Introduction

Discussion occurs in many different settings. It might take place in the boardroom, a conference room, a planning meeting, a city council meeting, or a classroom. Discussion is a fundamental part of how people exchange ideas and solve problems. In the classroom, a discussion uses dialogue, participation, and cooperation and is normally conducted with respect for all participants. Since discussion is the basic way we exchange ideas and broaden our perspectives, it is central to the academic process.

Because it allows us to test out ideas, discussion is also a fundamental part of the case study process. This process of talking through and testing ideas is another way to develop analytical thinking skills.

Discussion is one of the ways you and your classmates can work together to explore the case issues and discover counterarguments. In turn, this will help you to write your drafts.

Goals for Discussion

- Develop critical thinking skills
- Learn interpretation, analysis, and synthesis
- Understand the case and case issues
- Provide opportunities for the presentation of multiple viewpoints
- Combine your knowledge with that of your peers
- Challenge your ideas as well as those of your classmates
- Prepare you for writing
- Increase awareness of ambiguity and complexity
- Connect to topic
- Develop habits of collaborative learning
- Encourage respectful listening
- Include student voices and experiences

Don't worry if you feel uncomfortable with the idea of discussion. Discussion, like many other skills associated with academic and work contexts, can be learned.

There are four basic elements to a successful discussion:

- Preparation
- Participation
- Listening
- Group discussion settings
- Reflecting on discussion

Preparation

Before you ever walk into the classroom for a class discussion on a case study, you need to be prepared. Maybe you hadn't realized that discussions, like quizzes and papers, also need preparation ahead of time. Preparation is part of productive learning strategies and there are many advantages to preparing for class discussions. Being prepared makes you more confident and less stressed. You are able to participate more effectively and get more out of the class.

Coming prepared not only benefits you, it also benefits your peers. They benefit from your thoughtful contributions. Because a discussion is a dialogue, it is the responsibility of every member of the class. The advantages of being prepared for a discussion (benefits to everyone) include the following:

- There will be more participation and more contributions to the discussion.
- More points of view will be presented.
- More new ideas will be shared.
- A wider range of issues will be identified.
- More problems will be identified.

Steps for Preparation

1. Read the case scenario carefully and take notes.

Ask Yourself

Who are the stakeholders? What do they have at stake?
Which stakeholders will be making the decisions in the case?
What is the problem(s) facing the stakeholders?
What are the wider issues that relate to the problem in the case?
What is the significance of the problem?
When do the stakeholders need to act?
What are some possible solutions to the problem?
What are the consequences to the stakeholders?

2. Come to class mentally prepared to participate.

Think about the things you noticed as you were taking notes. These can be the foundation for your discussion points. Think as well about any questions that came up as you were taking notes. These can be the foundation for questions you ask in class. Come with things you can contribute, such as:

What did you notice about the case?
What are possible problems, or issues?
What are the implications you observed?

Come with questions to ask:

What other information do you need to know about the case?
What are some different perspectives?
What are possible solutions?

The more you prepare, the more you will get out the discussion. For example, say you have been assigned Case 4. You'll want to read the case scenario carefully and take notes. As you take notes, write your answers to the questions. Here are some possible answers to this example case:

- Who are the stakeholders? What do they have at stake?
  - The four students skipping class
  - The student whose car was vandalized
  - The journalism teacher
  - The principal
  - The mediator
  - The parents of the students
- Which stakeholders will be making the decisions in the case?
  - The journalism teacher, the principal, the mediator, and perhaps the parents
- What is the problem facing the stakeholders?
  - There are two problems: (1) deciding whether it is ethical to read the students' emails and (2) how best to discover who vandalized the car.
- What are the wider issues that relate to the problem in the case?
  - Wider issues might include privacy and the internet, students' rights, race relations, bullying.
- What is the significance of the problem?
  - What is the expectation of privacy that website users should have?
- What are the responsibilities of the school administration to its students and to its faculty?
  - Issues of safety
  - Possible issues of bullying
- When do the stakeholders need to act?
  - There doesn't appear to be a deadline in the case. The boy's parents might have a deadline for filing an insurance claim.
- What are some possible solutions to the problem?
  - Violate the students' privacy and read the emails.
  - Have an outside person like the mediator read the emails using a keyword search feature.
  - Ask the students' permission to read the emails.
  - Don't read the emails.
  - Search for the perpetrator another way.
- What are the consequences to the stakeholders?
  - There could be a loss of trust between the students and the school administration.
  - The wrong students might be singled out.

- The boy whose car was vandalized might have to pay for the car repairs himself.
- The relationship between the teacher and the principal might be damaged.

Discussion Contributions

Based on the sample answers, here are some questions or points that could be raised in class discussion:

- The journalism teacher is in a bad situation, caught between his boss and his students. What are his options?
- What rights, if any, do students have on school property?
- What roles should the parents have in this situation? Could they keep the principal from reading their children's emails?
- Why was Devon's car targeted? Who might want to hurt him? Is he being bullied? Did he even know the four students suspected of the vandalism?
- Are there problems or issues to consider in addition to the ones already raised?

In addition, your instructor may also give you an assignment to help you prepare for discussion. Be sure you do any assignment carefully using a critical thinking approach. Being prepared will give you the confidence to speak up in class.

Participation

In the classroom, a discussion is talking with a purpose, approached with intent. It is more than just a bunch of people chatting about a topic or talking about a book they've read. A discussion is a shared effort that provides an opportunity for students to dialogue with each other in order to reach a greater understanding of the case issues. For a discussion to be successful, it must be conducted in a respectful manner. Use these suggestions for respectful discussion as a guide.

Guidelines for Respectful Discussion

- Don't monopolize the discussion. Allow everyone who wants the chance to speak.
- Be courteous. Don't interrupt. Don't carry on private conversations or text on your phone during the discussion.

- Listen respectfully and carefully consider other people's opinions.
- Respect the right of others to hold opinions and beliefs that are different from yours.
- Direct any criticism to the ideas presented, not the individual.
- Respectfully challenge the ideas of others.
- Support your statements with evidence and reasons. Say why.
- When appropriate, use your personal experience, but recognize its limitations, too.
- Think about the effect what you are saying may have on other people.
- Avoid blame, speculation, and inflammatory language.
- Keep in mind that body language and nonverbal responses can be just as disrespectful as words.
- Keep any confidential and personal information shared in the discussion to yourself. Don't discuss it outside of class.
- Remember that a discussion is not a debate. Its focus is on learning, not winning.
- Keep in mind that the goal of the discussion is a deeper understanding of the case study.
- Include your voice. Share information. Each participant has a perspective and a responsibility to contribute to the whole.

In addition to these suggestions, your instructor might also want to develop a set of guidelines specific to your class.

Guidelines for Effective Participation

Effective participation means active engagement with the case scenario as well as with your classmates in the discussion process. It involves both active listening and active speaking. How can you get the most out of a case study discussion? Use the following suggestions to help you plan what to say in a discussion.

You can start with questions or comments that:

- Ask for evidence
- Ask for clarification
- Ask hypothetical questions to explore different solutions or consequences
- Ask for a synthesis or summary of ideas
- Explore the case issues or problem with open-ended questions
- Explore connections between different parts of the case
- Explore ideas in more depth
- Explore the cause and effect of stakeholder actions, or possible solutions

If you are uncertain how to phrase your remarks, you can use some of the following phrases (fill in the X's and Y's with details from the assigned case):

- If I were X stakeholder, I would take Y action because . . . [If I were one of the students, I'd resent the teacher reading my emails because . . .]
- I believe the key issue is X because . . . [I believe the key issue is students' rights because . . .]
- My take on the case suggests that X is the best solution because . . . [My take on the case suggests that not reading the emails is the best solution because . . .]
- I would like more clarification on X point [I would like more clarification on the students' legal rights]
- The information in X article suggests Y.
- These are some steps X stakeholder might consider because . . .
- I would like to propose X solution for Y reasons.
- I think we need to pay attention to X aspect for Y reasons.
- I think we need to spend more time on X point.
- We should hear from X because . . .
- We should talk about Y next.
- How does X connect to Y?
- How does X's comment fit with Y's comment?
- How does X's idea challenge what the group has been saying?
- What are the most important ideas raised so far?
- Why do you think X is important?

Remember, an important goal of the discussion is to engage in dialogue with your fellow students, not just the instructor. Share your ideas and respond thoughtfully to your peers' ideas and comments. Talk directly to your classmates. Address your questions and comments to them whenever possible.

What happens when the discussion isn't going so well? Check out the following list and see if any of these might be contributing to some of the lackluster discussions you may have participated in the past.

Characteristics of Ineffective Participation

- Students not prepared
- Being disrespectful to other participants
- Repeating case facts
- Just summarizing the case (unless asked to)
- Repeating someone else's comments
- Inconsequential interjections (for example, "I agree with so-and-so" without saying why)

- Deflecting the discussion off topic
- Monopolizing the discussion and not giving others the chance to share their ideas
- Not paying attention (playing with your phone, surfing the net, reading, doodling)

Check Yourself

Use these questions to help you evaluate your approaches to discussion:

Do your contributions reflect preparation?
Did you use references to the case scenario, background sources, or other evidence?
Were the ideas you offered substantive?
Did your contributions move the discussion forward?

Listening

Are you listening or just waiting to talk? Are you filling the silences in a discussion with thoughts or just anticipating your next turn to speak without really paying attention to what is being said by others? Or are you focusing attentively on what your peers are saying?

In any discussion, speaking is only part of your job; the other part includes listening carefully in order to better understand. In an active listening approach, listening is acting rather than not acting. In other words, listening is not just not talking. It is an act of understanding. The benefits of engaged listening include the following:

- Broadens your perspective
- Increases your knowledge
- Builds trust with peers

Listening and listening skills are an often-neglected aspect of discussion and critical thinking. Like discussion skills, good listening skills are transferable to other settings beside the classroom.

Ways to Convey Engaged Listening

- Paraphrase or summarize your peers' remarks.
- Ask for clarification.
- Keep an open mind.

- Ask questions.
- Discuss similar experiences.

Nonverbal Cues

- Eye contact
- Posture
- Head nodding
- Not acting distracted (texting, doodling, etc.)

Some sample phrases to use when practicing engaged listening include the following:

- I understand that . . .
- I like that solution; tell me more.
- Can you explain more why you think . . .?
- So you're saying that . . .
- I'm not sure I understand . . .
- This is the point I hear you making . . .
- I noticed that. . .

Listening with a willingness to understand the other ideas of others, especially when you don't agree with them, will help you to expand your perspectives on the case issues. Poor listening tends to bog the discussion down in repetition, mediocre points, and circular reasoning. Nobody benefits from a discussion derailed by ineffective listening.

Group Discussion Settings

In your classroom, the discussion setting may vary. For instance, you might be placed in a small group and given a topic, task, or text to discuss. This might serve as preparation for sharing with the larger group or might be a task in and of itself. On the other hand, your instructor might choose to start off the case with a large group discussion so that everyone can contribute and everyone can hear what is said.

Small Group Discussion

A small group discussion has certain advantages. There are fewer people, which gives everyone a chance to speak. Usually there is a specific task, which gives the group a starting point. If you are shy or reluctant to speak up in class, it might be easier to share your ideas in a small group rather than in the whole class. A small group can provide a better opportunity for you to contribute. Some of the benefits of small group discussion include developing communication skills, building confidence, and learning to recognize good ideas.

Ask Yourself

When preparing for small group discussions:

What can I bring to the group?
What should I take away from the assignment?
How can I help the group to work together effectively and stay on task?

Large Group Discussion

Large group discussion can be intimidating for some students, but once you get to know your classmates and your instructor, you may start to feel more comfortable contributing to class discussions.

Different instructors have different styles when it comes to class discussion:

- The instructor might start off the discussion but then put the rest of the responsibility on the students.
- The instructor might "cold call"—that is, call on students who aren't raising their hands in order to include everyone's ideas in the discussion. Thus, it's best to be prepared!
- The instructor might ask one student to respond to another student.
- The instructor might appoint a student to lead the discussion.
- The instructor might ask a student to sum up the discussion.

But whatever the instructor's approach, your responsibility to be prepared and to participate remains the same. Don't fall into the trap of letting a small group of students do all the work for everyone else in the class.

Reflecting on Discussion

Since it's often hard to take notes in the midst of the discussion itself, take a few minutes at the end of class to jot down what you want to remember from the class discussion. For example, you can summarize your observations and write down any insights, solutions, or counterarguments that were mentioned. Don't wait until later. It's easy to forget once you go on to the next class, have lunch with friends, or start your research in the library.

Check Yourself

Use these questions to help you evaluate your participation:

What did I contribute? Did my contribution move the discussion forward?
Did I provide ideas on the topic?
Did I listen with intent?
What new understandings of the case and the case issues did I come away with from the discussion?
Did I come up with ideas for writing or research?
Did I contribute any idea for a solution?
What could I have done better?
How can I improve my participation and listening skills?

Discussion fosters analytical thinking skills. Practice these skills by comparing your ideas with the ideas of others, by evaluating and critiquing the information shared, and by listening respectfully with intent to gain a greater understanding of the case.

CHAPTER SUMMARY

Discussion is an important resource used in academic and non-academic settings to explore multiple perspectives on issues and problems. Because it facilitates the exchange of different viewpoints, it is an important part of the case study process. In the classroom, discussion usually takes place in either a small or large group setting, each of which has different advantages and disadvantages. While there are effective and ineffective ways to participate in a discussion, several factors contribute to the success of discussions in the classroom setting. These include preparation, participation, listening, and reflection. In turn, discussion helps develop analytical thinking skills.

5 CONDUCTING RESEARCH AND EVALUATING SOURCES

What is the value of finding research sources as a student? How does one go about it? What is the difference between citation styles, and why do they matter?

Learning objectives for this chapter

- Understand ways of identifying, evaluating, and representing research sources
- Identify differences between primary and secondary sources in different fields
- Recognize ways to evaluate the credibility of an academic source
- Recognize aspects of research articles
- Differentiate common documentation styles in academic writing

Key concepts addressed in this chapter

- Academic research
- Primary source
- Secondary source
- Credibility
- MLA style
- APA style

Introduction

Researching and evaluating research are key to thinking and writing. Since we never think and write in a vacuum, we have to learn to find and evaluate already-existing sources. This chapter is designed to get you started by introducing you to research basics and helping you feel more comfortable with finding and considering research sources. More specifically, this chapter addresses several technical parts of identifying and evaluating research sources, while the next two chapters on the writing process will address engaging with research sources as you think about and write a specific assignment.

Why Do Research?

All research begins with a question—with a desire to know more about something, about a topic, an idea, an image, a TV program, a song, or a historical figure.

Research, like argument, is an essential part of many fields, including business, advertising, government, and, of course, academics. Businesses research markets and do feasibility studies. Advertisers research consumer behavior with focus groups and data mining. Governments conduct research in a variety of fields, from political science to the weather. Academics also conduct research on a variety of topics in many different fields, including the ones found in our case studies. The research skills you learn in college will be valuable to you in your professional life after college.

Like many aspects of arguing case studies, research involves making decisions and solving problems. You will need to tackle the problems of coming up with ideas, addressing the different issues and stakeholder needs, and finding sources to support your claims. As you research, you make decisions about what sources to use, what things to quote, and what types of evidence will convince your reader. Research lets you see and hear what others have thought—what solutions they've proposed and how your ideas or solutions for the case fit with theirs. It also adds to your credibility and gives your readers reasons to act on your recommendations.

Like writing, research is a recursive process, a cycle like the one below.

In the first chapter, we talked about writing and argumentation as parts of a conversation. This conversation metaphor applies here, too: Research is a part of that larger knowledge (academic) conversation, which helps you learn and also helps you locate your ideas within a larger dialogue of existing ideas and research. Developing successful strategies for locating and evaluating research sources is thus a key part of your development as a critical thinker and writer.

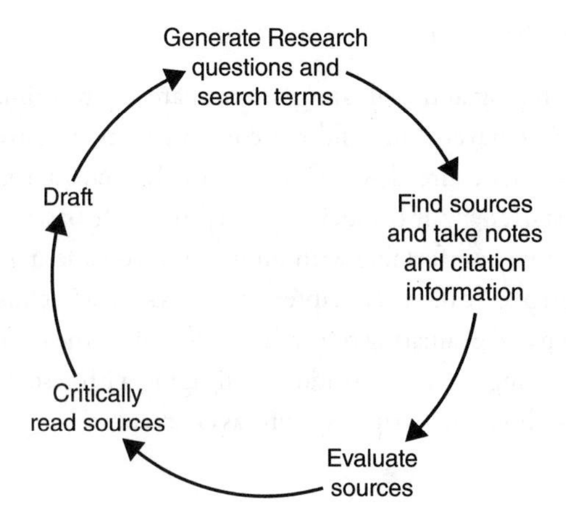

When writing arguments based on case studies, as this textbook asks you to do, research will help you better inform yourself on relevant case issues as well as on the types of actions you may end up recommending as part of your solution. Analyzing research sources, for instance, will help you critically think about the issues, understand what others have thought and proposed, and also build your own credibility as you craft your proposed solution to a case.

Research is part of the rhetorical shaping of the text. It is centered on both the reader and the writer.

For the reader it provides:	**For the writer it provides:**
Background information on issue	Expertise on topic
Supporting evidence for claim	Clarification of your position on issue
Counterarguments for claim	Credibility and authority

As writers, we want our message to be heard. How do we get our readers to be engaged with what we have to say? One way is by establishing our expertise, our authority, with credible and relevant information. Doing quality research allows you to build your expertise and create ethos (credibility) for your writing. It establishes you as someone worth listening to, as someone who is knowledgeable on the topic, or who has interesting ideas.

Critical Thinking and Research Preparation: Asking Questions When You Research

As you may have begun to realize, critical thinking is an integral part of every aspect of the argument writing and case studies process. This is true for research as well. Research plays a key role in the exploration part of the writing process. It is especially important when considering the different perspectives found in the case studies. You want to be asking critical questions at every stage of the research process.

Part of every investigative process is asking critical questions and making connections. Each new piece of information is connected to other pieces of existing information already recorded. Think of a giant web, a computer network, or a bunch of hyperlinks. There is a vast network of information available to you, both in print books and journal articles and in online sources. Your task is to tap into that network and use it to help you on a number of levels:

- Building knowledge: Increase your knowledge on a topic.
- Questioning knowledge: Explore multiple points of view on a topic or issue.
- Contextualizing within the broader field: Place your ideas within the wider discussion on your topic or issue.
- Supporting knowledge: Use what you've learned to support your ideas.

Research connects old information (general knowledge about the topic, or information others have already said about the topic) with new information (your claim, your perspective on the issue) for the reader. Successful research is a combination of preparation, persistence, and luck. Like other aspects of the writing process, the amount of planning and preparation distinguishes experienced writers from developing writers.

In the next part of this chapter, we will introduce these critical approaches for getting ready to do research:

- Time
- Preparation
- Formulating a research question
- Note taking
- Thinking critically about evidence
- Evaluating sources

Time

Like many other aspects of the writing process, research takes time. You might find that different stages of the research process might take different amounts of time. You might find you need time to do a lot of general reading on the issue or you might find searching the library's database takes up the most time. Remember to plan enough time to carefully and critically read the sources that you decide to use for your paper. Understanding your sources is just as important as finding them.

Preparation

Effective research strategies begin with preparation, and preparation for research, like for many other activities and skills, is partly mental and partly attitude. Before you start researching, ask yourself the following questions:

What interests me most about the case study?
What aspects of the issue do I feed the strongest about?
What is my purpose for doing research?
What is the purpose of my argument?
Is my purpose to inform or persuade?
What goals do I want to accomplish?
Who is my audience?
What questions would my readers ask?
What is the most effective way to reach my audience?
What types of information will convince my audience?

What does my audience already know about my topic?
What do I already know about my topic?
What claims have already been made about my topic?
What are the counterarguments I need to investigate?

As you research, you might also keep a research log. This can help you keep track of the sources you've found, where you found them, and what you still need to locate.

Another step in the preparation process is narrowing your focus and coming up with a research question(s). You don't necessarily have to have a research question before embarking on research for a paper. You do need to narrow your focus, however, and a research question can be helpful because it can lead you to your thesis and, thus, help focus your research process.

Ask Yourself

Use these questions to help you narrow your focus:

Use what you already know about the case topic (for example, climate change in the Arctic).
Use what you already know about the case issue (for example, village relocation options).
Use the information in the case scenario.
Do background reading on the case topic and use that information to decide on your approach to the case issue.
Consult with your instructor.

Formulating a Research Question

A research question is a specialized kind of question that helps focus and direct your research process. Research questions are usually open-ended.

Ask Yourself

Use these categories to consider what needs to be addressed in a research question:

The problem(s) raised by the case
Wider issues raised by the case
Possible solution(s) to the case

It's helpful to have already done some background reading on your topic before trying to come up with a research question. To generate a research question, you can use different techniques or sources of information such as free writing, class reading, class discussion, or lectures, or you can brainstorm ideas with peers.

Do	**Don't**
Explore different associations and relationships	Repeat only what has already been said
Ask "how" and "why" questions	Ask yes/no questions
Use aspects of the case that interest you	Use questions that are not debatable
Narrow the focus	Be too broad

Check Yourself

A good research question should be clear and focused. As you select a principal research question, ask yourself the following:

1. Is the research question interesting to you?
2. Is it researchable? Can you find enough sources to adequately answer the research question?
3. Does the scope of the research question line up with the scope of the paper?
4. Is the question too broad? too narrow?
5. Is it relevant to the case study?

Note Taking

Taking good notes will save you a lot of trouble and time later. Use your notes to keep track of (1) ideas and examples, (2) citation information, search histories, and keywords, and (3) quotes (be sure to know the citation information and page number for all quotes).

There are many different options for note taking. Some people keep all their information on 3 × 5 note cards, others use a double-entry format in a notebook, while others keep their notes on their computer or an app like Evernote. Figure out what option works best for you.

Keeping careful track of citation information will also help avoid any plagiarism problems caused by improper or incomplete citations. This is especially helpful if you are searching on the web. Keep track of the websites you visit. Write down, copy, or bookmark the URLs of the sites you've decided are reliable and that will be useful for your paper.

Always note where something came from in your notes. Don't underestimate the value of good note-taking skills. You don't want to be asking yourself, "Now where did I read that?" the night before the paper's due and waste time searching back through all of your sources for that one quotation.

To take good notes, do the following:

- Reflect critically about the source content.
- Reflect critically about the possible use of source(s) for evidence.
- Record content information accurately.
- Record bibliographic information accurately.
- Record page numbers for quotes and paraphrases.

Check Yourself

Notes should be helpful. Use these questions to help you evaluate your note-taking process:

How organized are they?
How effective are they?

Compare your note taking with the suggestions here. How did you do?

Thinking Critically About Evidence

The type and amount of evidence you use directly impacts your credibility. For your arguments to be believable, you need to support your ideas with credible evidence. Supporting ideas or positions in an argument with evidence is a cornerstone of academic writing and professional writing. Your long-term success both in and out of college will be greatly enhanced by your ability to develop successful research strategies.

What counts as evidence depends on your audience, your message, your purpose, and the type of paper you are writing. For evidence to be credible, it must come from sources where the information can be independently verified. The more credible your evidence is, the more credible you are, the more your reader will believe you, and the more likely your argument will succeed.

Types of evidence include the following:

Primary evidence: evidence you've collected yourself; systematic observations of a situation; surveys, interviews, or experiments
Personal experience: is experiential; tends to be personal and not systematic
Secondary evidence: comes from sources you've found in the library's databases

You can combine types of evidence in your paper. Keep in mind that some fields value different types of evidence over others. When determining what types of evidence to use, you need to consider the rhetorical situation (inform, describe, persuade), the situational context, the needs of your case stakeholder(s), and the needs of your audience.

Ask Yourself

Use these questions to help you identify the best type of evidence for your paper:

What types of evidence will best support my argument?
What types of evidence will be the most effective with my audience?
What kinds of data are preferred (statistics, facts, experimental results, personal experience, analogies, analyses)?
Which are more effective, primary or secondary sources?

After you've determined the types of evidence you are going to use, you need to decide how much evidence you will need to persuade your readers, and how you are going to present it in your paper. Even the best evidence won't help you if the reader doesn't understand how it support your claims.

Check Yourself

Which sources are the most credible?
Which sources will build ethos?
What did you decide, and why?

Evaluating Sources

We live in a digital age, and this is a mixed blessing. There is so much information available at a keystroke. There is interesting, thought-provoking, accurate information. There are also inaccurate, unsubstantiated rumors and disinformation. This glut of information requires all of us to be critical consumers of all the information we encounter.

Don't fall victim to what is called the *leveling effect*.[1] This happens because all the information on the Web is, for the most part, equally accessible, giving the

1. Burbules (1998) as cited in Miriam Metzger, "Making Sense of Credibility on the Web: Models for Evaluating Online Information and Recommendations for Future Research," *Journal of the American Society for Information Science and Technology* 58, no. 13 (2007): 2078–2091.

impression that the information is equally factual and the authors are equally credible. This impression can lead the internet user to unconsciously place all the information found on the internet on the same level. This, of course, is not the case.

Therefore, you need to apply critical habits of mind to evaluating your sources. Question your sources. Ask questions about each source you find, both those you find through the library databases (which may include non-scholarly sources) and those you find through the Web. It is crucial to evaluate any information you find, especially sources on the Web. Don't assume that just because it's out there, it's credible or relevant to your topic.

Ask Yourself

Use these questions as a guide to help verify the accuracy and reliability of information:

Does more than one source make the same claim?
Are the sources both scholarly?
Does more than one website on the same topic make the same claim?
Does each website list any references?
Is the site merely duplicating the original source?

As part of the critical thinking approach to doing research, evaluating sources should become automatic. This is important because no source is objective. All texts reflect the differing, sometimes contrasting perceptions, beliefs, perspectives, and underlying assumptions of their authors. As a reader, you need to be aware of these biases and how they might work to reinforce or undermine the credibility of the author.

You want to evaluate your sources from two perspectives: (1) Is the source credible? and (2) Is it relevant to your topic?

Evaluating for Credibility

Authority

1. Who is the author?
2. What are the author's credentials and affiliations?
3. Is it published by a reputable publisher?
4. Who sponsored the website? Are they reputable?

Currency

5. What is the date of the source?
6. Is the information current?

7. How recently has the website been updated?
8. Is the source the most current version or edition?

Accuracy

9. Is the information reliable?
10. Is the information free from errors?
11. Does the source contain a list of references?
12. Can this information be corroborated by other reliable sources?

Objectivity

13. What is the purpose of the information and website?
14. Who is the intended audience?
15. Is the information fact or opinion?
16. Is the information supported by evidence?
17. Does the information have a bias?
18. How many points of view are represented?
19. Is there a conflict of interest between the content of the information and the publisher of the website?
20. What is the relationship between the information and the sponsored (commercial) links on the website?

Coverage

21. How comprehensive is the information?
22. How in-depth is the information?
23. Is the information general or specific to the issue?
24. Is this a primary or secondary source?

Stability

25. How likely is it that your reader will be able to find the source on their own?
26. How long will the weblinks be active?
27. How long will the website be available?

Evaluating for Relevance

Is the content what you expected from the title or abstract?
Does the content relate to your topic?
Is this a key resource? Or does it just provide supplemental information?
Is it written by a major scholar on your topic?
Does it analyze the case issues you are researching?
Is it a general overview or an in-depth analysis?

Does the source provide you with ideas to use as a jumping-off point for your solution(s) to the case problem?
Does the source provide you with examples, evidence, or support for your ideas?
Does it provide counterarguments for your argument?

Table 5.1 provides a sample evaluation.
What do you notice about the differences between the two sources?

Table 5.1 Non-scholarly and Scholarly Sources: Citation Information

Non-scholarly Source	**Scholarly Source**
Citation information	Citation information
Carrington, D. (2016, December 1). Climate change will stir "unimaginable" refugee crisis, says military. *The Guardian*. Retrieved from https://www.theguardian.com/environment/2016/dec/01climate-change-trigger-unimaginable-refugee-crisis-senior-military	Marino, E. (2015). *Fierce climate, sacred ground*. Anchorage, AK: University of Alaska Press.
Authority	Authority
1. Daimien Carrington 2. Unknown 3. Yes. *The Guardian* newspaper is an award-winning British newspaper. 4. From the newspaper's website	1. Elizabeth Marino 2. Assistant Professor of Anthropology, Oregon State University-Cascades 3. Yes. University of Alaska Press is a respected academic press. 4. N/A (not applicable)
Currency	Currency
5. Dec. 1, 2016 6. It's two years old—perhaps a little out of date? 7. The website itself updates daily because it's a newspaper, but the information in this article has not been updated since 2016. 8. No	5. 2015 6. Fairly recent 7. N/A 8. Yes

(*Continued*)

Table 5.1 Non-scholarly and Scholarly Sources: Citation Information (*Continued*)

Non-scholarly Source	Scholarly Source
Accuracy	Accuracy
9. He uses terms like "senior military figures," "the generals," and names three different high-ranking military officials from the armed forces of three different countries: UK, US, Pakistan. Sources of information are the opinions of these military figures. They may be reliable in that they believe what they are saying, and perhaps there is military research to back them up, although no such research is cited in the article.	9. Yes, the book is based on the author's fieldwork and research in the Alaskan community of Shishmaref. It contains both primary and secondary sources, and supporting evidence.
10. Unknown	10. Yes, the information is error-free.
11. No list of references is given.	11. There is a 12-page list of references.
12. Unknown	12. The information can be corroborated with the references listed, other articles on the topics.
Objectivity	Objectivity
13. The purpose of newspaper is to inform the general public on issues both national and international.	13. The purpose is to analyze the effects of climate change on the community of Shishmaref, an Inupiaq community in Alaska.
14. General public	14. The book contains a lot of references but is written in order to be intelligible to a more general public. It would also interest other anthropologists, other scholars, and students.
15. It looks like it's just opinion.	15. The information is a combination of factual information, theoretical analysis, and first-hand interviews with community members.
16. No. The information is not supported by evidence.	16. Yes. The information is supported by a variety of evidence from both primary and secondary sources.

Table 5.1 Non-scholarly and Scholarly Sources: Citation Information (*Continued*)

Non-scholarly Source	Scholarly Source
Objectivity	Objectivity
17. Yes, everything is biased in some way. The underlying assumption here is that climate change is real and will have an impact on national security.	17. Yes, everything is biased in some way. Although ethnographies are supposed to represent the lived experience of the community, this book, like all texts, is shaped by the choices of the author. She foregrounds the complexity of the issues and the need to hear and respect indigenous people's voices and opinions on this issue.
18. No, only one point of view is represented.	18. Yes, different points of view are represented. She includes the views of the native people, other scholars, government organizations, as well as environmental and scientific perspectives.
19. Unknown	19. No
20. There are no longer any ads, but there are links to related stories at the bottom of the page.	20. N/A
Coverage	Coverage
21. It gives the opinions of three different military figures, but they all have the same opinion.	21. The book contains seven chapters. The chapters discuss theoretical frameworks, historical background, the background and history of Shishmaref's struggles with climate change, the typical responses of government agencies, the community's perspective on future actions and solutions.
22. It's not very in-depth. Some events are mentioned, like the Arab Spring or the Boko Haram uprisings, but no explanation or evidence is given for any links between these events and climate change.	22. The book is very detailed. It includes tables, figures, and illustrations and extensive references.

(*Continued*)

Table 5.1 Non-scholarly and Scholarly Sources: Citation Information (*Continued*)

Non-scholarly Source	Scholarly Source
Coverage	Coverage
23. The information is very general. It does provide a point of view not generally talked about in relation to climate change but it's not very detailed.	23. The information is specific to the topic.
24. Secondary source	24. Primary source
Stability	Stability
25. The article will probably continue to be available through a database like LexisNexis.	25. The book is available in the library, through interlibrary loan, or it can be purchased from a bookstore or online.
26. Unknown. Online newspaper cited older articles, but after a while the links are no longer active.	26. N/A
27. The website will be there as long as the newspaper is in business, but that does not mean the article itself will always be accessible.	27. N/A
Summary	Summary
While the author is listed, his qualifications to write the story are unknown. He relies heavily on the opinions of various mostly unnamed military experts. The experts he consulted all agree, so no dissenting opinion is given. The experts do not cite any verifiable facts or studies to back up their opinions. Instead, their opinions are taken are factual. Nor do they address the issue in any depth. There are no references given, so there is no way from the article itself to corroborate the information. The article is useful in that it raises the issue of a connection between climate change and military security, but it doesn't provide evidence for the claims made by the "experts." In order to include this information in a paper, more research would have to be done to independently corroborate the information in order to find out how factual the article actually is.	It is a well-written and well-documented book. It is one of the few books available that documents what is currently happening in Alaskan villages that are struggling with the effects of climate change. She discusses the challenges the community faces dealings with government agencies as well as the ongoing effects of climate change on the village itself. She also discusses the community's struggles to maintain their heritage, language, and sense of identity in the face of their ongoing effort to keep their community safe and intact. The book provides a lot of important background information on the larger issue of climate change in Alaska as well as background on this history of this specific community.

Types of Sources

There are two basic types of sources: credible and noncredible. The information in credible sources can be independently verified. When you are writing, you always want to use credible sources. To check to see if a source is credible, ask the following questions:

- Who wrote it?
- What are their qualifications?
- Was it published by a reputable source?
- How timely is the information?
- Who is the intended audience?
- What was the purpose (to inform or to entertain)?
- Who sponsored the publication or website?

Credible sources can further be subdivided into scholarly and non-scholarly (Table 5.2).

A source is considered scholarly if:

It's written by an expert in a field.
Its audience is other scholars.
It includes citations.
It has been reviewed by a panel of experts—usually the author's peers—before being published.

Scholarly sources are considered the most credible type of source to use in college writing. It's likely that your instructor will ask you to use some or only scholarly sources as part of your paper assignment.

Non-scholarly sources can be credible or noncredible depending on factors such as the author, publisher, currency, relevancy, bias, and sponsorship. Websites, like non-scholarly sources, may be credible or noncredible depending on who is sponsoring them, their purpose, who writes and double-checks the information on them, how current they are, and how stable they are.

Table 5.2. Non-scholarly and Scholarly Sources: Examples

Scholarly	Non-scholarly
Academic journal articles	Newspapers
Books published by an academic press	Magazines
Conference proceedings	Reviews
	Websites
	Trade publications

Whether you should use scholarly or non-scholarly sources depends on the following:

Your purpose
Your audience
Your assignment
Your assignment's requirements
Your topic

For some assignments, you may want to combine scholarly and non-scholarly sources. For example, in writing about Case 5, you might use webpages set up by the different communities undergoing climate change in the Pacific or Alaska, the webpages of different organizations set up to help communities undergoing climate change, scholarly articles or books, and policy initiatives compiled by government agencies.

Primary and Secondary Sources

Another way to classify sources is to categorize them as primary or secondary. Be aware that different fields may define these two categories slightly differently. A primary source (Table 5.3) is one that records a first-hand experience of an event, object, work of art, or a scientific study, while a secondary source (Table 5.4) comments on or interprets a primary source. Media like film and the internet can be used as sources in both the humanities and the sciences.

Table 5.3. Primary Sources

Humanities	Sciences	Other
Diaries, journals, letters	Research study results	Internet communication: email, blogs, Twitter, chatrooms, etc.
Government records	Scientific experiment results	Audio and video recordings, DVDs
Newspaper and magazine accounts	Clinical trial results	Film, TV, and radio shows
Speeches	Conference proceedings	Documentaries
Interviews	Technical reports	
Oral histories	Fieldwork	
Literary arts: songs, fiction, drama, poetry	Surveys	
Visual arts: painting, photography, sculpture	Statistical data	

Table 5.4. Secondary Sources

Humanities	Sciences	Other
Biographies Histories Literary criticism Book, art, and theater reviews Editorials	Reviews of research Commentary on and analysis of research results	Reference resources: dictionaries, encyclopedias Textbooks Abstracts

You might use a primary source like a survey or a poll if you want to find out what a group of people think on an issue, or you might use a primary source like an interview to get the perspective of an individual. You might use secondary sources like a newspaper or magazine to establish an overview of an event or to see how an event was represented in the media. You might use a secondary source like a journal article to get at the questions being asked about your issue or to find in-depth knowledge on your topic. You might find it appropriate to use both primary and secondary sources in your paper, depending on the rhetorical context and your assignment.

What Type of Source Is It?

With more and more resources for research papers available digitally, how do you tell what type of source you have? What kind of source it is can be blurred, especially if you are accessing a digital version rather than a traditional print version of the same source—for example, an online version of the newspaper instead of the print version.

It is important to be able to identify the source type because that will affect how you document it in your in-text citations and your list of references or works cited. Many newspapers, magazines, books, and scholarly journal articles can now be accessed online. However, you need to cite them as if they were print sources and not as if they were websites. (Since this varies by documentation style, consult your handbook for citation guidelines.)

Check Yourself

Use these questions and examples to help you decide what type of source you have:

If you found it on *The New York Times* or *The Washington Post* website, then it's a newspaper article.

(Continued)

If you found it on the *Smithsonian*, *Scientific American*, or *National Geographic* website, then it's is a magazine article.
It you found it on a government website, then it's probably a report.
What designation does the database give the source (book, academic journal, periodical, or report)?
What clues does the citation information give? If the citation gives a place and publisher, then it's a book. If the citation gives a volume number, an issue number, and page numbers, then it's a journal article.

How did you do? If you are uncertain about what type of source you have, always ask. Your instructor or a librarian will be happy to help you.

Check Yourself

Avoid these pitfalls:

Don't cite (quote or paraphrase) an abstract, especially a dissertation abstract, as if it were the full text. Many dissertations are not available as full-text files; they usually have to be obtained through interlibrary loan (although some are now available online). Your instructor will know that you didn't read the actual dissertation.
The same thing goes for a book review. Don't cite (quote or paraphrase) a book review as if it were the book. Again, your instructor will be able to tell.

Using book reviews and abstracts as a source instead of the actual book or dissertation will undermine your credibility as a writer since it looks like you were cutting corners or waited until the last minute to write your paper. Again: If you are uncertain about the type of source, ask your instructor or a librarian.

Search Strategies

Search strategies influence your preparation. Answers to your preparation questions as well as your research questions will all influence which search strategies you might use.

Before you begin your actual search, it's helpful to prepare a list of key words and subject terms. These are terms you will use to do searches in the library's databases (or Google Scholar). Use a thesaurus if you need help coming up with synonyms for your key terms. Look for repetition of terms, ideas, and names to help you zero in on fundamental texts written about that case issue or problem. As you search, you can add to your list by checking the subject terms of the articles and books you find.

Ask Yourself

Use these questions to help you plan your research strategies:

What am I looking for?
What types of information do I need (background information, new ideas, support for claim)?
Where can I find credible sources that answer my research question?
Which types of sources will build my credibility as a writer?

You want to find the sources that are the most relevant to your claim, and the most convincing to your readers. Be a curious searcher. Use multiple resources to find your information, such as the library, the library databases, primary sources, and the Web. Use multiple types of sources: books, journals, newspapers, and magazines.

As you search, don't settle for the first five hits you find in the library's database or from a Web search engine like Google. Don't use sources that were easy to find but don't really fit into your argument. This strategy will just confuse or frustrate your reader. It will lower your credibility, weaken your argument, and reduce your ability to convince your reader (and probably lower your grade). Your ideas and your sources should fit together like puzzle pieces, not like blocks strewn randomly on a pathway.

When you research, follow the example of experienced researchers. Tap into what is called the "citation network." When you find the ideal source, the one that fits your argument perfectly, use its bibliography, works cited, or reference page to identify other sources on the same topic. The "cited by" and "related articles" links in Google Scholar can also lead you to similar sources. Experienced researchers also rely on key names (names that are repeated in different sources) and key terms to help them find similar sources on the same topic. Your instructor or the reference librarian can help you to identify key scholars in a field. Remember to search for sources on counterarguments as well as sources that support your claim.

Check Yourself

Use this activity to help you evaluate your search strategies:

List your search strategies. How organized are they? How effective are they?
Compare your search strategies with the suggestions listed here.
Come up with five ways to improve your search strategies.

Finding Sources

After you've done your preparation, after you've decided on what information you need, after you've formulated a research question, after you have your key words and search terms ready . . . then it's time to go out and find the actual sources.

For academic writing, you should start your search with the university library, which is your best resource for scholarly sources. Check the library catalogue. Once you've found the call number, go to the shelf where your book is and browse the books next to it. You many find hidden or unexpected treasures that way.

In addition, most university libraries subscribe to a number of different of databases that index articles, books, newspapers, book chapters, and other types of sources for different fields of study. All this information is at your fingertips. Some common databases are:

Academic Search Complete—general purpose
ERIC—education
MLA—humanities
Web of Science—natural sciences and social sciences

Using these databases you can select languages, search parameters, whether a source is peer-reviewed, full-text PDFs, a date range, and more to help you narrow your search. Many of these database use Boolean search methods, so read the help guide before you get started.

What if your instructor tells you that you can't use Web sources? Does that mean you can't use the library's databases? No. Although people generally use the terms "internet" and "the Web" interchangeably, the two terms do not actually mean the same thing. The internet is the links formed between computers. Your computer must be connected to the internet through a modem, Wi-Fi, LAN, Ethernet, or other type of network before you can access the content of the Web. The Web, on the other hand, is the content you access through search engines like Google or Yahoo. So when your instructor says not to use the Web for your research, you can still use the library's databases that you can access over the internet, but you shouldn't use the sources available through a commercial search engine like Google or Yahoo. One reason your instructor might limit your use of the Web for sources is that anything goes on the Web. Scholarly sites, reliable sites, heavily biased sites, commercial sites, and fake information sites all exist side by side. Remember that you need to critically evaluate any information obtained from websites.

The Worldwide Web (WWW)

The Web is a ubiquitous and an extremely convenient source of information. However, for both everyday use and academic use, it should be approached with caution. There are some solid academic resources available on the Web—for example, online journals and sites set up by governments, by universities, and by scholarly or scientific organizations. There may be websites that have credible information on your issue, and it may be appropriate for you to use those. Use the URL as a guide: Use ones that end in .gov, .edu, or .org and avoid the ones that end in .com. However, don't rely solely on a commercial search engine like Google or Yahoo to do your research. Always get your information from a variety of places, not just the Web.

When you do end up using the Web to search for information on your case issue, use your critical thinking skills to evaluate the information you find. Information in the sources that you find through the library and the library's databases has already been reviewed and been checked for reliability and accuracy by other experts. However, sources on the Web have not gone through that review process. Using the Web as a way to find information responsibly means extra work, since you are the one responsible for checking the reliability and accuracy of the information.

Furthermore, information on the Web is often duplicated; it seems to be cut-and-pasted into another site without referencing the original source. For example, the first four hits on the topic of "Druze women kidnapped in the Syria" contain the exact same wording to their story. You think you are going to learn something new when you click on the next link, but in reality it turns out to be exactly the same thing you just read. You can end up wasting time checking out a bunch of different sites when the information is essentially the same.

In Figure 5.1, all of the news links (a. duplicated sources) have repeated the same source—the story from the AFP, a French news agency (b. original source). Other sites often cut and paste from Wikipedia. So you are not really accessing new information and can face potential plagiarism issues because you don't know the original source of the information.

One of the biggest drawbacks to using the Web to find information is that much of what is on the Web is geared to a three-second attention span. This is fine when you are looking for information on your favorite TV show, but it's a disadvantage when you are writing an argument paper. Information on websites often lacks depth and usually only touches the surface of the issue. Such a small amount of information, no matter how accurate, will not give you enough to use to argue your points with. The limitations of the information will be very apparent to your readers, which in turn will limit your ability to be persuasive and

a. Duplicated Sources

Druze women, children kidnapped by IS in Syria's Sweida
The Islamic State group kidnapped dozens of Druze women and children when it attacked their village last week in Syria's Sweida, residents of the southern province and a monitor said Monday.
Y https://www.yahoo.com/news/druze-women-children-kidnapped... More results

14 Druze women kidnapped in latest ISIS atrocity in Syria ...
Druze in Israel march in solidarity after massacre in Syria
JP https://www.jpost.com/Middle-East/14-Druze-women-kidnapped-in-l...

Daesh kidnapped Druze women, children in Sweida | GulfNews.com
Beirut - Daesh kidnapped dozens of Druze women and children when it attacked their village last week in Syria's Sweida, residents of the southern province and a monitor said Monday.
https://gulfnews.com/news/mena/syria/daesh-kidnapped-druze-wom...

Druze women and children kidnapped by ISIS in Syria
ISIS kidnapped dozens of Druze women and children when it attacked their village last week in Syria's Sweida, it has been revealed.
m dailymail.co.uk/news/article-6006791/Druze-women-children...

b. Original Source

Beirut (AFP) - The Islamic State group kidnapped dozens of Druze women and children when it attacked their village last week in Syria's Sweida, residents of the southern province and a monitor said Monday.

Sweida, which is mainly government-held and populated with members of Syria's Druze minority, had been largely insulated from the conflict raging in the rest of the country since 2011.

But on Wednesday, a string of suicide blasts and shootings claimed by IS left more than 250 people dead in the provincial capital and nearby villages, most of them civilians.

During the attack IS jihadists also abducted several dozen women and children from one village, according to the Syrian Observatory for Human Rights and Sweida residents.

FIGURE 5.1. Duplicated Source Example

convincing. It's simply too easy to find counterarguments when the information is thin and lacks depth. Remember, there is a difference between doing research and just Googling a topic.

Google Scholar

Google Scholar is a specialized search engine that indexes scholarly texts from a variety of sources. It functions similarly to the databases available through your university library. Like the library databases, it also contains full-text links to journal articles. It has other useful features, like citation information and links to related articles and "cited by" pieces (Figure 5.2).

Google Scholar has its limitations and should not be used as a substitute for your library resources. As always, you should carefully evaluate any sources you find using it. Limitations include the following:

There is no way to limit searches by subject terms, titles, or synonyms.
No notice is given when materials are updated.
Many older articles are present (which can be both good and bad).
No criteria are given for what is considered "scholarly."
Results vary in quality.

Wikipedia

Wikipedia is incredibly convenient. It usually comes up first in a Web search on most topics. Should you use Wikipedia for an academic paper? Is Wikipedia a credible source? Unfortunately, it's not. There are two issues you need to consider when deciding whether to consult Wikipedia.

First, unlike other encyclopedias, Wikipedia is not compiled by experts. Since the editing process is communally based and anonymous, no one takes responsibility for the accuracy of the information. As a result the articles are missing information, often contain false information, and are subject to vandalism (the deliberate practice of inserting humorous, nonsensical, false, or offensive material into a Wikipedia article).

Migration or forced displacement?: the complex choices of **climate change** and disaster migrants in **Shishmaref**, Alaska and Nanumea, Tuvalu
E Marino, H Lazrus - Human Organization, 2015 - sfaajournals.net
This article compares migration options in **Shishmaref**, Alaska and Nanumea, Tuvalu as responses to increasing risk of disaster. In both communities, increasing hazards and risks are associated with **climate change**—making the communities some of the first to be ...
☆ 99 Cited by 19 Related articles All 4 versions

FIGURE 5.2. Sample Google Scholar entry

Second, Wikipedia articles are not free from bias. The point of view tends to favor the perspectives and beliefs of its contributors, who are predominantly young, male, Western, English-speaking, computer literate, and affluent.

That being said, Wikipedia can be useful in two ways. If you keep in mind its limitations, it can provide you with some general background and a basic overview of your topic. If the article is properly documented, there should be a bibliography at the end, which you can use to help you get started in your own search. If the article has a warning (Figure 5.3) or there's no bibliography, don't use the article.

Documenting Sources

Documentation is an integral part of writing research papers. It also should be an integrated part of the writing process—thinking about what sources to use, keeping track of citation information in the note-taking process, adding in-text citations, and compiling a works cited or reference list for every draft that you write. Using sources is part of how both students and scholars participate in the larger academic conversation.

Documentation is vital since it helps you and the reader keep track of whose ideas are being shared and where you found them. Essentially, a documentation style is just an agreed-on method of communicating basic information about sources.

Compiling a successful reference or works cited page will be easier if you remember to take good notes and keep track of your source citations as you research, including page numbers for quotes and paraphrases.

Proper documentation serves the interests of both the reader and the writer (Table 5.5).

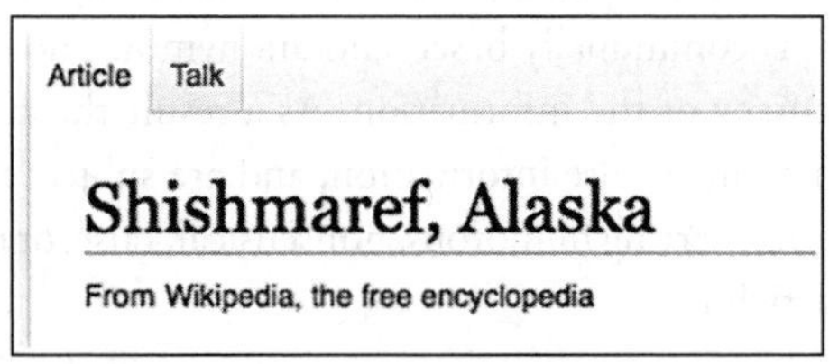

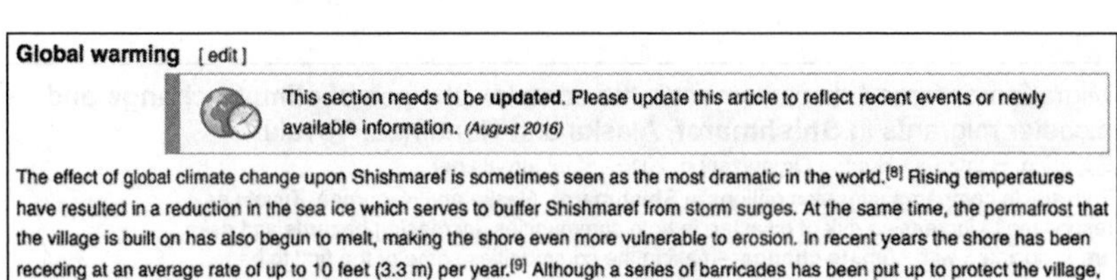
Global warming [edit]

This section needs to be **updated**. Please update this article to reflect recent events or newly available information. *(August 2016)*

The effect of global climate change upon Shishmaref is sometimes seen as the most dramatic in the world.[8] Rising temperatures have resulted in a reduction in the sea ice which serves to buffer Shishmaref from storm surges. At the same time, the permafrost that the village is built on has also begun to melt, making the shore even more vulnerable to erosion. In recent years the shore has been receding at an average rate of up to 10 feet (3.3 m) per year.[9] Although a series of barricades has been put up to protect the village, the shore has continued to erode at an alarming rate. The town's homes, water system and infrastructure are being undermined.[10][11][12][13][14] Currently, Shishmaref has obtained funds to construct seawalls that protect some of the shoreline.

FIGURE 5.3. Sample Wikipedia entry with a warning that the content needs to be updated.

Table 5.5. Documentation for Readers and Writers

The Reader	The Writer
Shows your reader you have done valid research	Allows the writer to give credit to the original author
Shows your reader you can support your argument with credible evidence	Allows the writer to create a strong ethos (credibility)
Provides your reader with research on the topic	Allows the writer to become an "expert" on the topic
Provides your reader with a means to double-check your interpretations	Helps the writer to avoid plagiarism

Documentation consists of two parts: (1) documenting sources in the actual text of your paper (in-text citations) and (2) compiling a list of the sources you used in your paper at the end of your paper. This list has different names, depending on the style (works cited, references, or bibliography).

All documentation styles ask for the same basic information:

1. Who wrote or edited it?
2. When was it written?
3. What is the title?
4. Who published it?
5. Where can it be found?

However, the information is arranged differently based on the needs of the field. Your job as a student is to be flexible. Learn how to read and apply the models for each style found in your handbook, guides from your university's writing center, or online guides like OWL Purdue. Online citation generators can be helpful, but be careful not to rely too heavily on them since they are not always correct—always double-check them against your handbook. Which style you are asked to use is usually specified in the assignment guidelines. If not, check to see if your instructor has a preference.

There are several commonly used styles of documentation (Table 5.6).

Many professional organizations, especially in the sciences and social sciences, have their own individual style.

Annotated Bibliography

An annotated bibliography is a special kind of bibliography that can have several different purposes.

Table 5.6. Common Documentation Styles

Style	Organization	Field(s)
MLA	Modern Language Association	Humanities
APA	American Psychological Association	Social sciences Behavioral sciences Education
CMS	Chicago Manual of Style	History, business, fine art
CSE	Council of Science Editors	Biology, sciences
IEEE	Institute of Electrical and Electronics Engineers	Engineering
AMS	American Mathematical Society	Mathematics
AIP	American Institute of Physics	Physics

Researchers might use it to:

Review the current literature on a topic
Provide examples of sources available on a topic
Explore a subject further
Evaluate research already done on a topic
Allow other readers to decide if a source would be useful to them

Students might use it to:

Show their progress on a research project
Illustrate the quality of research on their topic
Think critically about the content of their sources
Provide evidence that they have read and understood their sources
Evaluate research already done on a topic
Allow other readers to decide if a source would be useful to them

An annotated bibliography has two components: the citation information and a short summary or annotation (50–150 words) of each source. Like other lists of references, it is alphabetized. Often as part of the summary of the source, you may be asked to include a statement that evaluates each source for its usefulness to your paper and its contribution to your argument.

Think of the annotation as a summary. Things you can include in the annotation are as follows:

- Thesis or main claim of source
- Qualification(s) of the author(s)

- Purpose
- Audience
- Bias, point of view, or stance of the author on the topic
- Findings, results, and conclusion

Ask Yourself

Use these questions to help you evaluate the source's usefulness to your project:

What is your impression of the source?
Did it answer your research question?
How is it useful to you?
How does it compare with other sources you found?
How will it fit into your research paper?
How does it contribute to your argument?
Has it changed your thinking on the topic?

APA-Style Annotated Bibliography Example

Marino, E. (2015). *Fierce climate, sacred ground.* Fairbanks, AK: University of Alaska Press.

This book is an anthropological study of the effect of climate change on Native Alaskan villages. The book presents the case of Shishmaref, a village facing erosion and other problems due to rising sea levels, warmer temperatures, melting permafrost, shorter hunting seasons, and fiercer storms. Different chapters detail cultural issues, the difficulties dealing with government agencies, and the community's struggle to find a solution that will keep them together as a community and as a people. The book will be very useful for my paper because it gives a lot of detail on the many different issues faced by a real community struggling to relocate because of climate change. I will be able to use the examples from the book as part of my discussion.

MLA-Style Annotated Bibliography Example

Crane, Cody. "Climate Refugees." *Science World* 16–30 April. 2012:22–25. Print.

The article gives a brief overview of the connection between climate events such as drought, floods, typhoons, rising sea levels, and the displacement of people. These people are being called *climate refugees* and face many problems since they do not have the status of traditional refugees. The article is helpful in giving an overview of the problems people who are forced to migrate because of climate change face. It raises issues that I could include in my paper with more research.

Integrating Sources

While this section has focused on technical aspects of finding and using other sources, Chapter 7 will focus in detail on perhaps the most exciting part of engaging with other sources: integrating them into your ideas and writing during the writing process.

CHAPTER SUMMARY

This chapter has addressed many aspects of finding and evaluating sources, as well as technical aspects of reading and documenting them. This includes ways to identify, evaluate, and understand research sources, including identifying whether they are primary or secondary sources, evaluating whether they are credible academic sources, reading them for relevant information, and documenting and representing sources in different styles or in annotated bibliographies.

6 THE WRITING–THINKING PROCESS

ENGAGING WITH YOUR WRITING TASK

How do you know what a writing task is asking you to do? What do you when you begin to write? How do you make your writing better as you work through an assignment? How do you get and give good feedback in the process?

Learning objectives in this chapter

- Understand writing as a writing–thinking process
- Understand academic writing as a process
- Engage with and decipher a writing task
- Identify steps in the process, including idea generation, reading and research, drafting, organizing, collaborating, and rewriting
- Articulate the value of engaging with peers through collaboration and peer review

Key concepts addressed in this chapter

- The writing–thinking process
- Rhetorical goals
- Rhetorical moves
- Rhetorical appeals
- Peer review

Introduction

You have probably heard the phrase "the writing process" to describe the steps you take as you complete a piece of writing. A more apt way to put this is the *writing–thinking* process, since the process of writing records and stimulates thought. This is why many writers end up with their best ideas in the conclusions of their first or second drafts. The best thinking and writing often comes after many steps of the process. Though it takes time, that means that if we take more steps on a draft, we improve it.

On this note, it is good to remember that much of what we read came after a long process of thinking and writing. In published writing, we see the end result, not all the messy and discarded writing that helped along the way. In an interview with the *Paris Review*, the famous writer Maya Angelou said that during her writing process, she can usually use about two and a half or three of every nine pages she writes. The rest is not worth keeping. "That's the cruelest time, you know," she said, "to really admit that [the writing] doesn't work." Yet that is a crucial part of the writing–thinking process.

Of course, on some level, you already know this from both academic writing and the writing you do for other purposes. You have probably deleted a text message (or wished you could) and perhaps have completely rewritten a school paper. Academic writing is more extensive than many other types of writing: Good academic writing usually means good *rewriting*. The good news is that a multistep process is expected for academic writing—it is not meant to be successful in a first draft. Academic writing requires many steps of thinking, reading, writing, and revising like the ones we describe in this chapter.

The Writing–Thinking Process

Academic Writing as a Process

Academic writing is not all uniform, but we can think of it broadly as the written language often used in college and university settings by students and professors, and in written articles and books. Generally speaking, academic writing is devoted to demonstrating and growing knowledge within and across academic fields, by either developing new ideas or developing new ways of seeing and connecting existing ideas. Like other types of writing, academic writing tends to follow specific formats that correspond to the values of an academic field or academic writing more generally, and these influence the steps in the writing process. For instance, an academic research article in psychology usually has a clearly delineated methods section, because an expectation of the field is that a psychological study will have a valid methodology, with careful attention to study design and participants. Furthermore, researchers may want to replicate the study and so will need to know the steps that were taken. This expectation therefore affects the writing process, because the writer needs to think about how to choose and articulate clear methods during the reading and researching steps, the drafting and organizing steps, and the peer review and rewriting steps.

Along with delineating a credible approach, academic writing is expected to consider other writers' ideas and feedback. As we mentioned earlier, knowledge creation, knowledge building, and knowledge dissemination are all key values of academic writing. This means engaging in a writing–thinking process that appropriately responds to a particular writing task (a specific prompt, genre, purpose, assignment, etc.) and engages with peer feedback. This chapter addresses these two parts of the process—engaging with the writing task and engaging with peer feedback. Academic writing involves a recursive, or continual, process that moves back and forth across different steps of reading, writing, and revising.

One way to think about this recursive process is as a continuous decision-making process involving both big decisions (e.g., what is the contribution that I want to make?) and smaller decisions (e.g., what should this paragraph and sentence emphasize?). As you work through each writing assignment, consider the assignment expectations, your audience, and your purpose as you make those decisions, so that both the big and small choices you make cohere, or fit together.

Engaging with Your Writing Task

The following sections provide an overview of different components of the writing process, several of which are discussed in more detail in other chapters. Traditionally, the writing process has been broken down into seven components: prewriting, reading and research, drafting and organizing, collaborating, rewriting, copy-editing, and publishing. Again, these do not follow one by one in a linear fashion; rather, they overlap and repeat in something of a spiral.

Prewriting

Prewriting includes understanding the assignment, planning and goal setting, and idea generation.

Understanding the Assignment

Most writing assignments in your college classes begin with a writing description or prompt that includes a set of requirements and parameters. As you pay careful attention to the assignment description, consider why the instructor assigned this writing task:

> What kinds of knowledge and skills do you need to convey?
> What kinds of reading and research will you need to do, and when?
> What do you *not* need to do in this assignment?
> For whom are you writing?
> (Related to all of these) What kinds of questions do you need to ask?

For example, as you think about an imagined audience (beyond your instructor), you might ask about whether you are writing for an audience familiar with what you are writing about or not. If you are writing for a general, non–discipline-specific audience who is unfamiliar with your topic, you will probably need to define specialized terms and offer context for sources you cite (see Chapter 5 for more about contextualizing sources). But if it is for more of a discipline-specific audience, you may need to provide more specific and technical details, and fewer general definitions and contextual details. Ask questions so that you can be sure you understand what you are expected to do.

Planning and Goal Setting

One thing that often distinguishes experienced writers from novice writers is planning and goal setting. While many less experienced writers begin with a topic or thesis in mind, many more experienced writers begin with more detailed, rhetorical goals. Along these lines, we recommend that you consider two kinds of goals: (1) *rhetorical goals*, including the purpose, audience, genre, and writer's stance, and (2) *practical goals*, including timetables for planning and organizing, researching, drafting, getting feedback, and revising.

Ask Yourself

Rhetorical Goals

1. Purpose
   My purpose for this assignment is ___________
   To fulfill my purpose, I need to do ___________
2. Audience
   An appropriate audience to imagine is _______________
   My audience will need to know _____________
   My audience already knows _________________
3. The perspective from which I am writing is _______________
4. Research
   The aspects of the case I will need to research are_______________
   I need to know more about______________
   With this assignment, I hope to accomplish_______________

Idea Generation

The case scenarios give you a starting point for topics and argument positions, and assignments often lay out several parameters, so your challenge is to come up with creative ideas that also work within those parameters. In the writing you do in response to the case studies in this book, you don't have to come up with a topic, but you still need to come up with your own solution to the case's problem, the reasons for your solution, how to represent multiple perspectives, and how to connect all of these considerations in a clear way.

There are several strategies for generating ideas, and you are probably familiar with many of them. These include brainstorming, mind maps (spider graphs, association maps), free writing, and asking questions. Discussion is an excellent tool for figuring out what is interesting and confusing about a given issue or argument. Discussing the cases with your peers will help, and you can also consider calling up or texting a friend or family member to tell them about a case and asking them what they think. Another strategy is jotting down ideas and questions when they come to you, such as in your notebook, phone, or elsewhere. Many of these should come up as you read the cases and related research. Try noting questions and comments in the margins of your reading so that you already have a starting place for your later drafting.

Reading and Research

To be a credible writer, you need to know about relevant issues and perspectives. In the assignments in this book, this means knowing about key details and concerns in a given case, the stakeholders' positions, and the needs of your audience. Since no one can know everything, part of the process is researching and learning what you need to know and what you can leave out. Approaches to research are discussed in Chapter 5.

Drafting and Organizing

Many writers find a blank screen or piece of paper intimidating. How to start? The good news is that you've already begun the writing–thinking process by the time you begin to draft your paper, by going over the assignment, generating ideas, reading, and researching. For the assignments in this book, by the time you begin drafting your paper, you've gone over the assignment description and you've read the case, started collecting sources, and made notes. You've done collaborative work in class—discussing the case, bouncing ideas off of your peers, identifying the positions of different stakeholders, discussing the wider issues. These have all been laying the groundwork for writing your paper.

Using Rhetorical Moves

Some students find it helpful to write out their ideas in no particular order, and then go back and organize them. Other writers prefer to outline and organize their paper as they are drafting. Either way, consider the following introductory and development moves as you decide what to include and how to organize your ideas and evidence, whether that begins before or during your drafting. Research shows that these moves are common in advanced academic writing.

The first kind of moves are *introductory moves*. These were identified by John Swales, who saw that in academic writing across disciplines, there were three rhetorical moves that characterized the introductions to academic research articles. These three rhetorical moves help "create a research space" by moving the reader from a more general topic to the specific contribution that the writer will make:[1]

> Introductory move 1 "establishes a territory" by identifying existing research or views on a topic.
> Introductory move 2 identifies a gap or "niche" by showing a remaining question or problem in existing research of views.
> Introductory move 3 "occupies the niche" by suggesting how the writing will address said gap.

For instance, the following sample passage includes Swales's three introductory moves. This passage comes from a report written by a final-year undergraduate in economics.[2] The three introductory moves are labeled as they begin.

> [**Introductory move 1**] The business of insurance has long been established. In ancient times, insurance existed for life, fire, and marine. The need for health insurance came after the introduction of machine processes and factory technology in England. Dramatic types of industrial accidents coupled with a better system of communication to spread the knowledge of these events spurred the general public's desire for health insurance. [**Introductory move 2**] Modern-day health insurance institutions have taken on many forms. While other countries have compulsory national health insurance, the United States relies mostly on the private provision of health insurance. [**Introductory move 3**] This research paper will describe the economic reasons for the structure of the U.S. health insurance system.

Not all of your writing will necessarily have explicit introductory moves, but as you draft your introductory material for assignments in this book, try to make sure you introduce (1) the larger topic in a given case study, (2) the problem or lingering question in the case itself, and (3) the solution you propose.

---

1. John Swales, *Genre Analysis: English in Academic and Research Settings* (Cambridge: Cambridge University Press, 1990).

2. This paper is available for analysis along with hundreds of other A-graded, upper-level papers in the Michigan Corpus of Upper-Level Papers (MICUSP): http://micusp.elicorpora.info/search/view/?pid=ECO.G0.07.1.

The second kind of moves are *development moves*, or rhetorical moves that aid with the development of ideas. These four development moves will help you organize your evidence and analysis in a logical way:

Development move 1 introduces a particular idea or research trend that will be addressed in the subsequent paragraphs or section.
Development move 2 offers examples or evidence.
Development move 3 offers an interpretation of said evidence.
Development move 4 links the examples or analysis back to the original, broader topic of the paragraph or section.

These development moves progress from more general to more specific and back to more general, and a given paragraph or section may move back and forth between moves 2 and 3 before moving to the link in move 4.

For example, the following paragraph is the first body paragraph after the introduction in the student paper quoted earlier. The four development moves are labeled as they begin.

> [**Development move 1**] Before 1920, U.S. citizens' main financial concern of medical treatment was the lack of income from missing work, rather than the ability to pay hospital bills. [**Development move 2**] In 1919, the State of Illinois Commission Study estimated that lost wages for individual wage earners were approximately four times as great as the cost of medical care. [**Development move 3**] One reason for the low cost of medical care is that the North American population was widespread, and most people had the living space to treat ill family members at home. Instead of health insurance, most purchased sickness insurance. It was similar to today's disability insurance, since it was a supplemental income while the insured was unable to work. [**Development move 4**] Proposals for compulsory nationalized health insurance in the U.S. were unpopular because there was a lack of public demand for medical insurance coverage.

Audience Awareness: Engaging with Readers and Other Writers

Engaging with readers and other writers includes providing clear cohesion and organization through moves like those we have just discussed. It also includes clearly integrating and analyzing evidence. These aspects are especially important in academic writing because academic writing is most often approached as a conversation involving many different perspectives and sources. Thus, engaging with readers and other writers is addressed in detail in Chapter 7.

Collaborating

Discussion and peer review are important ways to generate ideas and to get feedback as you prewrite, draft, organize, and rewrite. Collaboration is therefore a part of many steps in the writing–thinking process, so we devote the second half of the chapter to addressing it. You will read more about it later.

Rewriting

Good writing is good revising, because when we first write, we are still working through our ideas. Rewriting involves changing and letting go of a lot of our writing—even well-written passages—because as our ideas develop, our writing must change, too. Here are some considerations as you revise; you will also use these as you analyze others' arguments in Chapter 8.

As you rewrite, consider both the context of your writing (the assignment parameters, your audience) and your own rhetoric (your word- and sentence-level choices). This will help you refine your writing to match your goals and purpose, your audience, and the requirements of the assignment. Of course, as Maya Angelou stated, this may mean getting rid of whole pages of your draft that are well written but just not relevant.

Check how well your writing matches the context of the writing task. **Assignment-based revision** focuses on the parameters of an assignment task. As you revise your writing, consider:

- What is the scope of the ideas I propose—in other words, to whom and to what do they apply? Does this scope seem reasonable? Too big or too small?
- If my audience is unfamiliar with the case, how well have I described the case? Where am I too broad or too specific?
- Overall, how well does my writing fit the assignment?

Idea-based revision, on the other hand, focuses on the details and evidence of the specific ideas you are developing. In many ways, this dimension is similar to how you will analyze cases, as addressed in Chapter 2: You look closely at details in order to determine who is involved and why, and to what end. Information analysis answers questions like the following:

- What is my main argument or contribution? Where do I state it, and how often do I link ideas back to it?
- What are the secondary arguments made to support the primary argument?

- What premises are used (or, what is the basis for any given claim), and are they reasonable? Why or why not?
- What warrants are used (or, what is the link or bridge between evidence and an argument made), and are they reasonable?
- What evidence or examples are used? Are they from credible sources? Are examples reasonable? Why or why not?
- What reasoning is used with the evidence? In other words, how is the evidence used? What is concluded about it?
- What are counterarguments? Or, what is a reasonable position (or multiple reasonable positions) that are not in agreement with the argument? What are the merits of each counterargument? Why, ultimately, is the alternative argument more reasonable?

  Is any evidence or reasoning missing? Are there flaws or logical fallacies in my reasoning? (**Flaws** and **logical fallacies** refer to breaches of logic or reasoning in a given claim or argument.)

Check Yourself

When working on an idea-based revision, ask yourself:

Have I looked back at the case, assignment description, and any other assignment materials throughout the process? Have I used them as I generated ideas?
Have I overlooked any major aspects of these assignment materials?
Have I used discussion to gain a fresh perspective on my own ideas?
Am I unsure of any of the logic or reasoning of my ideas? How can I resolve these? Whom can I consult? (See the section "Engaging with Your Peers" later in this chapter.)
Do I have any questions about the assignment that I have not asked my instructor or my peers?

Finally, **writing-based revision** focuses on how your contribution—a new idea, argument, or way of seeing something—is written (or spoken). It includes close attention to organization and language use. Some questions for your rhetoric-based revision include the following:

- What are the main parts or moves of my introduction? What is the general topic, what is missing or misunderstood, and what is this argument's contribution? Are all of these clear in my introduction?

- Where and how is evidence presented? Does any framing information include context, such as the credentials of a source, so that readers can tell why the evidence is credible? Do I analyze and link evidence back to my overall ideas?
- What is the purpose of each sentence and paragraph? Do all of these suit my purpose and audience?
- What is the level of certainty of my main idea? Does this level of certainty seem reasonable, or are their places where it seems overstated (e.g., via boosters like *clearly*, *obviously*, or *definitely*)? How can I offer a balance of appropriate caution and reasonable confidence?
- What is the register used: Is it informal, formal, colloquial? What is called for in this assignment?

Rewriting allows you to re-envision or re-see your words and ideas. Give yourself time to re-see your ideas and writing so you can make them better as you see them in new ways.

Check Yourself

What's your attitude toward rewriting/revising? Many writers don't enjoy rewriting, sometimes because it can feel like redoing something that's already done, and sometimes because it's hard to let go of passages that seem interesting or well written. The authors of this textbook experience both of these with our writing as well. We have to remind ourselves of two things:

First Draft ≠ The Best Draft
Interesting ≠ Relevant

By the first equation, *First Draft ≠ The Best Draft*, we mean that although it is difficult, you (and all writers) have to be willing to revise thoroughly, no matter how hard you have worked on an initial draft. Rethinking/rewriting gives you the chance to see and refine your ideas in ways impossible the first time you think about them and write them down. Put another way, taking a minimalist approach to revision by sticking with your first draft robs you of the discovery and improvement from rethinking the case, the issues, and your argument.

Copy-Editing

Editing is the last step before you turn in your work. It's the final spit and polish. It's the stage where you double-check and make final changes to spelling, commas and other punctuation, formatting, citations, and other technical concerns.

Be sure to proofread to catch any errors in the text; it is definitely not worth it to undermine your good ideas by failing to catch a typo or by misspelling the name of someone you cite. You want what you turn in to represent your best work and your attention to detail.

Publishing

Publishing is turning over that final draft to your readers. It's out of your hands and out into the world. Sometimes publishing will involve just turning the paper in to an instructor—other times it will mean sharing your writing on a class blog or wiki. Whatever the venue, it is the last step for your paper. Your paper has turned from process to product.

Engaging with Your Peers

Collaboration

What Is Collaboration, and Why Collaborate?

Writing is often thought of as an individual activity. Many people imagine great writers bent over desks, scribbling or typing away in attic rooms, emerging only to deliver a manuscript. The famous essayist Virginia Woolf wrote a long essay called *A Room of One's Own* promoting this very thing—solitude and space so that writers can write. In school, too, most of the grades you have received on your writing have likely evaluated your work as your own and no one else's. According to Lisa Ede and Andrea Lunsford, it is a "generally unspoken and commonsensical assumption" that writers work in solitude, addressing an unknown reader.[3]

While it is important to be able to concentrate and revise our thinking and ideas individually—and this is often what you are required to do in school—this version of writing as a solitary activity does not capture a great deal of writing in our world today. Particularly after college, the writing you do—creative, academic, informational, and otherwise—will regularly include group brainstorming, feedback from readers, and collaborative authorship.[4] Many public sources we read, such as dictionaries, news articles, and sources such as Wikipedia, are authored by many people without even indicating exactly who wrote which parts of the text.

---

3. See, e.g., Lisa S. Ede and Andrea A. Lunsford, *Singular Texts/Plural Authors: Perspectives on Collaborative Writing* (Carbondale, IL: Southern Illinois University Press, 1990).

4. See, e.g., Paul Benjamin Lowry, Aaron Curtis, and Michelle René Lowry, "Building a Taxonomy and Nomenclature of Collaborative Writing to Improve Interdisciplinary Research and Practice," *International Journal of Business Communication* 41, no. 1 (2004): 66–99.

In writing courses, collaborative thinking and writing are essential: You will regularly take into account your peers' and instructors' feedback as you draft and revise your ideas and writing. These practices are essential because it is very difficult to be objective about our own thinking and writing, even when they need improvement. Sometimes we can fail to see problems in our ideas or writing, and other times we can see problems but not know how to fix them. Furthermore, your work on the case studies in this book is inherently cooperative: As you think through the case studies and how to resolve them, you must consider multiple stakeholders' perspectives and multiple responses to possible solutions, and you must ultimately design compromises. Your practice of thinking and writing while responding thoughtfully to the ideas of others will help you gain different perspectives and will help prepare you for the collaborative tasks you will face in future academic and professional writing.

Collaborating on a Case

As we just noted, analyzing case studies and determining solutions to them involves a cooperative process: You must account for multiple perspectives to resolve an issue, and your resolution must show your attention to different stakeholders' distinct needs and perspectives. The solutions you design must facilitate fair consensus and coordination. As emphasized throughout this book, you have to consider several, often conflicting perspectives and consider the effect of different possibilities for different individuals and groups. Often the question is not just "Is this a good solution?" but rather:

> "Is this a viable solution for each stakeholder involved?"
> "Does any single stakeholder benefit more than another?"
> "If I were X stakeholder, what would I think?"
> "If I were Y stakeholder, what would I think?"

Peer Review

A common, collaborative practice in writing courses is **peer review**, in which students read each other's writing and provide feedback during the writing process. There are many different ways to conduct peer review. One common approach is the use of online tools or platforms in which students read and comment on each other's writing, sometimes by embedding comments in the text. Another common approach includes "writing workshop" opportunities, in which a group of three or four or more students read and comment on each other's work in class. Often students will read each other's work beforehand and will come together during the in-class writing workshop to go over their comments together. This can lead to collaborative discussion about issues in the text as well as how to resolve them.

The use of peer feedback—to incorporate a recommended change, or to thoughtfully decide not to—can strengthen the quality of ideas and writing. Research shows that many students find their peers' feedback even more useful than their instructors' feedback during the writing process. Furthermore, research shows that peer review between students is perhaps even more beneficial for the student *giving* the feedback than the one receiving it: Students' writing improves when they have opportunities to see and comment on their peers' work, because they learn to recognize places that are unsupported, unclear, or inconsistent.[5]

You may also hear the term *peer-reviewed* to describe research that you read and incorporate into your writing. This term refers to writing that is reviewed by other scholars in the author's research area (or, by the author's peers). Peer-reviewed articles and other forms of writing tend to be considered the highest-quality research and writing because of the constructive role of receiving and responding to feedback.

In sum, peer review is a valuable practice in writing courses for both those offering and those receiving feedback. It is also a common part of the academic writing–thinking process of collaborative thinking and writing. You will likely confront it and benefit from it in many academic and professional settings, even if the exact term "peer review" is not used.

Working Alone Versus Working in Teams

Working alone and working collaboratively are both useful. Ideally, practicing both can help develop your skills of independent and cooperative thinking and writing. Benefits of working alone include the ability to design a writing process and timeline that are familiar to you and fit with your schedule. Working alone can also be productive because it can challenge you to work with your own strengths and weaknesses as a writer. It can force you to tackle what is most difficult or most unfamiliar to you because you do not have a more experienced person to take over the task.

Benefits of working with others include being exposed to new ideas and also new ways of thinking. Research suggests that people come up with more creative solutions when they brainstorm and debate together. University of California Berkeley Professor Charlan Nemeth has shown that groups that freely propose ideas, and also constructively criticize ideas, come up with the most original solutions. Her research shows that both "authentic criticism" and exposure to

5. See, e.g., Kristi Lundstrom and Wendy Baker, "To Give Is Better Than to Receive: The Benefits of Peer Review to the Reviewer's Own Writing," *Journal of Second Language Writing* 18, no. 1 (2009): 30–43, and Joseph M. Moxley and David Eubanks, "On Keeping Score: Instructors' Vs. Students' Rubric Ratings of 46,689 Essays," *WPA: Writing Program Administration* 39 (2015): 53–80.

unfamiliar perspectives produce less predictable, more creative ideas.[6] Even though it can be hard to hear criticism, it is often the only way to push us beyond our initial ideas to discover better ones.

Here is one way to think about working alone versus working in a team. Imagine that you are on a coast, and your task is to describe the part of the ocean in that area. If you work alone, you can decide what you want to focus on. You can choose your approach on your own. You might want to stand on the beach and describe the ocean that touches the shore. Perhaps you want to wade in, or swim in shallow water, in order to better describe the water. This might lead to a clear, focused, and cohesive description of that part of the coast where it meets the water. You might feel that it is easier to showcase an original idea and to be evaluated for it.

Imagine now that you work collaboratively on the same task. On the one hand, it might be challenging to agree on an approach to the description, or on times to meet at the coast to do the work. On the other hand, imagine if one person has a boat, another has scuba-diving equipment, and another has a drone. In this case, you would have multiple vantage points: on the coast, on the water, under the water, and in the air. You would be able consider the best one or a blend of them, and you would surely discover new information in the process.

Working collaboratively is like this, even without different physical locations, because every person brings a different perspective or vantage point to a task. Both approaches, working alone and working with a team, have pros and cons. Ideally, you will practice both. But when you are working collaboratively, the process can be helped by do's and don'ts such as the following.

Collaboration Do's

DO: Keep an open mind. A key part of the creative and innovative power of group work is being open to the ideas and needs of others.

DO: Share the work evenly. Find ways to give everyone an equal say in ideas and plans, even if the group makes some choices based on different strengths. To facilitate this, make a clear, agreed-upon plan for how the work will be shared.

DO: Agree on shared goals. Make collective goals for the project, and set at least one goal for each meeting. Articulate these at the start of the project, and reiterate them periodically throughout the process.

DO: Make a plan and check in regularly. Make a plan for when, and how often, everyone will check in. Plan meeting times, and

6. See, e.g., Charlan Jeanne Nemeth and Margaret Ormiston, "Creative Idea Generation: Harmony Versus Stimulation," *European Journal of Social Psychology* 37, no. 3 (2007): 524–535.

also designate ways to contact one another and exchange ideas and resources. Make sure to plan for all stages of a project, including gathering information and evidence, reading, writing, revising, and editing. Make a clear timeline with deadlines for both small and big steps.

DO: Communicate when there is a problem. Sometimes group tensions arise not from actual problems but from misunderstanding. If a peer is not following through, communicate with them. Try to determine what the problem is and how other team members can help. If it is not possible to resolve the issue within the group, communicate with your instructor about what to do well in advance of big deadlines.

Collaboration Don'ts

DON'T: Try to control the group. Remember that the point of collaboration is to find creative, collaborative approaches and ideas. If you try to make everyone follow your plan and your thinking, you will miss out on the opportunity to consider multiple perspectives and to rethink your own.

DON'T: Let one person dominate. The flip side of not dominating the group yourself is also helping to ensure that no one else dominates the group. Domination by one person can stifle ideas and needs. Try to find ways to ensure that everyone feels comfortable sharing ideas, disagreeing with ideas, and voicing concerns.

DON'T: Be disrespectful of unfamiliar or different ideas. Remember that creative and imaginative ideas are fueled by being forced to think in different ways. As in the studies described in the last section, diplomatic and constructive criticism—not disrespectful or needlessly harsh critique—is beneficial to everyone in a group.

DON'T: Plagiarize your peers' ideas. If an idea or example clearly originates with one of your peers, make sure to check with them before using it, and give credit to your peer where appropriate.

Check Yourself

Have I been open-minded to feedback and other forms of collaboration?

Have I contributed to and used discussion and other forms of collaboration in my writing–thinking process? Do I have good reasons for rejecting any peer ideas or feedback I did not follow?

Have I been thorough but not overbearing in my own peer feedback? Have I offered the kind of feedback I hope to get for my own writing?

CHAPTER SUMMARY

The writing–thinking process is an important part of in-depth writing tasks. It is certainly part of academic writing, because a thoughtful, recursive process of idea generation, reading and research, drafting, organizing, collaborating, and rewriting makes our ideas and writing better. Three important parts of the writing–thinking process are (1) understanding your writing task—what is expected, what probably won't work, what questions to ask; (2) understanding and attending to your audience; and (3) engaging with your peers through collaboration and peer review.

7 THE WRITING–THINKING PROCESS

ENGAGING WITH READERS AND OTHER WRITERS

How do we engage readers? How do we anticipate what a reader might question or want to know?

Learning objectives in this chapter

- Recognize and label ways that writers engage with readers, including through rhetorical appeals
- Recognize and label ways that writers engage with other writers, including integrating and analyzing evidence

Key concepts addressed in this chapter

- Rhetorical appeals
- Evidence
- Paraphrasing
- Analysis

Introduction

In the previous chapter you read about writing process steps that relate to the two topics in this chapter, engaging with readers and engaging with other writers. In this chapter, we further discuss engagement because it is such an important part of academic writing as a conversation.

Engaging with Readers

Rhetorical Strategies

Rhetoric is usually defined as the art of using spoken or written language to effectively persuade an audience. The foundations of rhetoric can be traced back to the ancient Greeks and the study of oratory. In Greek culture, oratory prepared students to communicate effectively as they entered the fields of law, politics, and teaching. These insights into oratory and persuasion still have relevance for students today.

Philosophers like Aristotle analyzed speech in order to come up with effective ways of persuading others. He felt that speech involved three basic components: speaker, message, and audience. Each component works in relation to the others: The audience influences the speaker, the speaker influences the message, and the message influences the audience. In order to influence an audience, Aristotle recommended analyzing the situation in order to figure out the best means of persuasion. He identified three appeals of rhetorical persuasion: ethos (character), logos (logic/reason), and pathos (emotion). Speakers must determine which combination of appeals will help them best accomplish their purpose. The relationship between these three appeals is often represented as a triangle—usually called the rhetorical triangle.

Historically the guidelines for rhetoric were developed for spoken language, for oral speeches, in three specific contexts: deliberative (concerned with what is advantageous), judicial, and ceremonial. As a culture, our focus has shifted from oral language to written language. However, when applying a model from oral language to written texts, we need to keep in mind that spoken language and written language have different characteristics:

Speech	**Writing**
Oral	Graphic
Intonation	Punctuation
Dynamic	Static
Immediate feedback	Delayed feedback/no feedback
Dependent on context	Lacks an immediate context

Despite these differences, we can adapt some of the central principles of oral rhetoric to creating written texts, since some of the basic fundamentals of communication apply to both oral and written communication. The biggest difference between the two that we can observe from this list is the difference in the immediacy of the response—when you are talking to someone, you know immediately if they understand you, if they realized that your remark was sarcastic or not. In contrast, when you're writing, you don't know if your readers will understand your true intentions; they may misinterpret your tone and think that your satirical remark was serious, for example. Because of this difference, written texts require more planning and more thinking about what the audience needs than oral texts.

Writing involves a series of decisions. Long before we put words down on a page, we've consciously or unconsciously started the writing process. Decision making in the writing process, like the critical thinking process, begins with a series of questions: what, why, who, and how. These questions can be matched to the elements of Aristotle's traditional rhetorical triangle, ethos, logos, and pathos (speaker, message, and audience). In addition to the foundational components of Aristotle's triangle, modern writers also must consider context and medium.

Context is the situation the writing is a part of. Examples of situational context include a history class, a business meeting, or a poetry reading. Context can also mean the body of knowledge the text belongs to—in other words, how the text relates to all the things already written about that topic in a specific field. The context influences the genre as well as other choices.

The **medium**, or means of communication, also plays a role in the construction of texts. In Aristotle's day, the medium was the spoken word; later, graphic symbols or writing was invented and the medium of communication could be either oral or written. Now we have digital means of communication, which often mix the visual, oral, and written. This textbook concentrates primarily on strategies for the written medium, but your instructor may expand the case scenarios, classroom activities, or writing assignments to include digital media.

Planning how to use these rhetorical strategies usually starts at the beginning of the writing assignment, but you should keep them in mind at all stages of the writing process. Aristotle's appeals are a key resource at your disposal to organize your text in the best way to persuade your audience. The following sections discuss each component in more detail.

Rhetorical Appeals

Logos

The Greek word *logos* means word, speech, or reason. It is derived from the verb "to say." Our word *logic* has its roots in *logos*. In rhetoric, logos is an appeal to the rational side of our audience. In many types of academic writing, logos dominates over the other rhetorical appeals. Writers concentrate on presenting their readers with solid, credible evidence.

Usually students assume that logos just refers to the type of evidence used to convince a reader; however, it also refers to the internal consistency of an argument: How clear is the claim, how logical are the reasons given for the claim, and how effective is the support for the claim? All of these things should hold together in a logical fashion. The argument should be able to stand on the strength of its rational foundations.

Pathos

The Greek word *pathos* means suffering, emotion, and passion. It is derived from the verb "to suffer." Our words *sympathy* and *empathy* are all derived from the same verb. Both sympathy and empathy are qualities you want to use in persuasion because in persuasion, it is the emotional impact of the message that moves the reader to action.

Often a paper will catch a reader's attention with a story. An appeal to pathos is an effective way to hook your reader. Once you've gotten their attention, then you can dazzle them with your logic. For an academic audience, an entire paper written using only appeals to pathos wouldn't be viewed as credible. However, don't neglect pathos in academic writing: We need to engage our readers' feelings as well as their minds in order to persuade them.

But pathos is not just about appealing to the emotions of the audience; it is also about appealing to their imagination. Pathos can be used to create a positive image of the audience, one the audience will want to identify with. An audience that identifies with what you are saying is more likely to be persuaded. Alternatively, pathos can be flipped: It be used to express the writer's feelings, which can serve as a bridge to connect to the reader.

Ethos

The Greek word *ethos* means custom, usage, disposition, character, or delineation of character. Our word *ethics* is related to *ethos*. In Aristotle's triangle, the writer is connected to ethos. He lists three components of ethos: good sense, good moral character, and goodwill. These characteristics are meant to inspire the audience's trust in the writer. Our perceptions of a speaker or writer influence how willing we are to believe what they have to say. Their background, education, and past experiences all contribute to our perceptions of their ethos, their credibility.

Goodwill in a writer means the writer has the audience's best interests at heart, not their own self-interest. One way the writer shows goodwill is by respecting the intelligence of the audience. In academic writing, good character means being credible, having some claim to authority or expertise. But how do you create a persona of authority as a college student? How do you enter the conversation of other academic writers? One way you can build your expertise is through your research on the case issues and the stakeholders, so that you can analyze their points of view and expertise the same way you analyzed your audience's characteristics and needs. The next section addresses how you can engage with other sources in order to build ethos in your writing.

Engaging with Other Writers

Integrating Sources

Reading source texts on a topic we are investigating helps our writing–thinking process. It can also provide examples, ideas, and direct quotes to use in our writing. Academic writing tends to include a lot of examples from outside sources because it shows that writers have been diligent in their reading on a topic and because building knowledge depends on learning from many different ideas, perspectives, experiments, etc.

When you have identified ideas and/or quotes in source texts you read that are relevant for a paper you are writing, you will make choices about how to integrate them into your paper. You don't want to just drop them in out of nowhere, so-called hit-and-run quotes (what the linguist John Swales calls "parenthetical plonking"). You want to have a rhetorical reason for where you include a source text and whether you use a quote or paraphrase. You also want to make sure it is clear to your reader which ideas and words are yours and which ones come from your source material. (This will also help you avoid any problems with accidental plagiarism.) And you don't want to overuse quotes: Using too many quotations will give the reader the impression that you have no ideas of your own or that you don't understand what you read.

There are three common parts to an integrated source or sources:

1. The introduction, contextual information, and/or signal phrase
2. The quote, summary, or paraphrase
3. The follow-up analysis or commentary

Introducing and Contextualizing Source Material

Introducing the quote means letting your reader know that source material is coming. This can be in the form of contextual information such as *cognitive scientist Lera Boroditsky* or a signal phrase or transition such as *for example*. For instance, in the following two sentences, the student writer offers context for the research cited by indicating what the researchers studied, how they studied it, and what their results were:

> In their study of glaciers in Greenland, Jones and Davis (2001) took over 300 core samples. The analysis of these samples showed a greater loss of glacier ice in the last twenty years than the last one hundred years.

By contrast, the following example offers the general results of the cited study but does not offer readers information that will help them decide the validity of the results:

> Jones and Davis (2001) found that there was a greater loss of glacier ice in the last twenty years than the last one hundred years.

Placing sources in conversation can also be a good way to introduce and contextualize cited material, such as in the following example:

> Jones (2011) claims that rising sea levels will submerge low-lying islands. Yet Warne (2015) claims that islands may grow in size or change in shape in response to shifting soil and rising sea levels.

Providing Commentary and Analysis on Source Material

Students often find that selecting source material, and even explaining it, are easier than *analyzing* it. Writing the analysis or commentary that *follows* a quote, summary, or paraphrase is challenging. That analysis or commentary needs to interpret the source material for your readers, telling them what's important about it and how it supports your ideas. Some hints for commenting on cited material are as follows:

- Build on the main ideas stated in the quote, summary, or paraphrase.
- Connect the ideas in the cited material back to the sentence(s) before the cited material.
- Connect the ideas in the cited material back to the main idea of the paragraph.
- Connect the ideas in the cited material back to your overall thesis..
- Help readers understand why you included the specific cited material. How does it relate to your main idea? How does it relate to other sources you are using?

Examples of Quotation Use

Here are some examples taken from student papers written on the climate change case. The words in **bold** indicate a transition or signal phrase, and *italicized* words indicate follow-up commentary.

Signal Phrase, No Follow-Up Comment

> The government is already providing them with help in the form of food and water, but now it is crucial that they help with protection: protection of the island, and protection of themselves while relocating to a safer place. **Applegate** (2016) talks about the different ways how protection is crucial to the islanders because of tradition. Protections should include "individual buildings and sites from flooding, damage to infrastructure, shore erosion and the loss of natural resources" (p. 515). **Applegate** also talks about how the retreat approach can be crucial: "The retreat approach attempts to reduce the hazards created by sea level rise ... (p. 515).

In this example, the name of the author signals to the reader that the writer is offering a paraphrase and, later, a quote. The student quotes a list that would be hard to paraphrase, so the use of a quote makes sense. However, the student does not include any comment or evaluation of the quote; instead the writer immediately introduces another quote and shifts the topic from protection to retreat.

To better integrate this quote, the student could add a comment explaining the quote and provide a transition to help ease the topic shift. For instance, the student could provide commentary like the following after the first quote:

> Building sea walls to prevent flooding, planting mangrove trees to help stop erosion, and maintaining access to fresh water would all be protective measures the government could do in addition to their current actions. Furthermore, Applegate discusses the retreat approach ...

Signal Phrase, Weak Follow-Up Comment

> The location of our village has been good to us because of how easy it is to get food from the sea and land. Our culture has been around for centuries and for the longest time it has been all we know. **According to the GAO [Government Accountability Office] Reports**, "For generations, these Alaska Natives have used the surrounding waters and land to hunt, fish, and gather wild plants for food. These subsistence activities are intricately woven into the fabric of their lives" (p. 5). *It is now becoming hard to focus on our culture because the hunters are having to travel farther to get food for their families and it is becoming more dangerous.*

In this example, we see a different signal phrase being used, not just the author's name. Here also the student has made an attempt to explain the quote by linking back to the idea of culture mentioned just before the quote. However, culture is not mentioned in the quote itself. The sentence also introduces the dangers of traveling to hunt—an idea also not mentioned in the quote. Possible solutions:

- Add sentences.
- Make ideas less broad. In this case, build on the idea of subsistence and location and culture.

Signal Phrase, Strong Follow-Up Comment

> As the ice melts, marine animals that we hunt for food are forced to relocate to colder waters that are further than we can travel to hunt. The loss of food has been catastrophic in the Maggak village. **Roberts and Andrei** (2015) state, "Sea ice, which provides transportation routes to link communities and provides access to hunting grounds, is thinning, which increases the danger associated with travel" (p. 262). *Because of thin ice, we cannot travel to hunt, or seek help from neighboring communities.*

In this example, the authors' names serve to mark the boundary between the student's description of village conditions and the quote. The student's follow-up comment connects the quote to the sentences before the quote and to the larger topic of the paragraph, the melting of the permafrost.

Examples of Paraphrasing

No Signal Phrase, Follow-Up Comment

However, the recently increased exposure of Pacific communities, such as those on both the Fiji and the Lilo islands, to global contact, modernization, urbanization, and other such factors that tend to separate younger generations from traditional knowledge systems, have reduced the ability of some communities to reproduce this cultural knowledge system. Greater majorities of island communities are unable to properly recognize and prepare for natural disaster, thus also limiting the extent to which communities can recover from extreme damage caused by environmental threats (Campbell, 2014, p. 1315). *This follows to show that Pacific Island communities may currently be more structurally vulnerable to these environmental threats, ones that have only gown more serious with the progression of climate change, than they have been in the past.*

The first two sentences of this example imply that all of these ideas come from the cited source rather than the student. This makes it difficult to decipher the writer's analysis and ideas, if any are offered. Here, the student does use the final sentence to provide a commentary to the paraphrase that ties the ideas back to earlier claims about the use of traditional knowledge in the paragraph.

Writing Hint: Some readers find that the use of *this* alone, as in *this means,* is less clear than using *this* with a noun, such *this fact means, this trend means,* etc.

Signal Phrase and Follow-Up Comment

Villages like Maggak have a difficult lifestyle to accommodate, and because government workers have not been sensitive to Maggak's desires, the villagers of Maggak feel their needs are not being met. **For example**, Kivalina is a village going through the same circumstances as Maggak, and the Army Corps of Engineers has provided a plan with six potential relocation options. The village chose one of the Corps' options, which the Corps researched further and eventually found to have unsuitable living conditions. The villagers disagreed with the Corps' findings and requested a third-party investigation regarding the potential of their selected site (Alaska Native Villages, 2009, p. 32). *Even if the villagers' doubts of the Corps prove fruitless, they feel that their voices are being silenced.*

In this example, the student marks the boundary of the paraphrase with a transition (*for example*), which also serves to tell the reader the function of the paraphrase—that the paraphrase provides an example of the claim made in the prior sentence. The follow-up comments reinforce the paraphrase as an example and link the ideas back to the notion of native voices being silenced in the relocation process.

CHAPTER SUMMARY

This chapter has explored two important aspects of your writing, engaging with readers and engaging with other writers. These relate to steps in the writing process you read about in the previous chapter, but this chapter addressed these aspects in more detail because they are such important parts of academic writing as a conversation.

8 ANALYZING ARGUMENTS

What makes an argument effective? How can you tell what will make your arguments more successful?

Learning objectives in this chapter

- Differentiate observations, opinions, and arguments
- Identify how to analyze the elements and effectiveness of your own and others' arguments
- Understand three dimensions of argument analysis: context analysis, rhetorical analysis, and information analysis

Key concepts addressed in this chapter

- Context analysis, including analyzing audience and purpose
- Rhetorical analysis, including analyzing moves, appeals, and language
- Information analysis, including analyzing evidence and conclusions

Introduction

You may have encountered arguments that you can tell are effective, but you can't tell exactly what makes them convincing. Sometimes, too, you may see evidence for different perspectives and not know which is most credible. This chapter discusses steps for critically analyzing arguments. These include three overlapping dimensions of analyzing arguments: context analysis, rhetorical analysis, and information analysis.

We will briefly describe these dimensions of analysis, listing the sample questions that each one helps to answer. We will go through strategies for each one, with examples to illustrate. As you can see in the representation below, these dimensions overlap and combine to help us analyze arguments.

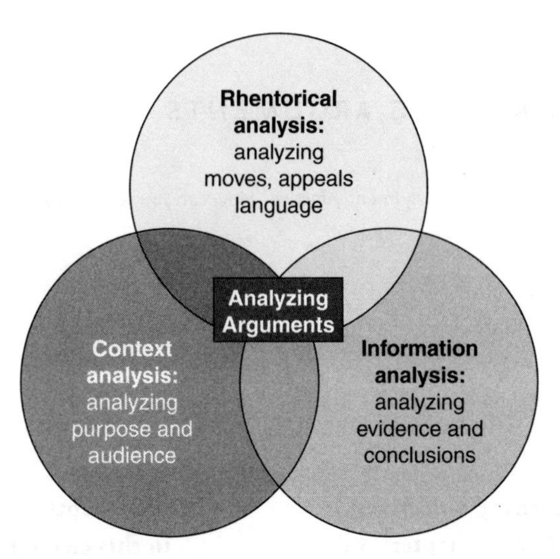

FIGURE 8.1

Context Analysis: Analyzing Purpose and Audience

Context analysis focuses on whom and what an argument is for—for example, whether it is for a general audience or a specialized audience, and whether the audience is already invested in the topic or not. Analyzing the purpose of an argument helps you determine whether it is identifying a problem, offering an interpretation, or proposing a solution—or more than one of these at once. Context analysis allows you to answer questions such as:

Who is the argument written for? What is the primary audience? Who are any secondary audiences? What are likely the interests or goals of the audience(s)?

What is the purpose of the argument? Is there a clear, primary purpose or aim? What are any secondary aims?

What is the overall genre (e.g., report, advertisement, essay)? How and in what circumstances is this genre generally used? Is the genre informal, formal, interpersonal?

Is any audience or stakeholder (someone who will be affected by the outcome of the argument) prioritized in the argument? Is any audience ignored?

Rhetorical Analysis: Analyzing Moves, Appeals, and Language

Rhetorical analysis focuses on how the argument is written (or spoken). It includes close attention to organization and language use. This kind of analysis will give you insights into the other kinds of analyses as well. Some questions that rhetorical analysis answers are:

What are the main parts or **moves** of the argument? What is the general topic, what is missing or misunderstood, and what is this argument's contribution?
What is the **scope** of the argument—in other words, to whom and to what does it apply? Does this scope seem reasonable? Too big or too small?
What is the level of **certainty** of the argument? Does this level of certainty seem reasonable (e.g., via boosters like *doubtless, clearly, definitely*)? Does the author note exceptions or potential qualifications (e.g., via hedges like *perhaps, might, possible*)?
What is the **register** used: informal, formal, colloquial?
Where and how is evidence presented? Does any framing information (e.g., *unfortunately, correctly*) show how the writer reacts to the evidence?
What are the appeals of the argument? *Pathos* is described as an appeal to values; *logos* is described as an appeal to logic.

Information Analysis: Analyzing Evidence and Conclusions

Information analysis focuses on the details and evidence of the argument being made. In many ways, this dimension of analyzing arguments is similar to how you analyze cases, as addressed in Chapters 2 and 4: You look closely at details in order to determine who is involved and why, and to what end. Information analysis answers questions like the following:

What is the main argument?
What are secondary arguments made to support the primary argument?
What premises are used (or, what is the basis for any given claim), and are they reasonable? Why or why not?
What warrants are used (or, what is the link or bridge between evidence and an argument made), and are they reasonable?
What evidence or examples are used? Are they from credible sources? Are the examples reasonable? Why or why not?
What reasoning is used with the evidence? In other words, how is the evidence used? What is concluded about it?
Is any evidence or reasoning missing?
What are counterarguments? Or, what is a reasonable position (or multiple reasonable positions) that are not in agreement with the argument? What are the merits of each counterargument? Why, ultimately, is the alternative argument more reasonable?

Like writing, these three dimensions are recursive: You will go back and forth between them rather than doing them in a linear order. But we will focus on one at a time in order to illustrate what each dimension can help us analyze. We'll use the same written and visual argument to demonstrate these analysis steps. We'll start with context analysis, since you probably look for context clues before you even start reading an argument, though we will also learn more about context as we go through the other dimensions.

Context Analysis of a Written Argument

To practice context analysis on a written argument, we will use an example that we will also use in our rhetorical analysis and information analysis later in the chapter. The example is Elizabeth Kolbert's "Paying for It," which ran in the comment section of the *New Yorker* magazine in December 2012.[1] Remember that context analysis focuses on audience, genre, and purpose, though the other dimensions help clarify all of these. One way to begin is to consider who a piece is written for, and to what end.

Even before we read it, the source of this piece gives us some clues. Think back to your prereading strategies in Chapter 3. One detail is that it is from the *New Yorker*, a magazine that tends to be written for a general audience of well-educated adults rather than a specific or specialized audience (for example, it is not a travel magazine or a magazine for medical practitioners). Within the *New Yorker*, this piece ran in the general comment section, which contains short editorial pieces. This general comment section is not under another, specific section, such as "culture" or "news." This, too, might have led you to believe that it was written for a general audience, who may or may not already be interested in the topic.

The fact that it is an editorial tells us something, too: The purpose of the piece is argumentative. It is not, for example, aiming primarily to tell a story or to report an event. Without reading it, however, we don't yet know the nature of the argument; we do not know, for example, if it is arguing for a particular conclusion or a particular solution (or both).

Other questions about audience and purpose can help us examine the piece more closely, such as whether any audience is appealed to more than others. We will continue to think about this as we begin our rhetorical analysis and information analysis. These, too, help us further identify the audience and purpose of the writing.

---

1. Elizabeth Kolbert, "Paying for It," *New Yorker*, December 10, 2012, http://www.newyorker.com/magazine/2012/12/10/paying-for-it.

Context Analysis of a Visual Argument

Let's try one more example, this time of a visual argument. If you encountered an image like the one in Image 8.1 on a billboard or a bus, what might you conclude about the audience and purpose?

Here, the young person in the image might lead you to believe that it is aimed at young people. The young person is smoking a cigarette. The smoke forms an image of a gun, something that causes death, pointed at the smoker's head. It seems reasonable to conclude that it is making an argument about the fatal dangers of smoking, and that it was developed as part of an initiative promoting wellness and health awareness aimed at young people. But closer analysis of the image can tell us more, as we will see in our rhetorical analysis.

> **Check Yourself**
>
> Try your hand at context analysis. Pick a written or visual argument to practice on. It could be an editorial like the *New Yorker* example or one of your readings for a case study. When you are doing your context analysis, use the following questions to help you get started:
>
> What contextual clues can you discover?
> Who is the audience?
> What is the purpose?
> What is the genre?

IMAGE 8.1. Visual argument. *Source*: thetruth.com

Rhetorical Analysis

Rhetorical Analysis of a Written Argument

The concept of **moves** is often used when analyzing written academic arguments. In academic writing, moves refer to the rhetorical steps that writers make to order their ideas in readable and convincing ways. For instance, writers commonly move from a more general idea to a more specific idea in the introduction to an argument; this helps lead readers into the argument. In another example, writers often move from introducing an example, to explaining an example, to showing how the example links back to the argument. Both the order of the moves and the information in the sentences, therefore, help to make the information accessible and persuasive.

In academic writing, there are three introductory moves that are common in introductory paragraphs (we already mentioned these in Chapter 6). John Swales[2] identified these in academic research articles, regardless of academic field or discipline:

Move 1 is called **establishing a territory**. In this move, writers provide **background**, such as by noting the importance or urgency of the subject or reviewing existing views or research.

Move 2 is called **establishing a niche**. In this move, writers indicate a **gap or lingering question**—something interesting we still need to know.

Move 3 is called **occupying the niche**. In this move, writers note their own **claim or contribution** and often briefly indicate what their paper or article will include.

These moves are not always in this order, though they often are.

Let's see these three moves at work in the introduction to Kolbert's *New Yorker* editorial:

> [**Move 1**] It's been almost a century since the British economist Arthur Pigou floated the idea that turned his name into an adjective. In "The Economics of Welfare," published in 1920, Pigou pointed out that private investments often impose costs on other people. Consider this example: A man walks into a bar. He orders several rounds, downs them, and staggers out. The man has got plastered, the bar owner has got the man's money, and the public will get stuck with the tab for the cops who have to fish the

2. John Swales, *Genre Analysis: English in academic and research settings*. Cambridge: Cambridge University Press, 1990.

man out of the gutter. In Pigou's honor, taxes that attempt to correct for this are known as Pigovian, or, if you prefer, Pigouvian (the spelling remains wobbly). Alcohol taxes are Pigovian; so are taxes on cigarettes. The idea is to incorporate into the cost of what might seem a purely personal choice the expenses it foists on the rest of society.

[Move 2] One way to think about global warming is as a vast, planet-wide Pigovian problem. In this case, the man pulls up to a gas pump. He sticks his BP or Sunoco card into the slot, fills up, and drives off. He's got a full tank; the gas station and the oil company share in the profits. Meanwhile, the carbon that spills out of his tailpipe lingers in the atmosphere, trapping heat and contributing to higher sea levels. As the oceans rise, coastal roads erode, beachfront homes wash away, and, finally, major cities flood. Once again, it's the public at large that gets left with the bill. **[Move 3]** The logical, which is to say the fair, way to address this situation would be to make the driver absorb the cost for his slice of the damage. This could be achieved by a new Pigovian tax, on carbon.

In this example, Move 1 is long: the full first paragraph. This paragraph gives background information, introducing the general topic, which is the challenge of what to do about individual choices that also affect the societies people live in. You might already see some appeal to pathos here, or the appeal to the value of a cooperative collective society, rather than appealing to individual values at the expense of others.

Move 2 begins at the start of the second paragraph. It begins to narrow the scope of the topic to global warming, and here the writer makes a *secondary argument*—one that is not her main argument but is necessary in order to make the main argument in Move 3. This secondary argument is that global warming can be thought of as a Pigovian problem, meaning that it can be thought of as something in which individual choices about the environment ultimately have an impact on everyone in that environment. This is a *premise*—that environmentally dangerous substances used by individuals can be thought of as a Pigovian problem. Also in Move 2, we can see some ethos and logos. Specifically, we can see narrative ethos in statements such as, "Meanwhile, the carbon that spills out of his tailpipe lingers in the atmosphere, trapping heat and contributing to higher sea levels." We can see logos in Move 2 in this cause-and-effect statement: "as the oceans rise, coastal roads erode, beachfront homes wash away, and, finally, major cities flood." After making this move, the writer then makes her main argument in Move 3, that individuals should pay a tax on their own carbon emissions. In this case, a warrant is implied here, between Moves 2 and 3: that because global warming is a problem caused by many individuals and affecting everyone on the planet, it should be subject to a Pigovian tax.

As you can see, rhetorical analysis of introductory moves can help answer many questions addressed in context analysis, such as audience and purpose. For example, the fact that Move 1 includes a definition of Pigovian tax in non-technical language suggests that the piece is written for a general, educated audience, rather than an audience of tax specialists. Rhetorical analysis can also identify details addressed in information analysis, such as the primary argument (in this case, in Move 3) and the secondary argument (in Move 2).

In addition to moves, your rhetorical analysis should pay close attention to language use, as you may have already done. You may have already noticed clues about the register of the language—how formal or colloquial it is—that let us know that the piece is written for a general audience and is not highly formal or technical. The sentences "Consider this example: A man walks into a bar. He orders several rounds, downs them, and staggers out" are written in accessible, non-technical language. At the same time, the piece is not very informal, either; the writer does not use slang or nonstandard grammar throughout it.

We may also notice that the author does not use exaggerated or emphatic language in this argument. For example, she writes, "One way to think about global warming is as a vast, planet-wide Pigovian problem." Kolbert does not suggest that this is the *only* way to think about global warming but, rather, is *one* way to think about it. When analyzing arguments, looking for these kinds of clues—and using them in your own writing to avoid exaggerated claims—can help you practice identifying the elements of arguments.

To help heighten your awareness of language use in arguments, let's look at three types of language commonly used: hedges, boosters, and generalization markers.

Words that qualify or downplay claims are called **hedges.** Writers use hedges to make a claim without arguing that it is true in every case. Hedges include words such as *perhaps*, *seems*, *possible*, and *likely*—for instance, "a carbon tax is a *possible* solution to climate change."

By contrast, **boosters** are words that intensify or show full certainty about a claim, such as *clearly*, *truly*, *only*, *definitely*, *must*, and *should*—for example, "a carbon tax is a *definite* solution to climate change."

Finally, there are words that mark **generalizations** or that extend a claim across many contexts. Words such as *always*, *never*, *everyone*, and *everything* indicate generalizations—for instance, "*everyone knows that* a carbon tax is a solution to climate change."

All three of these (hedges, boosters, and generalizations) modify a claim with language and therefore change the claim. In other words, all of them change the following claim that is neither hedged, nor boosted, nor generalized: "a carbon tax is a solution to climate change."

As you probably know, academic writers need to be careful not to use too many boosters or generalizations to avoid making claims they cannot support. In fact, linguistic research on academic writing shows that academic arguments almost always include more hedges than boosters, regardless of the academic discipline or type of writing (such as an article versus an essay). This is because hedges help academic writers leave room for alternative perspectives while still making their claims. Research shows that experienced academic writers use hedges to do the following:

1. Show that a conclusion is based on reasoning rather than certain fact
2. Tone down risky claims
3. Acknowledge other research
4. Account for a critical reader who may have an opposing view.[3]

At the same time, academic writers still need to show conviction and emphasis at certain points in their arguments. In these cases, boosters or generalizations can be useful for intensifying a claim, such as when the writer has clear evidence to support the claim and wants to emphasize it. Therefore, experienced academic writers tend to use both hedges and boosters, and occasionally generalizations, to balance caution and conviction in their arguments.

To help you analyze and use these language features in arguments, we will consider four examples below: two by first-year college writers and two by published academic writers. In the examples, *hedges* are italicized and bolded, **boosters** are underlined and bolded, and *generalizations* are italicized. As you read, consider how these features help support the writer's credibility and develop the writer's argument.

First-Year Writing Examples

(Example 1) The current standards used for hiring teachers are not producing adequate results. An economist at Stanford, Eric Hanushek, calculates that "if you rank the countries of the world in terms of the academic performance of their schoolchildren, the U.S. is just below average." This is due *in part* to how possible teachers are evaluated during the interview process. Jacob Kounin, an educational researcher, states that exceptional teachers demonstrate a characteristic called withitness. This is a teacher's ability to communicate to the children by his/her behavior, not verbally. Withitness is an ability that **cannot** be measured in an interview. However, interviewers look *mainly* at credentials and if the interviewee

3. See e.g., Ken Hyland *Metadiscourse: Exploring Interaction in Writing* (New York: Bloomsbury Publishing, 2018).

meets the frequently rising standards. If the set standards do not incorporate what matters most in a classroom, then what is the point in raising them? What matters **most** *in a classroom* are elements that can **only** be judged through observation.

(Example 2) *Part of* what makes us *human* is our ability to emotionally connect to each other and offer an empathetic ear in times of need. Brian Christian also proposes a **radically** different idea in regards to what makes us *human* when he introduces the reader to a computer that would be *unlikely* to have many friends were it human. This computer was set up by its programmer and left overnight to respond to questions from outside users regarding technological difficulties. One man ended up having a heated argument that lasted over an hour, eventually becoming frustrated with the argumentative and insulting responses. At one point, the user commented on how very computer-like the "person" on the other end of the conversation was. As negative as it *may* sound, the argument that Christian makes through this example is the idea that what makes us *human* is our *tendency* to be argumentative and arrogant.

In these first-year college writing passages, the paragraph featured in Example 1 uses boosters and hedges as well as a generalization ("across all classrooms"). Example 2 also uses hedges and boosters, and it considers the generalized question of what makes *us*, or everyone, *human*. The claim at the end of the paragraph is boosted twice. The second example shows a bit more caution, though it also uses the booster "radically" for emphasis. The four hedges in Example 2 convey caution and conviction, and they help the writer show that she can't answer what "makes us human" and that her argument may not apply for all people.

Experienced Academic Writing Examples

(Example A) Researchers have known about CRF's effects since the 1980s. Roberto's study's contribution, however, was a discovery about the second peptide, nociceptin: It negates CRF, and thereby prevents the negative mood-inducing effects. It also blocks some of the effects of alcohol itself. According to Roberto, Scripps researchers are now investigating compounds that *might* either adjust a recovering alcoholic's nociceptin levels or act like nociceptin and neutralize CRF. Roberto *hopes* that such future treatments *could blunt* recovering alcoholics' alcohol cravings before they turn into relapses.[4]

(Example B) Thus, although the evaluation score was more highly correlated, both scores *appear* to have contributed significantly to the

4. Rick Docksai, "Chemical Tools for Treating Alcoholism," *Futurist*, September 3, 2017.

> composite score. The correlation between the sub-scores themselves was r(529) -.38, which is also a significant coefficient, here at the .01 level. The lower correlation coefficient indicates that the two sub-scores were contributing *somewhat* different information to the composite. Thus, results showed that these measures, especially the composite index, captured significant differences in the scores of stories throughout this age range. There was **strong** developmental growth from ages 4 to 9 years and a **significant** impairment of knowledge of these four elements in the stories of LI children of both dialect groups.[5]

In these examples by published academic writers, the writers use many written clues to adjust their commitment to particular claims. For instance, Example B uses both hedges and boosters: the hedged claim "somewhat different information" and the boosted claim "strong developmental growth."

You Do It!

Now it's your turn to try doing rhetorical analysis. Use the text you picked for your contextual analysis. Try analyzing the moves and see what the language use tells you about what the writer or artist is telling you and how. See if you can identify the moves in the introduction. Look for hedges, boosters, and generalizations. Pay attention to details about where the writer or artist is "moving" the argument, your eyes, your ears. The movement from one detail to another can also be a move from one claim to another, or from one detail to a conclusion.

Rhetorical Analysis of a Visual Argument

Let's return now to the visual argument made in the antismoking ad in Image 8.1. Without language or written moves, how do you analyze a visual argument like this? You can consider similar concepts in new ways by asking the following:

> What is the scope of the argument?
> To whom does it apply, and how do you know?
> Are there any exceptions implied in the image?
> What is most emphasized about the argument?
> What is urgent in the argument?

5. Frances Burns, Peter Villiers, Barbara Pearson, and Tempii Champion, "Dialect-Neutral Indices of Narrative Cohesion and Evaluation," *Language, Speech, and Hearing Services in Schools*, 43, no. 2 (2012): 132–152.

First, let's consider the visual moves the image makes. You may be drawn first to look at the young person smoking, then to the cigarette, and then to the smoky image of the gun. This same movement mimics a similar development, perhaps, in someone's life: First there is a young person, that young person decides to smoke, and that decision can eventually lead to the person's death. Also in this progression, you may have first locked eyes with the young person—his eyes may have been what you noticed first. This is because he is not looking at the source of danger, though it is pointed at him.

What about the scope of the argument? Because the image contains only one person smoking, and that same person is threatened by the pointed gun, you could conclude that the argument implies that anyone who smokes is in danger. You could also suggest that the image is aimed specifically at young people, as discussed earlier.

You may also be thinking about logos and pathos here. Logos relates to cause-and-effect claims implied, so you might have thought that the logos of this image suggests that cigarette smoking will lead to death. Since pathos appeals to viewers' values, you might have thought that the pathos of the image of the young man implies that a young person's life is especially valuable and should not be endangered or cut short.

Information Analysis

Information Analysis of a Written Argument

To practice information analysis, let's return to our previous sample text, the *New Yorker* editorial by Elizabeth Kolbert. The opening two paragraphs that we analyzed earlier are followed by this paragraph:

> [**Sentence 1**] In the past several weeks, as New York and New Jersey have continued to dig out from under the debris left by Hurricane Sandy, the possibility of a carbon tax has come to seem more likely than ever, that is, not very likely, but also not entirely out of the question. [**Sentence 2**] The reason for this is not so much the terrible cost of the storm, now estimated at more than sixty billion dollars. (The other day, Governor Andrew Cuomo said that Sandy had caused forty-two billion dollars' worth of damage in New York State alone.) [**Sentence 3**] It's that, as Washington edges toward the fiscal cliff, it has become obvious to just about everyone, except maybe House Republicans, that Washington needs more revenue.

In this paragraph, we can see that the writer presents both evidence and an interpretation (or use of) that evidence. For example, Sentence 1 cites the damage caused to New York and New Jersey by Hurricane Sandy, and because we can tell that the piece came out in the weeks following the hurricane, we can see that the author probably viewed this as a meaningful time for making the argument she wants to make (the Greeks called this *Kairos*, a kind of timeliness for arguments). In Sentences 2 and 3, the writer suggests a way to interpret this example. Specifically, in Sentence 2, the writer tells us what is true—the specific cost of damage—but suggests that even this high cost *is not* the key interpretation. In Sentence 3, the writer tells us what *is* the key interpretation. Many writers of arguments use this move—"it's not x; it's y" or "it's not only x; it's also y"—to help explain how they are using evidence. Also in Sentence 3, we get a hint as to a potential audience: This writer appears to disagree with Republicans in the U.S. House of Representatives on whether Washington DC needs more revenue. At the same time, this sentence is hedged twice: "it has become obvious to *just about* everyone, except *maybe* House Republicans." Here, by hedging, Kolbert avoids stating that *everyone* sees the issue the same way; she also avoids definitively stating that House Republicans hold a certain conclusion.

Information Analysis of Writing in Different Disciplines

The Kolbert example comes from a magazine written for a general audience. In writing aimed at a specific academic discipline, however, the type of evidence and how it is used will vary.

Different academic disciplines represent different modes of thought, and thought and knowledge are intrinsically linked. These disciplinary differences are often clear in choices about evidence: Even flipping through a philosophy article versus an engineering article will show you these differences. The article from philosophy, a humanities discipline, is likely to use hypothetical examples and quoted passages as evidence, and it is likely to showcase the writer's interpretation and reasoning as the basis for a credible argument. That means you are less likely to see tables or figures, and you are unlikely to see sections like "methods" and "results." On the other hand, engineering is a physical science discipline. In the engineering article, you are more likely to see elements, diagrams, and figures, and the basis for a credible argument is likely to be experimental procedures and results. In both the philosophy and engineering articles, you are likely to see research reviewed, a gap or lingering question identified, and an argument for how the research can be continued.

Information Analysis of a Visual Argument

We hope that by now you are noticing how recursive your analysis is. You have probably already picked up on information in your context and rhetorical analysis of a visual argument. In an information analysis, you want to record descriptive details.

For example, in an information analysis of the visual argument in Image 8.1, you might note the following:

1. The ad appears in black, white, and gray hues rather than other colors.
2. It includes a human individual who appears to be male, light-skinned, and young.
3. The individual appears to be looking out at the reader or witness of the image.
4. The individual appears to be smoking.
5. The smoke forms the shape of a gun, and the gun is pointed back toward the individual.

You Do It!

Try doing an information analysis of the antismoking ad. In the rhetorical analysis of this ad, you were probably already thinking about evidence. Information analysis focuses specifically on the evidence used in arguments and where it comes from—the examples and the source of those examples. For instance, using the evidence we have just listed, see if you can determine:

What reasoning is used with the evidence? In other words, how is the evidence used?
What is concluded about it?

Check Yourself

In this exercise we will ask you to analyze arguments using all three types of analysis we have discussed in this chapter: context, rhetorical, and information.

The following essay was written by a first-year student in a college composition course. The students were asked to read Brian Christian's article "Mind vs. Machine"[6] and to write an evidence-based argumentative essay about the role of machines in human lives, using the article for evidence.

Read and consider the essay, using context, rhetorical, and information analysis. Consider the audience and purpose of the piece. Label the main argument and any examples (or evidence) and how they are used. Number where you see the rhetorical moves we have discussed. Circle any hedges and

6. Brian Christian, "Mind vs. Machine." *Mind* 7 (March 2011): 46.

underline any boosters or generalizations you see. As you read, consider how the writer develops the argument, whether you think it is effective, and what could be done differently.

> As the information age progresses, technological achievement seems to be increasing exponentially. Knowing this, it is not unreasonable to conclude that computers will, in the not-so-distant future, surpass humans in every measurable way. However, as Brian Christian argues in his article "Mind vs. Machine," this is not the case. While computers may be able to imitate humans in a believable matter, the human race will always be superior by being adaptive and innovative.
>
> In 1950, a test known as the Turing Test, named after its creator, was conceived to test how intelligent a computer program is. This test required several judges to conduct conversations with unseen participants through a computer terminal. Some of these participants were human while the others were computer programs. Based on the conversations, the judges needed to tell them apart. While Turing thought that by the year 2000, a computer would be able to fool thirty percent of the judges, so far this has not come true. What Turing failed to realize is the limitless potential that humans have.
>
> The human race is constantly changing to combat new threats to its existence. We can solve our problems by either figuring out the solution in our head, or by inventing a tool that can solve it for us. In this sense, we always find a way to continue onward. This is not to say that computers cannot solve problems. From solving complex math problems to interpreting what the Turing judges are saying and coming up with an appropriate response, solving problems is what computers do best. However, what computers fail at is persevering through a problem to come up with a solution.
>
> Consider a logic problem known as the "dot problem." In this problem, nine dots are placed in a 3 × 3 grid. These nine dots must be connected by drawing exactly four lines without lifting the pencil from the paper and going through each dot only once. Initial efforts of going from dot to dot will not work and will just lead to a dead end. However, by literally going "outside the box" and extending the lines beyond the 3 × 3 grid, the participant can discover the answer. In this aspect of problem solving, computers fall far behind humans. A program called "Catherine" who competed in the 1997 Turing test showed this lapse of logic. After engaging in a deep discussion about the Clintons and Whitewater, Catherine was asked the simple question if she wanted some water. At this point the computer could not understand what the judge was asking and erupted into complete gibberish. Even after the judge tried to engage the program further, it was unable to recover. This brings the key difference between computers and human minds. Computers are simply unable to see the

(*Continued*)

> bigger picture. While computers will simply crash when they cannot figure something out, humans will seek out additional data while also using their current data to come up with multiple solutions.
>
> It is in this sense that computers will never be equal to humans. What humans have that computers cannot imitate is that creative spark. It is these "ah-ha moments," when an intuitive leap creates a new creative insight, that computers utterly fail in comparison. It is this sudden burst of thinking that has saved our lives in our prehistoric days and will continue to enable us to solve any problem that we might come across. While the Turing Test may have a valid method of measuring intelligence, it fails to measure what it is to be human.
>
> As Christian said, "We're not going to take defeat lying down." The human race will always be willing to stand up against the odds and face any challenge. We can adapt to sudden changes and see the overall picture. While computers may advance to be able to compute equations at unfathomable speeds, they will never be as innovative as the human race.

Overall, this student did a good job, writing a well-ordered argument with examples that were linked back to the overall argument. The student's instructor did comment that the student could have used fewer boosters, which were not needed and made the argument seem overstated at times.

The fact that this was an essay written for a first-year college composition course told you something about the audience and purpose. You could reasonably conclude that it is written for a generally educated audience, and because it is an evidence-based academic essay, you could reasonably conclude that the purpose is to argue for a specific position using evidence. You also saw that a purpose was to use a reading source. Reading the essay, you probably saw that these were reasonable conclusions based on the language and evidence used.

Next we provide a sample annotation, noting many annotations based on rhetorical analysis and information analysis. The bracketed numbers indicate the introductory moves that follow them. ***Hedges*** are italicized and bolded. <u>**Boosters**</u> are underlined and bolded. **Generalizations** are in bold. Use of evidence is indicated in brackets.

> [**Move 1**] As the information age progresses, technological achievement ***seems*** to be increasing <u>**exponentially**</u>. Knowing this, it is ***not unreasonable*** to conclude that computers will, in the not-so-distant future, surpass **humans** in **every** measurable way. [**Move 2**] However, as Brian Christian argues in his article "Mind vs. Machine," this is not the case. [**Move 3—Main argument**] While computers ***may*** be able to imitate **humans** in a

believable matter, the **human race** will **always** be superior by being adaptive and innovative.

[Evidence] In 1950, a test known as the Turing Test, named after its creator, was conceived to test how intelligent a computer program is. This test required several judges to conduct conversations with unseen participants through a computer terminal. Some of these participants were human while the others were computer programs. Based on the conversations, the judges needed to tell them apart. While Turing thought that by the year 2000, a computer would be able to fool thirty percent of the judges, so far this has not come true. **[How to understand evidence]** What Turing failed to realize is the limitless potential that **humans** have.

The **human race** is **constantly** changing to combat new threats to its existence. **We** can solve **our** problems by either figuring out the solution in **our** head, or by inventing a tool that can solve it for **us**. In this sense, **we always** find a way to continue onward. **[Potential counterargument]** This is not to say that computers cannot solve problems. From solving complex math problems to interpreting what the Turing judges are saying and coming up with an appropriate response, solving problems is what computers do best. **[Refutation of potential counterargument]** However, what computers fail at is persevering through a problem to come up with a solution.

[Evidence] Consider a logic problem known as the "dot problem." In this problem, nine dots are placed in a 3 × 3 grid. These nine dots must be connected by drawing exactly four lines without lifting the pencil from the paper and going through each dot only once. Initial efforts of going from dot to dot will not work and will just lead to a dead end. However, by literally going "outside the box" and extending the lines beyond the 3 × 3 grid, the participant can discover the answer. **[How to understand evidence]** In this aspect of problem solving, computers fall far behind **humans**. **[Another example]** A program called "Catherine" who competed in the 1997 Turing test showed this lapse of logic. After engaging in a deep discussion about the Clintons and Whitewater, Catherine was asked the simple question if she wanted some water. At this point the computer could not understand what the judge was asking and erupted into **complete** gibberish. Even after the judge tried to engage the program further, it was unable to recover. **[How to understand evidence]** This shows the key difference between computers and **human minds**. Computers are **simply** unable to see the bigger picture. While computers will **simply** crash when they cannot figure something out, **humans** will seek out additional data while also using their current data to come up with multiple solutions.

It is in this sense that computers will **never** be equal to **humans**. What **humans** have that computers cannot imitate is that creative spark. It is these "ah-ha moments," when an intuitive leap creates a new creative insight, that computers **utterly** fail in comparison. [**Example**] It is this sudden burst of thinking that has saved **our** lives in **our** prehistoric days and will continue to enable **us** to solve any problem that **we** might come across. [**How to understand example**] While the Turing Test may have a valid method of measuring intelligence, it fails to measure what it is to be **human.**

[**Support**] As Christian said, "We're not going to take defeat lying down." The **human race** will **always** be willing to stand up against the odds and face **any** challenge. **We** can adapt to sudden changes and see the overall picture. While computers ***may*** advance to be able to compute equations at unfathomable speeds, they will **never** be as innovative as the **human race.**

CHAPTER SUMMARY

Language and moves give us clues about the writer, audience, and purpose of a piece of writing. In our own writing, we want to use clues to help convey relevant information about our purpose and our attention to audience. As you continue to read and write critically, consider the context, rhetoric, and information in each argument. As you do so, you will become more practiced at identifying audience, purpose, moves, language, arguments, and evidence. These abilities will improve both your analysis of others' arguments and how you craft and revise your own.

9 AVOIDING PLAGIARISM

What is plagiarism? How do most people define it, and how can you avoid it?

Learning objectives in this chapter

- Define plagiarism, including overt and subtle forms
- Practice recognizing plagiarism
- Analyze a real-world case study involving plagiarism
- Identify strategies for avoiding plagiarism

Key concepts addressed in this chapter

- Plagiarism
- Cheating
- Attribution and non-attribution
- Patch writing

Introduction

First, see what you think. Which of the following count as plagiarism?

a. Submitting someone else's writing as your own
b. Copying paragraphs from a source text without using quotation marks
c. Copying paragraphs from a source text without using an in-text citation
d. Copying from a source text and then deleting or replacing some words or grammatical structures

The answer is in the footnote.*

* For most institutions in North American and Western Europe, all four of the above constitute plagiarism and require punitive action on students.

Here are some terms used to describe acts of plagiarism:

a. **Cheating**: submitting someone else's writing as your own
b. **Non-attribution**: copying paragraphs from a source text without using quotation marks
c. **Non-attribution**: copying paragraphs from a source text without using an in-text citation
d. **Patch writing**: copying from a source text and then deleting or replacing some words or grammatical structures

These expectations are not always clear to students or followed by them. Some students understand only A, "cheating," to be plagiarism, while many instructors, as well as plagiarism detection software packages, treat all four as plagiarism.

In the first part of this chapter we define plagiarism and offer some guidelines for avoiding it. Then we turn to a case study, a real-world case of plagiarism by a college student who tried for a long time to repeal her case, on the grounds that she was not guilty of plagiarism and that the consequences of her case adversely affected her future opportunities. For the assignment in the chapter, you will use both the overview of plagiarism and the case study to inform your writing.

Defining Plagiarism

Many universities use a multilayered definition like the following to define plagiarism.[1] Some universities, such as the University of Wisconsin, require that students sign a contract acknowledging their understanding of this definition when they enroll.

Plagiarism is:

- Using someone else's words or ideas without proper documentation
- Copying some portion of your text from another source without proper acknowledgment
- Borrowing another person's specific ideas without documenting their source
- Having another person correct or revise your work (versus getting feedback from a peer or tutor that you then try to implement)
- Turning in a paper written by another person, from an essay "service," or from a website

---

1. R. M. Howard, "A Plagiarism Pentimento," *Journal of Teaching Writing* 11, no. 3 (1993): 233–246, and Rebecca Moore Howard, "Plagiarisms, Authorships, and the Academic Death Penalty," *College English* 57, no. 7 (1995): 788–806.

High schools also have plagiarism definitions and policies. According to the Common Core Standards for Writing adopted by most U.S. school districts, being able to avoid plagiarism is an important skill when using other sources. The Common Core Standard for Writing in 11th–12th Grade states[2]:

> W.11-12.8 Gather relevant information from multiple authoritative print and digital sources, using advanced searches effectively; assess the strengths and limitations of each source in terms of the task, purpose, and audience; integrate information into the text selectively to maintain the flow of ideas, avoiding plagiarism and overreliance on any one source and following a standard format for citation.

Now that you know how many institutions define plagiarism, how can you prevent it?

Three Tips for Preventing Plagiarism

First, clarify with your instructor what you can practice and watch for. For example, you could ask questions such as: Is it necessary to cite the textbook when I mention an example from it, if it isn't a direct quote? How should I proceed if I'm not sure about when or how to cite something?

Second, be able to summarize based on your understanding. After reading source materials, practice summarizing them without looking at them. This will help you develop your ability to summarize according to your understanding, rather than by attempting to reword what you read. This is not a simple task, but it gets easier as you practice.

Finally, double-check texts using self-detection services. Before submitting your papers to instructors, try using one of the following self-detection plagiarism tools to double-check it:

- http://www.plagscan.com/
- http://www.grammarly.com/Plagiarism_Checker
- http://www.smallseotools.com/plagiarism—-checker/
- http://www.plagiarisma.net/

---

2. See more Common Core State Standards here: http://www.corestandards.org/ELA-Literacy/W/11-12/8/.

A Case Study of Plagiarism

Case Scenario

The Setting

Rutgers University, New Jersey, USA

The Characters

Amanda Serpico, a senior at Rutgers at the time of the case
Mrs. and Mr. Serpico, parents of Amanda Serpico
Leon Laureij, Rutgers doctoral student serving as the "Argumentation" course instructor
Attorney hired by the Serpico family
Edward Sponzilli, a Bridgewater attorney hired by Rutgers
Rutgers University administrators

Case Study Readings

- Jonathan Bailey, "Lessons from the Amanda Serpico Plagiarism Case," *Plagiarism Today*, December 5, 2011, https://www.plagiarismtoday.com/2011/12/05/lessons-from-the-amanda-serpico-plagiarism-case/.
- Jonathan Bailey, "Follow-Up Updates on the Amanda Serpico Plagiarism Case," *Plagiarism Today*, December 8, 2011, https://www.plagiarismtoday.com/2011/12/08/follow-up-updates-on-the-amanda-serpico-plagiarism-case/.
- Kelly Herboer, "Former Rutgers Student Says Software Detecting Plagiarism Was Wrong When It Flagged Her Work, Caused Her to Fail," NJ.com, December 4, 2011, http://www.nj.com/news/index.ssf/2011/12/former_rutgers_student_says_so.html.

Assignment

After reading the introduction to plagiarism in this chapter, read the case study materials on the Amanda Serpico and Rutgers University case. Then, write a paper in which you take a position on how Serpico and representatives of Rutgers (e.g., the instructor and administrators) handled the issue. Could they have handled the case better, or is there no way in which the proceedings could have been improved? Provide your reasoning, regardless of your position. Your writing should show your understanding of plagiarism, the case, and the stakeholders' perspectives.

This assignment is a little different from the ones in the case study chapters because it asks you to show your understanding of plagiarism as a writing issue, and also to analyze and respond to a case study. But it is similar in that you will show your knowledge of the issues and stakeholders in the case study. For your audience, write to university and high school administrators who are drafting plagiarism policies and considering plagiarism cases.

The format is as follows:

- The paper should be a minimum of 1,000 words long. It can be longer. Type the word count at the end of the paper.
- Typed, double-spaced, one-inch margins
- APA documentation style
- A minimum of three sources, two of which must be peer-reviewed. You may use the sources listed in the "Case Study Readings" for one of these sources, but you should have at least two additional sources. In other words, the sources given can serve as one of your three required sources but not more than that. (Wikipedia will not be accepted as a source.)

CHAPTER SUMMARY

This chapter addresses plagiarism and various ways to define and identify it. The chapter also outlines a case in which a student was suspected of plagiarism and faced serious consequences as a result. Take your time with assignments and be careful in your use of sources to help avoid any possible suspicion of plagiarism. And don't hesitate to ask your instructor, librarians, or other faculty and staff questions so that you can be sure you understand how to recognize and avoid plagiarism.

10 REFLECTION

Why reflect? How can reflection help you as a thinker and writer?

Learning objectives in this chapter

- Reflection as an important learning tool to take charge of your writing and learning processes
- The three stages of reflection: monitoring, evaluating, and adjusting
- The use of reflection with case studies
- A list of sample reflection questions

Key concepts addressed in this chapter

- Reflection
- Monitoring stage
- Evaluating stage
- Adjusting stage

Introduction

Reflection is an important part of learning. To reflect on your learning means to think critically about your learning successes and failures, to connect the content you are learning to information you already know, and to devise ways to apply your new understanding to future learning situations. Reflecting on your learning promotes self-awareness and encourages self-assessment. Reflective writing helps you reflect on your learning experiences—not only **WHAT** you've learned, but **HOW** you learned it. Reflecting specifically on why you made certain choices in the process of writing (or any other task) can help you build your mental toolkit.

For example, you might reflect on the best way to study for an exam: by yourself or with a study group. As part of your reflective process, you might consider the advantages and disadvantages of each situation:

> When you study by yourself, you can control where, when, and how long you study.
> When you study with a group, you have to meet at a certain time, but you can pool resources and get help from the group with questions you might have about the material.

Thinking about these factors could help you decide which option is the best use of your study time.

When you study, you are usually not aware of the mental processes and strategies you are using. You might not realize which of your current learning strategies work for you and which don't. Reflection is one way you can make these mental processes and learning strategies visible. Identifying and evaluating the effectiveness of your learning strategies can give you more control over them and guide you to make more informed choices about the way you learn best and the way you write best. Further, the insights you gain can help you tackle similar writing and learning tasks in the future.

Like critical thinking, reflection can become a habit of mind—one that will benefit you since the reflection process encourages you to take charge of your learning. But, like many other learning habits, getting good at reflection takes practice.

Reflection can be fairly simple, like our example about studying, or it can be more involved. It is often a three-stage process:

1. Check-in or monitoring (*How am I doing?*)
2. Evaluating (*How well am I doing?*)
3. Adjusting or making changes to your actions (*How can I do better?*) based on the results of Steps 1 and 2.

Thus, reflection is often an umbrella term for a series of recurring actions. In this chapter, although we are breaking down reflection into a series of stages, it is really more of a recursive process: You might find yourself doing all the stages together or moving back and forth in the same reflective writing between more than one stage. You'll want to figure out the best way reflection works for you. While the approach we describe here involves asking and answering questions as a guide for reflection, that's not the only way to approach reflection. Other ways to reflect on your thinking and writing progress might include writing logs, journals, blog entries, error logs, and free writing.

We recommend that you get into the habit of writing short reflections (150–500 words) to check your progress as you work through your paper assignments. Let your creativity flow as you think over and ask questions about how things went, what worked, and what didn't work as you progressed through the steps of the case study. You can do the reflection on your own, use the questions at the end of the chapter as a guide, or use prompts assigned by your instructor.

Check-In or Monitoring Stage

Reflection provides you with a way to check in and monitor your progress when you are in the middle of an assignment. In this stage, your reflections might sound more descriptive since you are trying to identify or describe your prewriting, research, and drafting processes. Descriptions might look start out like these:

> For this paper I used lots of sources such as ...
> I think I did a good job on this paper because ...
> My research process included ...

You might also answer questions. For example:

> Did you find enough research for the case study?
> Did you contribute your best effort to the small group discussion?
> Did you understand the issues of the case?

Checking in periodically during the different stages of the case discussions and writing process will allow you to make any changes necessary to improve your performance while you are still working on the assignment rather than after you are done. Checking in through reflection lets you set new writing goals, alter existing drafts, or adjust your writing strategies if something isn't working. Later, after you have completed the assignment, you can review your reflections and apply what you've learned to the next case study or writing assignment.

Reflection can also help you overcome writer's block, or when you feel stuck. Use reflection questions to push beyond the "this isn't working" feeling to get at why you are stuck.

For example, let's say you've been assigned to do a reflection on your research process. You've picked the following questions to help you write it:

> Did I have a solid research question to guide my research?
> How did I find my sources?
> Where did I find my sources?

Here's what you might write:

> For my first draft, instead of using a research question, I generated search terms from the main points in my thesis: the lack of health care resources on campus, the need for less expensive health care insurance options, and more coverage for mental health care. After I'd come up with a list of terms, I located my sources online. I Googled some of the key words from my topic and checked out the top hits for each of the search terms. I was lucky and found sources for each of my sub-points. I found newspaper articles on campus health care, an article from a university website on student heath and absenteeism from their policy institute, and a PDF of a journal article on mental health care concerns. I was able to download all of my sources. Since I found my sources so quickly, I only spent 10% of my time on research and the rest on drafting.

Evaluating Stage

Reflection, like critical thinking, involves asking questions. When you reflect on your learning process, you are thinking critically about your experience and your knowledge as well as course or case study content.

For reflection to be valuable in the long term, you need to do more than just describe what you did. Description is only the beginning—the surface of reflection. You can take the descriptions you generated in the monitoring stage and use them to go beneath the surface and dig deeper and evaluate what you've observed. Think about the difference between "I did this" and "Why did I do this?" Which asks you to think more? The question will lead you to a more critical understanding of your learning and writing processes.

Evaluation is probably something you already subconsciously do on your own. It's also something you do in class, for example with your peer editing group. To jump start your reflective evaluation process, you could always use criteria generated in class or guides given to you by your instructor.

Some questions to help you dig deeper are:

- What does it mean?
- What am I going to do now that I know this?
- What are the advantages and disadvantages to the research and writing approach I used?
- Why did or didn't my argument convince my readers?

As a writer, you want to develop a critical faculty as well as a set of strategies you can use to evaluate your own writing. Evaluative reflection can help you build the critical and creative habits of mind necessary to reimagine and revise your drafts. Ultimately you will need to become your own best critic and your own best advocate of your writing.

Let's say that after you get your draft back with comments from your peers and your instructor, you are asked to reflect on how you used your sources and their effectiveness. For this reflection, you decide to take a more evaluative approach. You start with the following questions:

> What were the advantages to the sources I used?
> What were the drawbacks to the sources?
> Why didn't my research help support my argument in a way that was convincing to my peers?

Here's what you might write:

> The main advantages of the sources I used were that they were easy to access and easy to read since they were all written for a general audience—well, except for the journal article. Since they were aimed at different audiences (the general public, a university community, and a scholarly audience), they were also able to provide different points of view on my topic. But it seems like one of the advantages turned out to be a kind of disadvantage: Being short turned out to be both an advantage and a disadvantage since the two shorter sources didn't contain a lot of information on the topic, so I was only able to get one quote or example from each of them. This limited the claim I could support for each of my sub-points. Also, each of the non-scholarly articles only presented one point of view and didn't include any counterarguments. The journal article potentially had lots more information in it, but I found it hard to read and only skimmed it, just picking out a few quotes from the conclusion. I guess I got so focused on finding sources to support my points that I forgot about counterarguments. I discovered that just having three sources can be limiting since it breaks down to one source per sub-point and if that source isn't strong, it can weaken the argument for that point. The comments I got made me realize that the sources I selected were kind of random, since I just picked the first ones that came up in Google. Perhaps that's not the best approach. Even though they were on my topic, it wasn't clear to my readers how they related to the points I was trying to make. So while my sources seemed good to start with, and the perspective of different audiences was useful, they just didn't provide enough information in the end to convince the other students in my peer editing group.

Adjusting Stage

Lastly, reflection provides you with a way to improve your writing and learning processes. The answers from your monitoring and evaluative reflections will let you pinpoint areas in your writing and learning processes that might need adjustment. Sometimes the changes you might want to make are obvious; other times you can use the reflection questions to help you generate new ideas, alternative plans, or new strategies. Here are some reflective questions for adjustment:

- What could I have done differently?
- How can I apply this in the future?
- What changes will improve my writing process?
- What strategies will help me to be better at discussion, research, drafting, and rewriting?

Adjustment represents the final stage in the reflection process. It allows you to be proactive about your writing and learning. It gives you the tools you need to become more aware of how you write and the information you need to adjust your process so you can become a more successful writer and learner.

Let's say you've been asked to turn in a reflection on changes to your research process as part of your revision plan for your next draft. You used the following questions to start your reflection:

> What could I have done differently?
> What changes to doing research can I make to improve my next paper?

Here's what you might write:

> Thinking about the comments I got and what I can do to improve, the first thing I think I need to do is to give myself more time to do research. Another thing I should think about is what I need from my sources. What am I looking for in a source? Am I just looking for sources I can use to quote or am I looking for something that will help me better understand the topic? Or both?
>
> Another thing to consider might be not to use the first hits in the search engine, but to explore a little further. I might also search other places besides Google, like the library databases. From my peer editing comments, it seems like longer sources with more information might help my argument, so I might want to use more scholarly sources in the future. I guess this means I will need to come up with a better strategy for reading journal articles since I'll probably be reading more of them. Using only the

> minimum required number of sources seemed like a good idea at the time, but now I see that adding more sources could help my argument and also give me a better way to include counterarguments. Mostly, I need to think about who my audience is and what evidence will convince them. This means paying more attention to the types of sources that will convince my readers instead of just using the first ones I find. One thing I've realized is that even for a short paper the quality of the sources is an important factor in convincing a reader.

You should use the insights gained from the final reflection to add to your revision plan a list of the changes you plan to make to improve your use of sources.

Reflection and Case Studies

Reflection can enrich your experience of the case study on two levels: (1) understanding the case content and (2) understanding your writing process. Case studies are designed to teach you communication skills, collaboration, analytical thinking, and problem solving. Each case asks you to get personally involved in the story by stepping into the shoes of the stakeholders and trying out different perspectives and points of view. You can use reflection questions to help you think about the needs of the stakeholders as well as the needs of the audience. Since reflection asks you to think critically about your learning experiences, it can be a good tool to see if you are where you want to be.

Check Yourself

Use these questions to help you reflect on your progress:

- What have you learned from this case study?
- What is significant about the case study and its issues?
- How can you apply what you learned to the next case study, or to another class?

Reflection can also help you to be better prepared as you move through the steps of the case study. The better prepared you are, the more you will get out the class discussions and small group work on the case. You will have more ideas and will have an easier time doing research and drafting your argument paper.

Next we will offer some questions you can use as a guide for reflections on different parts of the case study. Your instructor may provide specific reflection questions for you as well. You don't need to restrict yourself to these questions; include any other relevant aspects of your experience in the class as it relates to your awareness of the "what" and "how" of your learning process. As you get more practiced at it, you will come up with your own approaches and questions to guide your reflections.

To get started, pick one or two of these guided reflection questions to focus on for a short reflection, or pick a topic you need help with or want to explore. As you write, allow your thoughts to flow.

Case Scenario and Case Issues

- What are some ways that critical reading techniques can increase my understanding of the case?
- What should I be looking for in the case scenario?
- What is the best way for me to identify the case issue(s) and solution(s)?
- What information about the case (stakeholders, issues) is important to remember?
- What did I learn that was new about the case topic?
- Why is the case issue(s) important?
- Why do I feel strongly about one side or another of the issues?
- What can I do if I don't understand the case?
- What can I do if I don't understand the supplementary readings?

Class Discussions and Group Work

- How can I use the class discussions and group work to identify other points of view?
- How can I learn to become comfortable with uncertainty and multiple points of view?
- What are some of the benefits of thoughtfully and critically considering the different points of view in the case?
- In what ways do I try to see the case from the perspectives of different stakeholders?
- How carefully am I listening to my peers in class discussions?
- What new things did I learn from listening to my peers' opinions?
- How do my contributions to the class contribute to my peers' understanding of the case?
- What are the consequences to my peers and me if I am unprepared to discuss the case?
- What could I have done to contribute more to the group discussion?
- What would make me change my mind about the case issues or solutions?
- What can I do if I don't understand the issues raised in the case during discussion?

Research and Drafting

- What will help me to effectively research my paper?
- What are the best ways to use my time wisely?
- What gaps in my knowledge do I need to fill in order to write my draft?
- In what ways would researching multiple points of view on the case help me write my argument?
- What is the relationship between research and persuasion?
- How do class discussion and group work help prepare me to write my draft?
- How can I use my notes from classwork to generate counterarguments?
- How can I incorporate insights from the classwork into my drafting process?
- How can I incorporate insights from stakeholder interviews into planning and writing my draft?
- What will help me to effectively draft my argument?
- Why do some writing techniques work better for me than others?
- What direction should I take my draft?
- How did I arrive at my take on the argument?
- Is my draft where I want it to be?
- What changes do I need to make to my draft?
- In what ways does my solution to the case's problem challenge my reader beyond the obvious?

Final Reflection

- What did you learn about the issues of the case?
- What did you learn about process of constructing an argument and counterarguments for an issue?
- What did you learn about doing research, both how to do it and why it is important to argumentation?
- Now that you have done one case study, what approaches will you use for the next one? For instance, what will you do differently and what will you do the same?
- What did you like about doing the case study? What didn't you like about it?
- What are any other responses or reflections that you had on the case assignment?

CHAPTER SUMMARY

Reflection is a learning tool commonly used to help students understand and evaluate their writing process and other learning strategies. Understanding the mental processes and techniques that you use will enable you to make any necessary adjustments to improve how your learn and write. The process of reflection is broken down into three recursive stages: monitoring, evaluation, and adjustment.

These stages can be used to examine any aspect of the writing process or the case study assignment. While reflection can be applied to all learning situations, it is especially relevant to case studies because it helps you focus on preparation, critical thinking, audience awareness, and problem solving. As you continue to work on case studies and your other coursework, consider how you can use reflection in this class or other classes to help you become a better learner and a more successful writer.

II CASE STUDIES

Part Two of the textbook consists of eight complete cases. Each case includes the case scenario as well as other instructional materials including prewriting activities, discussion questions and assignments. Instructors can select the cases most appropriate for their classes.

1 CENSORSHIP IN THE PUBLIC SCHOOLS

Case Scenario 1: The Harry Potter Books by J. K. Rowling

The Setting

A medium sized middle school with a diverse student population in a midsized U.S. town

The Characters

Greg Hartmann, language arts teacher at MacArthur Middle School
Logan Davis, a seventh-grader in his class
Anna Davis, Logan's mother
Carla Rivera, the principal of MacArthur Middle School
Hanna Larson, the school librarian
Oliver Voss, Paul Norton, Sharon Tuttle, Clara Alvarez, and Maria Vega, school board members
Mr. and Ms. Randolph, parents who complain about the principal's policy

The Issues

Meeting with an Upset Parent

Anna Davis set up a meeting with Greg Hartmann, her seventh-grade son Logan's language arts teacher, to discuss one of his class assignments. Logan was an average student; he did his work but didn't participate very much in class discussions. The door opened and Ms. Davis came in.

"Ms. Davis, it's good to see you," Greg said. "Won't you sit down." He indicated a chair by his desk, and then sat in a chair opposite her.

"Mr. Hartmann, thank you for seeing me."

"What did you want to talk about?"

She reached into her large bag and pulled out a book covered in brown paper and an essay assignment sheet. "This." She thrust them at him.

He took them from her and looked at the assignment sheet. It was the essay assignment on characterization he'd given this week using *Harry Potter and the Sorcerer's Stone* by J. K. Rowling.

"I cannot allow my son to do this assignment," she said. "My husband and I are good Christians. We do not allow our children to read books glorifying witchcraft."

"Ms. Davis, the book is a fantasy rather than real. I'm using it to teach the class to analyze characters in fiction."

"The book is immoral, Mr. Hartmann. I don't think any of the children in the school should be exposed to its teachings. I want the book taken out of the classroom and school library. "

"You want to ban the use of the book in the school?"

"Yes, I do." She nodded emphatically.

"I see." Greg was flabbergasted. To him, it was a great book. All the kids seemed to love it. He'd never imagined that this would happen. "Well, Ms. Davis, in order to do that you will have to fill out the American Library Association challenge forms. The school librarian has them."

"Very well, I'll stop by the library and get them. But I expect you to quit using the book in your classroom." She stood up to leave. Greg walked her to the classroom door and said goodbye.

As soon as she was gone, he headed for the principal's office. He hoped that Principal Rivera was still there. He needed her advice.

He knocked on the door frame of her office and stuck his head in.

"Carla, got a minute?"

She looked up from the pile of forms on her desk. "Sure, come in," she said. "Sit down. What do you need?"

"I've got a situation with a parent."

"Oh?"

"Ms. Davis, the mother of one of my seventh-graders, came in today to complain about a writing assignment that I'd assigned using one of J. K. Rowling's books. She felt the book was anti-Christian and she wants it pulled."

"Just from your classroom?"

"No, from the school library as well."

"Can she be talked out of this?"

"I don't know. She seemed pretty adamant."

"Well, we'll just have to go through the steps and see if we can find a solution that works for everyone. Did you give her the challenge forms?"

"I sent her to Hanna to get them."

"Good. Next, we'll arrange a meeting with you, Hanna, and Ms. Davis. Hanna can serve as a mediator. Greg, see if you can come up with some kind of compromise."

"I'll try."

"Don't worry, Greg. These things usually get worked out."

"Thanks, Carla," Greg said as he stood up to leave.

Meeting Between the Upset Parent, the Teacher, and the Librarian

Principal Rivera arranged for Ms. Davis to meet with Mr. Hartmann and Hanna Larson, the school librarian, the following Tuesday. She offered the use of the small conference room next to the main office.

Hanna started off by saying, "Ms. Davis, we're glad you're meeting with us today, and we want you to know that we appreciate you bringing this concern to Mr. Hartmann. The school wants your son's learning experience to be a good one."

"I just want the best for Logan," Ms. Davis said. She turned to Mr. Hartmann and asked, "What are you going to do about the assignment?"

"Well," he said, "Logan needs to complete a writing assignment or lose points, which wouldn't be fair to him. So I propose that he do a similar assignment using a different book."

"That sounds fair," Ms. Davis said, "depending on what book, of course."

"Is *Treasure Island* by Robert Louis Stevenson acceptable?" he asked.

"That's fine," she said.

"Good. I'll give him the assignment tomorrow." Greg was relieved. That part had gone well; he just hoped the rest of the discussion would go as well.

"What about the other children? Are you going to change the assignment for them?" Ms. Davis asked.

"No, Ms. Davis, I wasn't planning on it," he replied.

"They shouldn't be exposed to that book either."

"Ms. Davis, until your challenge to the book has gone through the process, Mr. Hartman can still use the assignment," Hanna pointed out. "You are the only parent who has complained about the book."

"I'm the only one with guts, you mean. The school should not be a place of godlessness."

"Ms. Davis, the purpose of education is the free exchange of ideas. Young people should be introduced to different perspectives on many topics," Greg explained.

"Witchcraft is not an acceptable topic for young children, Mr. Hartmann, and you know it. It will only lead to worse things."

"Ms. Davis, while we at the school respect your religious beliefs, the Constitution guarantees a separation of church and state in the First Amendment," said Hanna. "One of the things this means is that the public schools, since they are funded by the state, cannot teach or endorse any particular religious views. I'm sure you understand that we need to be fair to all our students and their parents. Our school represents a wide variety of backgrounds and religions. The First Amendment is designed to protect their rights as well as yours."

"Ms. Larson, I understand the First Amendment just fine. If the schools would stick to teaching the basics, we wouldn't be having this conversation."

Greg sighed and looked at Hanna: This was going to be harder than he thought.

"Ms. Davis, have you read the book?" Greg asked.

"Of course I have. How do you think I know it teaches immoral things? Witchcraft and divination go against the Bible's teachings. The Bible is quite clear on that, Mr. Hartmann. And it's especially troublesome that you want your students to look at the characters' behavior in your assignment. The characters in that book are not good role models. They lie, break rules, and are disobedient. What's more, they get rewarded for this kind of bad behavior! Surely you can't argue that children should be taught it's good to lie! Would you want your students to disobey you?"

"No, I wouldn't. But, Ms. Davis, in my opinion, seventh-graders are quite capable of telling the difference between reality and fantasy. And I could always use the book to promote a discussion of appropriate behavior."

"It would be easier if you just had them read a book where the characters acted morally," Ms. Davis said.

"'Acted morally' according to whose standards, Ms. Davis?" asked Greg. "There are different ways that people can act morally. I put a lot of thought into picking the books and designing the lessons for my classes in order to expose my students to different ways of thinking. What you are asking me to do amounts to censorship. It also undermines my authority as a trained professional in the classroom."

"Mr. Hartmann, I'm sure you're a fine teacher. Logan enjoys your class. What I'm asking you to do is not censorship. As adults we have a responsibility to protect our young people from inappropriate things. You wouldn't teach anything pornographic, would you?"

"Of course not. But *The Sorcerer's Stone* is not pornography."

"No, it's Satanism, which is just as bad."

"That is just one opinion of the book. Other people have very different interpretations of the book, more positive ones. For instance, it's viewed as a contest between good and evil, where Harry and his friends battle evil. Fighting against evil is moral, isn't it, Ms. Davis?" Greg asked.

"You can't trick me with word games! I know that you can't fight evil with evil."

"Ms. Davis, we're not trying to trick you," said Hanna. "We're just trying to show you another perspective on the book, which might explain why Mr. Hartmann is using it in his classroom. What you are asking us to do is censorship, since removing the book from use in the class denies students access to it—"

"And the library, too!" Ms. Davis interrupted.

"—and removing it from the library denies students the right to read the book and form their own opinion," Hanna finished.

"Ms. Larson, you're the librarian so you have to say those kind of things. But parents have rights and responsibilities, too."

"Of course, Ms. Davis," Hanna replied." I'm here to see that all the issues get raised and that you and Mr. Hartmann each get a say on this matter. Mr. Hartmann was hoping that a different assignment for Logan would satisfy your objections to the book."

"In my opinion, the whole class should have a different assignment."

"So you are unwilling to drop your objection to the book, even though Logan is no longer required to read it? You wish to continue your challenge to have the book banned?" Hanna wanted to make sure she understood Ms. Davis's wishes in this matter.

"Yes, I do. Mr. Hartmann, it's nothing against you; it's just that I have to stand up for my beliefs."

"Ms. Davis, I understand. I feel I need to defend mine as well. Unfortunately, our beliefs on this issue are very different," he replied.

"Do you have the challenge forms?" Hanna asked.

"Yes." Ms. Davis reached into her bag and handed them to Hanna.

"Since the three of us were unable to work out a solution, Ms. Davis, you'll need to set up an appointment to talk to the principal," Hanna said.

Meetings Between the Upset Parent and the Principal

Ms. Davis met with Principal Rivera several times. At the first meeting Ms. Davis presented her objections to the book and explained her reasons for wanting it banned, not just for her son but for the entire school. She genuinely felt it was her duty to protect the students from harmful exposure to what she felt were anti-Christian ideas about witchcraft.

Principal Rivera needed to find a compromise that would work for the school and at the same time would protect the First Amendment rights of all the students. Banning a book was a very serious issue. Although she hoped that she and Ms. Davis could find a solution, she'd sent a report to the school board, alerting them that a book challenge was in progress.

At her first meeting with Ms. Davis, Principal Rivera suggested that the book's use in the school be considered by a challenge committee made up of the school librarian, the other seventh-grade English teachers, the seventh-grade level leader, and another parent. Ms. Davis agreed to the committee review if the parent on the committee was "a churchgoing Christian." Otherwise, she was concerned that her objections would not get a fair hearing. Principal Rivera said she would do her best but legally could not ask anyone who volunteered to serve on the committee about their religious practices. The principal was able to assemble a committee, and they were given two weeks to review the challenge.

At the end of the two weeks, Principal Rivera notified Ms. Davis that the committee had made its decision. As part of reviewing her complaint, the committee looked at the American Library Association's guidelines as well as the policies of comparable school districts in the state. The committee saw no reason that the book could not be used by teachers in the school.

Ms. Davis was very disappointed with the decision and threatened to go to the school board with her concerns. Principal Rivera then proposed a compromise. J. K. Rowling's books would be restricted from use in the classroom. They would still be available in the school library, but students would need their parents' permission to check them out. Reluctantly, Ms. Davis agreed to the compromise; she couldn't tell other parents what to do, after all.

While the principal felt the solution was not a perfect one, she hoped it was one the school as a whole could live with. However, those hopes dissipated when she received phone calls several weeks later from irate parents who objected to the policy of requiring permission slips for the Harry Potter books. They accused the principal of censoring what their children were allowed to read. When the principal tried to explain about Ms. Davis's complaint, she was accused of allowing one person to railroad school policy. At this point, all the principal could do was tell the unhappy parents to take the matter to the school board.

The School Board Meeting

On Thursday evening, the regularly scheduled school board meeting took place in the Education Service Center's meeting room. When the chair of the school board, Oliver Voss, arrived early to set up the mikes, he noticed that the room was filling up. He glanced at his watch. It was 5:40 p.m. and the meeting wouldn't start until 6. By the looks of things, they'd need more chairs. Normally, not many people attended the school board meetings, even though they were open to the public.

It's probably because of the book controversy, Oliver thought. Each set of parents had submitted a letter outlining their concern, and they would each be speaking at tonight's meeting.

At 6 p.m., Oliver checked with the other board members, Paul Norton, Sharon Tuttle, Clara Alvarez, and Maria Vega, for any last-minute business and then called the meeting to order. The meeting droned on as they worked their way through the agenda. Finally they came to the agenda item concerning the Harry Potter books.

Ms. Tuttle summarized the situation: "The board has been asked to make a final decision about the case of using books from J. K. Rowling's Harry Potter series at MacArthur Middle School. The case so far is that one parent, Ms. Davis, complained about the use of the book for a classroom assignment. A committee reviewed her complaint about the book and decided it was fine to use in school. As a compromise solution, the principal put in place a policy whereby students must get their parents' permission to check out any of the Harry Potter books from the school library. According to the principal, several parents complained about that policy, and Mr. and Ms. Randolph wrote a formal letter of complaint to the school board, asking the school board to rescind the principal's policy. Ms. Davis and the Randolphs will be given time to present their sides of the issue, and then we will open the mike up for comments. Ms. Davis, you can begin."

Ms. Davis rose and went to the mike facing the board. She reiterated her reasons for banning the book, stating that it glorifies witchcraft and divination, which goes against the teachings of the Bible. She stated that it also glorifies lying and disobedience, which goes against sound moral principles of behavior and leads children to hatred and rebellion. Because children should not be exposed to immoral and satanic ideas, she argued, and because it is the school board's job to protect the values of the community, she was asking the board to ban the books from use in the classroom and from the school library.

After Ms. Davis spoke, Mr. Randolph got up and addressed the school board: "My wife and I, as well as several other parents of children at the school, object to the present restrictions in place that keep our children from having easy access to the books of J. K. Rowling. We feel that this is blatant censorship and a violation of our First Amendment rights. We request that the school board rescind the school principal's current policy. For the record, I want to state that my wife and I are also Christian and attend our church regularly. J. K. Rowling's books do not threaten our Christian beliefs."

He continued, "The Harry Potter books fit into a long tradition of fantasy and fairytale books. Does Ms. Davis want to ban Grimms' fairy tales or the Chronicles of Narnia? Our children are old enough to tell fantasy from reality. These are engaging books that encourage our children to read. Ms. Davis is welcome to, and indeed has the right to, restrict what her son reads, but she doesn't have the right to restrict what our daughter reads. We urge the school board not to let the voice of one parent dictate to the majority. It is the school board's job to protect the rights of our children and allow them to be exposed to many different viewpoints so they will be prepared for the real world."

After Mr. Randolph finished, Mr. Voss opened the floor up for discussion.

Several parents got up and spoke in support of the Randolphs, while others supported Ms. Davis's viewpoints. Several students spoke. They talked about how much they liked the books and how the books made reading fun. The discussion got heated, ending up with both sides calling each other names:

"A bunch of religious nuts can't tell my kids what to read."

"Godless liberals shouldn't be allowed the ruin this country."

"The religious right should just mind their own business. You all want our kids to be ignorant and bored."

"Our children should be exposed to the classics, not popular books."

When the debate disintegrated into name calling, Mr. Voss called for order and ended the discussion.

"The school board will rule on this matter at the next meeting," he told the agitated crowd.

Your Task

You decide: What should the school board do?

Case Scenario 2: *The Absolutely True Diary of a Part-time Indian* by Sherman Alexie

The Setting

A medium sized middle school with a diverse student population in a midsized U.S. town

The Characters

Greg Hartmann, language arts teacher at MacArthur Middle School
Logan Davis, a seventh-grader in his class
Anna Davis, Logan's mother
Carla Rivera, the principal of MacArthur Middle School
Hanna Larson, the school librarian
Oliver Voss, Paul Norton, Sharon Tuttle, Clara Alvarez, and Maria Vega, school board members
Mr. and Ms. Randolph, parents who complain about the principal's policy

The Issues

Meeting with an Upset Parent

Anna Davis set up a meeting with Greg Hartmann, her seventh-grade son Logan's language arts teacher, to discuss one of his class assignments. Logan was an average student; he did his work but didn't participate very much in class discussions. The door opened and Ms. Davis came in.

"Ms. Davis, it's good to see you," Greg said. "Won't you sit down." He indicated a chair by his desk, and then sat in a chair opposite her.

"Mr. Hartmann, thank you for seeing me."

"What did you want to talk about?"

She reached into her large bag and pulled out a book covered in brown paper and an essay assignment sheet. "This." She thrust them at him.

He took them from her and looked at the assignment sheet. It was the essay assignment on exploring identity through a character analysis he'd given this week using *The Absolutely True Diary of a Part-Time Indian* by Sherman Alexie.

"I cannot allow my son to do this assignment," she told Mr. Hartmann. "My husband and I are good, upstanding members of the community. We do not allow our children to read books that contain vulgar and obscene language."

"Ms. Davis, the book is told from the point of view of a teenager," Greg explained. "I'm using it to teach the class about racism and overcoming adversity."

"The book contains depictions of sexual acts, Mr. Hartmann! I don't think any of the students in the school should be exposed to sexually explicit material. That's just wrong! I want the book taken out of the classroom and school library."

"You want to ban the use of the book in the school?"

"Yes, I do." She nodded emphatically.

"I see." Greg was flabbergasted. It was an award-winning book and all the kids loved it. He'd never imagined that this would happen with one of his students.

"Well, Ms. Davis, in order to do that you will have to fill out the American Library Association challenge forms. The school librarian has them."

"Very well, I'll stop by the library and get them. But I expect you to quit using the book in your classroom." She stood up to leave.

Greg walked her to the classroom door and said goodbye.

As soon as she was gone, he headed for the principal's office. He hoped that Principal Rivera was still there. He needed her advice.

He knocked on the door frame of her office and stuck his head in.

"Carla, got a minute?"

She looked up from the pile of forms on her desk. "Sure, come in," she said. "Sit down. What do you need?"

"I've got a situation with a parent."

"Oh?"

"Ms. Davis, the mother of one of my seventh-graders, came in today to complain about a writing assignment that I'd assigned using Sherman Alexie's book. She felt the book was inappropriate and she wants it pulled."

"Just from your classroom?"

"No, from the school library as well."

"Can she be talked out of this?"

"I don't know, Carla. She seemed pretty adamant."

"Well, we'll just have to go through the steps and see if we can find a solution that works for everyone. Did you give her the challenge forms?"

"I sent her to Hanna to get them."

"Good. Next, we'll arrange a meeting with you, Hanna, and Ms. Davis. Hanna can serve as a mediator. Greg, see if you can come up with some kind of compromise."

"I'll try."

"Don't worry, Greg. These things usually get worked out."

"Thanks, Carla," Greg said as he stood up to leave.

Meeting Between the Upset Parent, the Teacher, and the Librarian

Principal Rivera arranged for Ms. Davis to meet with Mr. Hartmann and Hanna Larson, the school librarian, the following Tuesday. She offered the use of the small conference room next to the main office.

Hanna started off by saying, "Ms. Davis, we're glad you're meeting with us today, and we want you to know that we appreciate you bringing this concern to Mr. Hartmann. The school wants your son's learning experience to be a good one."

"I just want the best for Logan," Ms. Davis said. She turned to Mr. Hartmann and asked, "What are you going to do about the assignment?"

"Well," he said, "Logan needs to complete a writing assignment or lose points, which wouldn't be fair to him. So I propose that he do a similar assignment using a different book."

"That sounds fair," Ms. Davis said, "depending on what book, of course."

"Is *The House on Mango Street* by Sandra Cisneros acceptable?" he asked.

"That's fine," she said.

"Good, I'll give him the assignment tomorrow." Greg was relieved. That part had gone well. He just hoped that the rest of the discussion would go as well.

"What about the other children? Are you going to change the assignment for them?" Ms. Davis asked.

"No, Ms. Davis, I wasn't planning on it," he replied.

"They shouldn't be exposed to that book either."

"Ms. Davis, until your challenge to the book has gone through the process, Mr. Hartman can still use the assignment," Hanna said. "You are the only parent who has complained about the book."

"I'm the only one with guts, you mean. The school should not be a place where students learn about antisocial behavior," she declared.

"Actually, Ms. Davis, the purpose of education is the free exchange of ideas. Young people should be introduced to different perspectives on many topics," Greg explained.

"Vulgar language and alcoholism are not acceptable topics for young people, Mr. Hartmann, and you know it."

"Ms. Davis, while we at the school respect your rights as a parent, one purpose of education is to expose students to different experiences. Our school represents a wide variety of backgrounds and it's important that all voices be heard," Hanna said.

"Ms. Larson, if the schools would stick to teaching the basics, and leave teaching about values to the parents, we wouldn't be having this conversation."

Greg sighed and looked at Hanna: This was going to be harder than he thought.

"Ms. Davis, have you actually read the book?" Greg asked.

"Of course I have! How do you think I know it contains references to sex, profanity, and depictions of bullying and alcoholism? By assigning a book like this, you are giving the impression that the school condones this type of behavior. It's especially troublesome that you want your students to look at the characters' behavior in your assignment. The characters in that book are not good role models: They drink, lie, abuse children, and use profane language. Surely you can't argue that children should be taught it's acceptable to beat up other students on the playground!"

"No I wouldn't," said Greg. "But, Ms. Davis, in my opinion, seventh-graders are quite capable of telling the difference between right and wrong. And I could always use the book to promote a discussion of appropriate behavior."

"It would be easier if you just had them read a book where the characters acted morally," Ms. Davis said.

"'Acted morally' according to whose standards, Ms. Davis?" asked Greg. "There are different ways that people can act morally. I put a lot of thought into picking the books and designing the lessons for my classes in order to expose my students to different ways of thinking. What you are asking me to do amounts to censorship. It also undermines my authority as a trained professional in the classroom," he said.

"Mr. Hartmann, I'm sure you're a fine teacher. Logan enjoys your class. What I'm asking you to do is not censorship. As adults we have a responsibility to protect our young people from inappropriate things. We have a responsibility to uphold the values of the community. You wouldn't teach anything pornographic, would you?"

"Of course not! But *The Absolutely True Diary of a Part-Time Indian* is not pornography."

"No, it's racist, which is just as bad."

"That is just one opinion of the book. Other people have very different interpretations of the book, more positive ones. For instance, it's viewed as a testament to hope. The main character is able to overcome some of the difficulties of his situation and maintain a positive outlook. Teenagers are able to relate to his struggles. That gets students interested in reading," Greg told her.

"Teenagers should not be encouraged to use profanity by their teacher," she replied.

"Ms. Davis, we don't use profanity in the classroom. We discuss the issues the main character faces as he tries to figure out who he is and where he belongs," Greg responded. "Something all teenagers have to do."

"The school feels it's important to expose students to different perspectives, which is why Mr. Hartmann is using it in his classroom," said Hanna. "What you are asking us to do is censorship since removing the book from use in the class denies students access to it—"

"And the library, too!" Ms. Davis interrupted.

"—and the library denies students the right to read the book and form their own opinion," Hanna finished.

"Ms. Larson, you're the librarian, so you have to say those kind of things. But parents have rights and responsibilities too."

"Of course, Ms. Davis. I'm here to see that all the issues get raised and that you and Mr. Hartmann each get a say on this matter. Mr. Hartmann was hoping that a different assignment for Logan would satisfy your objections to the book," Hanna said.

"In my opinion, the whole class should have a different assignment."

"So you are unwilling to drop your objection to the book, even though Logan is no longer required to read it? You wish to continue your challenge to have the book banned?" Hanna wanted to make sure she understood Ms. Davis's wishes in this matter.

"Yes, I do. Mr. Hartmann, it's nothing against you. It's just that I have to stand up for my beliefs," Ms. Davis told Mr. Hartmann.

"Ms. Davis, I understand. I feel I need to defend mine as well. Unfortunately our beliefs on this issue are very different," he replied.

"Do you have the challenge forms?" Hanna asked.

"Yes." Ms. Davis reached into her bag and handed them to Hanna.

"Since the three of us were unable to work out a solution, Ms. Davis, you'll need to set up an appointment to talk to the principal," Hanna said.

Meetings Between the Upset Parent and the Principal

Ms. Davis met with Principal Rivera several times. The first time they met, Ms. Davis discussed her objections to the book and her reasons for wanting it banned, not just for her son but for the entire school. She genuinely felt it was her duty to protect the students from harmful exposure to what she felt were antisocial ideas, sexually explicit material, and violence.

For her part, Principal Rivera needed to find a compromise that would work for the school and at the same time would protect the rights of all the students. Banning a book was a very serious issue. Although she hoped that she and Ms. Davis could find a solution, she'd sent a report to the school board, alerting them that a book challenge was in progress.

At her first meeting with Ms. Davis, she suggested that the book's use in the school be considered by a challenge committee made up of the school librarian, the other seventh-grade English teachers, the seventh-grade level leader, and another parent. Ms. Davis agreed to the committee review if the parent on the committee was a prominent member of the Parent-Teacher Association. Ms. Rivera was able to assemble a committee, and they were given two weeks to review the challenge.

At the end of the two weeks, Ms. Rivera notified Ms. Davis that the committee had made its decision. As part of reviewing her complaint, the committee looked at the American Library Association's guidelines as well as the policies of comparable school districts in the state. The committee saw no reason that the book could not be used by teachers in the school. Ms. Davis was very disappointed with the decision and threatened to go to the school board with her concerns. Ms. Rivera then proposed a compromise to Ms. Davis that the book be restricted from use in the classroom. It would still be available in the school library, but students would need their parents' permission to check it out. Reluctantly, Ms. Davis agreed to the compromise; she couldn't tell other parents what to do, after all.

While the principal felt the solution was not a perfect one, she hoped it was one the school as a whole could live with. However, her hopes were dashed when she received phone calls several weeks later from irate parents who objected to the policy of requiring permission slips for book. They accused the principal of censoring what their children were allowed to read. When Ms. Rivera tried to explain about Ms. Davis's complaint, she was accused of allowing one person to railroad school policy. At this point, all the principal could so was tell the unhappy parents to take the matter to the school board.

The School Board Meeting

On Thursday evening, the regularly scheduled school board meeting took place in the Education Service Center's meeting room. When the chair of the school board, Oliver Voss, arrived early to set up the mikes, he noticed that the room was filling up. He glanced at his watch. It was 5:40 p.m. and the meeting wouldn't start until 6. By the looks of things, they'd need more chairs. Normally, not many people attended the school board meetings, even though they were open to the public.

It's probably because of the book controversy, Oliver thought. Each set of parents had submitted a letter outlining their concern, and they would each be speaking at tonight's meeting.

At 6 p.m., Oliver checked with the other board members, Paul Norton, Sharon Tuttle, Clara Alvarez, and Maria Vega, for any last-minute business and then called the meeting to order. The meeting droned on as they worked their way through the agenda. Finally they came to the agenda item concerning *The Absolutely True Diary of a Part-Time Indian*.

Ms. Tuttle summarized the situation: "The board has been asked to make a final decision about the case of using to *The Absolutely True Diary of a Part-Time Indian* at MacArthur Middle School. The case so far is that one parent, Ms. Davis, complained about the use of the book for a classroom assignment. A committee reviewed her complaint about the book and decided it was fine to use in school. As a compromise solution, the principal put in place a policy whereby students must get their parents' permission to check out the book from the school library. According to the principal, several parents complained about that policy, and Mr. and Ms. Randolph wrote a formal letter of complaint to the school board, asking the school board to rescind the principal's policy. Ms. Davis and the Randolphs will be given time to present their sides of the issue, and then we will open the mike up for comments. Ms. Davis, you can begin."

Ms. Davis rose and went to the mike facing the board. She reiterated her reasons for banning the book. Because it used vulgar and profane language, depicted sex acts, and exposed students to bullying and alcoholism, she argued, it went against the moral standards of the community. She asked the board to ban the book from the classroom and the school library, saying it was the board's job to protect the values of the community.

After Ms. Davis spoke, Mr. Randolph got up and addressed the school board: "My wife and I, as well as several other parents of children at the school, object to the present restrictions in place that keep our children from having easy access to *The Absolutely True Diary of a Part-Time Indian* by Sherman Alexie. It is an award-winning book that heartwarmingly depicts the struggles of a teenage boy in a new environment. It also deals very straightforwardly with racism and the devastating emotional effects of poverty. These are conversations our children should be having. We live in a multiracial world. Ignoring injustice will not make it go away. What are the values that we want our children to learn? Should we teach them to ignore things because they don't fit some narrow view of the world?"

Mr. Randolph described the policy as "blatant censorship and a violation of our First Amendment rights" and asked the school board to rescind it.

"Ms. Davis is welcome to, and indeed has the right to, restrict what her son reads, but she doesn't have the right to restrict what our daughter reads," said Mr. Randolph. "We urge the school board not to let the voice of the minority, of one parent, dictate to the majority. It is the school board's job to protect the rights of our children and allow them to be exposed to many different viewpoints so they will be prepared for the real world."

After Mr. Randolph finished Mr. Voss opened the floor up for discussion.

Several parents got up and spoke in support of the Randolphs, while others supported Ms. Davis's viewpoints. Several students spoke. They talked about how much they liked the book, how they could relate to the main character, how they liked that the truth was presented straightforwardly, and how the book was engaging to read. One student even admitted to using worse language than was found in the book. The discussion got heated, ending up with both sides calling each other names.

When the debate disintegrated into name calling, Mr. Voss called for order and ended the discussion.

"The school board will rule on this matter at the next meeting," he told the agitated crowd.

Your Task

You decide: What should the school board do?

Exploring the Case: Prewriting

Prewriting assignments are a useful way to explore case problems and issues as well as brainstorm and test out solutions. In addition, you can use them as a way to "think through writing" in order to explore your own opinions and ideas about the case. In turn, what you discover in your prewriting process can be used as a starting point for your paper or in class discussions.

Prewriting assignments will vary in length depending on the requirements of your instructor. Use the following prewriting activities to help you: (1) Case Analysis, (2) Exploration Questions, and (3) Interview Activities.

1. Case Analysis

The Stakeholders

Who are the stakeholders?
What is at stake for them?
What do they have to gain or lose?
How does the case appear to the different participants/stakeholders?

Come up with two questions you would like to ask each stakeholder.

The Issues

What are the main issues in the situation?
How would you rank the issues (from most to least important)?
What reasons can you give for your rankings?
How does the immediate problem or issue tie into larger social issues?
What conflicts in values or belief systems form part of the issue?

Come up with two questions that explore the issues you've identified in more depth.

Solutions and Their Consequences

What are the possible courses of action and solutions?
How would you rank them?
What are the advantages and disadvantages for each one?
Is your solution a short- or long-term solution?
What are the consequences of your solution for each of the stakeholders?

Come up with two questions that explore the consequences of your solutions.

2. Exploration Questions

What are the larger implications of banning books in the public schools?
How should the school board balance the rights of the students and the interests of the community?
How should the school board respond to the parents' requests?
Discuss the risks and possible consequences of the school board's responses.
What compromises could be found besides the ones already tried in the case?

Read a chapter of the disputed book and answer the following questions:

What aspects of the chapter might support the claim of the mother who wants to ban the book?
What aspects of the chapter might support the claim of the parents who don't want the book banned?
Based on your reading of the chapter, what is your opinion of the potential risk to the students?

3. Interview Activities

See the "Interview Your Audience" and "Interview Your Stakeholder" prompts in the Appendix. These activities are designed to help you better understand the needs and goals of the case audience and stakeholders. This exercise of imagination and of empathy will help you step into the shoes of the audience or stakeholder so that you can identify with them, which will in turn help you to choose what arguments to make in your paper.

Arguing the Case: Writing Assignments

Paper Assignment 1

You are a member of the school board and want to persuade other school board members to vote the same way you are planning to vote on the issue of banning the Harry Potter books or Sherman Alexie book. You will need to state the actions you feel the board should take (your solution) and describe why those actions would be the best ones in this situation. As part of your proposal, you must consider the needs of as many stakeholders as possible.

In order to support your proposed solution, you will need to address the context of the wider issues involved in the case. This is the portion of the paper where you will need outside resources to provide you with evidence and other examples of similar cases.

You will need to consider the following stakeholders in your decision:

The teachers
The librarian
The principal
The parent bringing the complaint
The other parents and students
The student whose parent brought the complaint and his classmates

The audience is the school board, the principal, the parents, and the teachers.

Paper Assignment 2

Choose a stakeholder and write your paper from their point of view. Your goal is to persuade the school board members to either ban or not ban the Harry Potter books or Sherman Alexie book, depending on your stakeholder's position on the issue. You will need to state the actions you feel the school board should take (your solution) and describe why those actions would be the best ones in this situation. As part of your proposal, you need to take into account the needs of as many stakeholders as possible.

In order to support your proposed solution, you will need to acknowledge the context of the wider issues involved in the case. This is the portion of the paper where you will need outside resources to provide you with evidence and other examples of similar cases.

You will need to consider the following stakeholders in your decision:

The teachers
The librarian

The principal
The parent bringing the complaint
The other parents and students
The student whose parent brought the complaint and his classmates

The audience is the school board, the principal, the parents, and the teachers.

Alternative Assignments

1. Explore any local instances of book banning in your state or community. Describe the effect of potential or actual censorship on your community.
2. Interview local high school librarians for information on books that get challenged, and why, in your community. What do they think about the possibility of books being censored in your community? What do you think?
3. Design posters and/or set up an information campaign for Banned Book Week on campus. Work with your university librarians. Use the campaign and posters to present multimodal arguments for censorship awareness.

Reflecting on the Case: Looking Back

Reflection is an important part of the learning process. It gives you the chance to examine what you've learned, how you learned it, and how you can improve your learning strategies in the future. Here, you are being asked to reflect on what you have learned from doing this case study. Use the following questions to help you reflect on the case study process:

- What did you learn about the issues of the case?
- What did you learn about process of constructing an argument and counterarguments for an issue?
- What did you learn about doing research, both how and why it is important to argumentation?
- Now that you have done this case study, what approaches will you use for the next one? For instance, what will you do differently and what will you do the same?
- What did you like about doing the case study? What didn't you like about it?
- Do you have any other responses or reflections on the assignment?

2 VIOLENCE AND VIDEO GAMES

Case Scenario

The Setting

A courthouse jury room

The Characters

Plaintiffs: Emily and David Williams on behalf of their daughter Caitlyn
Offenders: Lucas Carter and John Nielson, high school seniors
Defendants: the makers and distributors of Doom, Medal of Honor, Call of Duty, and Grand Theft Auto: Id Software, Sega, NetherRealm Studios, Rockstar Games, Warner Brothers, Sony, Nintendo, Danger Close Games, Electronic Arts, Infinity Ward, and Activision
Judge: The Honorable Susan Graham
Several expert witnesses
Other jurors: your classmates
A juror: you

The Issues

You are a juror on a civil wrongful death suit, *Williams vs. Id Software et al.* Judge Graham has explained that a civil case decides whether or not the defendant is liable for the injuries sustained as part of the crime. It does not determine innocence or guilt. The standard of proof for a civil suit is different from that of a criminal case. In a civil lawsuit, the case must be proved by a "preponderance of the evidence"—that is, by enough evidence to conclude that it is more likely than not that the victim's claims are true. Also, civil lawsuits require only 10 of 12 jurors to agree on a decision instead of the unanimous decision required in a criminal trial. If found guilty, the defendant will have to pay the victim or the victim's family or benefactors monetary damages.

During the trial, you have heard various testimony. Here are the facts of the case:

Caitlyn Williams and her friends Chloe and Alyssa were shopping at the mall on Saturday, October 12. They were having lunch in the mall's food court when two teenage boys with guns appeared and started shooting. Caitlyn, her two friends, and 12 other people were killed. Twenty-four people were wounded. Hearing sirens in the distance, the boys ran out of the mall, stole a car, and attempted to flee. Trapped by the police at the end of the mall's parking lot, the two boys fired their guns at the police, killing one officer. The boys were killed in the shootout by the police. They were later identified as Lucas Carter and John Nielson, two seniors at Eastside High School.

Witnesses at the mall testified that the boys had spent several hours prior to the shooting playing video games in the mall's video arcade. The video arcade manager testified that they played games there regularly. On the day of the shooting one witness heard them laughing and boasting "that they were ready to take it to the next level." The witness testified that shortly after this statement the boys left the arcade, heading for the food court.

Officers testified that the boys had smuggled the weapons into the mall in their backpacks. Recovered at the scene, the backpacks contained 9mm semiautomatic handguns and a sawed-off shotgun. The police also recovered the 9 mm semiautomatic rifle and 12-gauge pump-action shotgun used in the shooting. Officers also testified that they found several violent first-person-shooter games, including Doom, Mortal Kombat, Wolfenstein 3D, and Grand Theft Auto, on their home computers. School counselors testified that the two boys were loners and obsessed with the video games.

Several expert witnesses testified for the plaintiffs. These experts—psychiatrists, pediatricians, and sociologists—told the court about their research on the relationship between video games and violence. They all claimed that studies show there is a link between media violence such as video games and real-life violence and aggressive behavior. Further, they stated that long-term exposure to such violent games promotes the acceptance of violence as a means to solve problems and promotes a desensitization to violent acts, with a corresponding decrease in the ability to feel empathy toward others. Correlational and experimental studies have shown links between playing violent video games and an increase in hostile feelings, hostile attitudes, and aggressive behavior.

In contrast, several equally qualified expert witnesses for the defendants testified that there is no causal link between playing video games and violent behavior. They stated that while some studies may show a correlation, the evidence is still inconclusive. Furthermore, many studies do not take into account other factors such as poverty, family issues, or mental illness, which would also influence behavior.

Your Task

You have received your instructions from the judge and retired to the jury room with the rest of the jury. The jury must decide: What is the relationship between playing violent first-person-shooter games and aggressive and violent behavior in teens and young adults? Did playing violent video games influence the behavior of the two young men? What side are you going to argue for? How will you persuade your fellow jurors to vote the same way?

Exploring the Case: Prewriting

Prewriting assignments are a useful way to explore case problems and issues as well as brainstorm and test out solutions. In addition, you can use them as a way to "think through writing" in order to explore your own opinions and ideas about the case. In turn, what you discover in your prewriting process can be used as a starting point for your paper or in class discussions.

Prewriting assignments will vary in length depending on the requirements of your instructor. Use the following prewriting activities to help you: (1) Case Analysis, (2) Exploration Questions, and (3) Interview Activities.

1. Case Analysis

The Stakeholders

Who are the stakeholders? What is at stake for them?
What do they have to gain or lose?
How does the case appear to the different participants/stakeholders?

Come up with two questions you would like to ask each stakeholder.

The Issues

What are the main issues in the situation?
How would you rank the issues (from most to least important)?

What reasons can you give for your rankings?
How does the immediate problem or issue tie into larger social issues?
What conflicts in values or belief systems form part of the issue?

Come up with two questions that explore the issues you've identified in more depth.

Solutions and Their Consequences

What are the possible courses of action and solutions?
How would you rank them?
What are the advantages and disadvantages for each one?
Is your solution a short- or long-term solution?
What are the consequences of your solution for each of the stakeholders?

Come up with two questions that explore the consequences of your solutions.

2. Exploration Questions

What are the larger social implications of violent video games?
How should the jury balance the needs of the parents and the interests of the video game companies?
What are the risks and possible consequences of not holding anyone responsible for the deaths?
What are the legal compromises available to the jury in the case?
How should the correlations between increased aggression and bullying and loss of empathy and playing violent video games factor into the jury's decision?
How do you make an informed decision on an issue when the research evidence is sometimes contradictory?

3. Interview Activities

See the "Interview Your Audience" and "Interview Your Stakeholder" prompts in the Appendix. These two activities are designed to help you better understand the needs and goals of the case audience and stakeholders. This exercise of the imagination and empathy will help you step into the shoes of the audience or stakeholder so that you can identify with them, which will in turn help you to choose what arguments to make in your paper.

Arguing the Case: Writing Assignments

Paper Assignment 1

You are a juror in a civil case where a video game company is being sued. You need to decide if the video game company is culpable, not culpable, or partially responsible. Your purpose for this paper is to state your decision and persuade your fellow jurors to vote the same way.

In order to support your argument, you will need to set it in the context of the wider issues involved in the case. This is the portion of the paper where you will need outside resources to provide you with scholarly evidence about the effects of violence on behavior and other examples of similar cases.

You will need to consider the following stakeholders in your decision:

The parents of the child killed
The video game company
The parents of the teenagers accused of the killing
The consumers of the video games

The audience is your fellow jurors.

Paper Assignment 2

Choose a stakeholder and write your paper from their point of view. Be sure it is clear in your introduction which stakeholder you have chosen. Your goal is to persuade your audience that video games influence or do not influence behavior, depending on your stakeholder's position on the issue. You will need to state the actions you feel your audience should take (your solution) and argue why those actions would be the best ones in this situation. As part of your argument, you need to take into account the needs of as many stakeholders as possible.

In order to support your argument, you will need to set it in the context of the wider issues involved in the case. This is the portion of the paper where you will need outside resources to provide you with evidence and other examples of similar cases.

You will need to consider the following stakeholders in your decision:

The parents of the child killed
The video game company
The parents of the teenagers accused of the killing
The consumers of the video games

Your audience is the other stakeholders.

Alternative Assignments

1. Research the connection between playing violent video games and behaviors like bullying, mean world syndrome, loss of empathy, other types of aggressive behaviors, and the use of violence to solve problems. Should consumers (players and parents) be made aware of the possible effects of playing these types of games? What solution could you offer?
2. Research the social effects, both positive and negative, of playing video games. How does video game playing affect social interaction and physical and mental health? What other factors did your research uncover that users should be made aware of?
3. Research the relationship between the First Amendment, entertainment products like video games, and consumer rights.

Reflecting on the Case: Looking Back

Reflection is an important part of the learning process. It gives you the chance to examine what you've learned, how you learned it, and how you can improve your learning strategies in the future. Here, you are being asked to reflect on what you have learned from doing this case study. Use the following questions to help you reflect on the case study process:

- What did you learn about the issues of the case?
- What did you learn about the process of constructing an argument and counterarguments for an issue?
- What did you learn about doing research, both how and why it is important to making a contribution on a topic?
- Now that you have done this case study, what approaches will you use for the next one? For instance, what will you do differently and what will you do the same?
- What did you like about doing the case study? What didn't you like about it?
- Do you have any other responses or reflections on the assignment?

3 STUDENT HEALTH CARE

Case Scenario

The Setting

A midsized state university in the Midwestern United States. The school primarily serves undergraduate students but has a small number of graduate programs. The students are drawn from the local region and from surrounding states. The student body reflects that of many universities today: Although a majority group exists, there are domestic and international students from many ethnicities, languages, and income levels.

The Characters

The students
The university administration
The health clinic on campus
The campus health care insurance provider
The faculty
The community

The Issues

In the past, the university has been able to provide all full-time students with health care as part of their tuition. This has been a great boon to students: They were able to have their medical care needs provided for at the campus health clinic at no extra cost to them.

However, the state legislature has drastically cut the university's funding. The university now must make some tough decisions in order to balance its budget. One of the things the university had to cut was its tuition-funded health care program.

Because the university wants all students to have health care coverage, they now require all students to purchase a health care package through the university. Unfortunately, this package is inadequate: It has a restricted provider network and it doesn't cover prescriptions, contraception, or mental health care. The health clinic is still operating on campus; however, students can't seek treatment there unless they are covered under the new university-required plan.

The new policy has raised many concerns. Many students are upset about the new requirements. The new plan is expensive, and it doesn't cover what the old plan covered or even what some of their parents' plans cover. Since some students no longer have access to preventive care at the campus health clinic, resident advisors in the dorms have noticed a growing number of students coming down with both simple illness like colds and more serious conditions that are interfering with their studies.

Faculty have noticed that more students are absent from class due to illness, which is adversely affecting their performance in the class. Faculty have also noticed a rise in the number of illnesses and depression among their students.

The director of the local hospital is also concerned since the hospital has seen more and more students showing up in the emergency room since the new regulations have gone into effect. The director is concerned about the financial effect this will have on the community, who will end up paying the bill.

Your Task

You are a representative of the student government. You are one of three representatives who have been chosen to meet with the university administration to try to address the problems facing students under the new health care regulations. You have a special interest/investment in seeing changes made to the health care situation since your roommate attempted suicide earlier in the semester and had to drop out and go home. You feel that if your roommate had had access to counseling under a good health care plan, the suicide attempt could have been prevented.

What changes are you going to ask the university to make?

Exploring the Case: Prewriting

Prewriting assignments are a useful way to explore case problems and issues as well as brainstorm and test out solutions. In addition, you can use them as a way to "think through writing" in order to explore your own opinions and ideas about the case. In turn, what you discover in your prewriting process can be used as a starting point for your paper or in class discussions.

Prewriting assignments will vary in length depending on the requirements of your instructor. Use the following prewriting activities to help you: (1) Case Analysis, (2) Exploration Questions, and (3) Interview Activities.

1. Case Analysis

The Stakeholders

Who are the stakeholders?
What is at stake for them?
What do they have to gain or lose?
How does the case appear to the different participants/stakeholders?

Come up with two questions you would like to ask each stakeholder.

The Issues

How would you rank the issues (from most to least important)?
What reasons can you give for your rankings?
How does the immediate problem or issue tie into larger social issues?
What conflicts in values or belief systems form part of the issue?

Come up with two questions that explore the issues you've identified in more depth.

Solutions and Their Consequences

What are the possible courses of action and solutions?
How would you rank them?
What are the advantages and disadvantages for each one?
Is your solution a short- or long-term solution?
What are the consequences of your solution for each of the stakeholders?

Come up with two questions that explore the consequences of your solutions.

2. Exploration Questions

What are the larger implications of lack of access to health care for students?
How should universities balance the health care needs of students and the costs of health care to the university?
How might the university respond to student requests for health care?

What are the risks and possible consequences of lack of access to mental health care for both students and the wider community?
What compromises could be worked out in this situation?
What are some long-term solutions to student health care needs?

3. Interview Activities

See the "Interview Your Audience" and "Interview Your Stakeholder" prompts in the Appendix. These two activities are designed to help you better understand the needs and goals of the case audience and stakeholders. This exercise of the imagination and empathy will help you step into the shoes of the audience or stakeholder so that you can identify with them, which will in turn help you to choose what arguments to make in your paper.

Arguing the Case: Writing Assignments

Paper Assignment 1

You are a representative of the student government. You have been asked to negotiate with the university administration for better health care for students at your university. You will need to come up with a better plan for health care for students and provide reasons why the university administration should adopt your plan. You need to consider the financial pressures the university is under as well as the physical and mental health of the student body. What is the best way to meet the needs of both groups?

You will need to consider the following stakeholders in your decision:

The students
The university administration
The health clinic on campus
The campus health care insurance provider
The faculty
The community

The audience is students, other universities facing the same problem, parents, university administrators, and health care providers.

Paper Assignment 2

Choose a stakeholder and write your paper from their point of view. Be sure it is clear in your introduction which stakeholder you have chosen. Your goal is to present your stakeholder's arguments and solutions for better access to health care on campus. You will need to come up arguments for why the university administration should adopt your stakeholder's plan. As part of your argument, you need to take into account the needs of as many stakeholders as possible.

In order to support your argument, you will need to set it in the context of the wider issues involved in the case. This is the portion of the paper where you will need outside resources to provide you with evidence and other examples of similar cases.

You will need to consider the following stakeholders in your decision:

The students
The university administration
The health clinic on campus
The campus health care insurance provider
The faculty
The community

The audience is students, other universities facing the same problem, parents, university administrators, and health care providers.

Alternative Assignments

1. Design posters or brochures to advertise the health center or counseling services on your campus. (This could be a service learning project.)
2. Research the health care needs of students on your campus. Focus on either mental or physical health. Come up with solutions for better access to health care for students at your campus.
3. Research student activism either locally or on a particular issue. How have student actions and/or protests made a difference to issues in the past? How could similar activism by students make a difference on this issue?

Reflecting on the Case: Looking Back

Reflection is an important part of the learning process. It gives you the chance to examine what you've learned, how you learned it, and how you can improve your learning strategies in the future. Here, you are being asked to reflect on what you have learned from doing this case study. Use the following questions to help you reflect on the case study process:

- What did you learn about the issues of the case?
- What did you learn about the process of constructing an argument and counterarguments for an issue?

- What did you learn about doing research, both how and why it is important to argumentation?
- Now that you have done this case study, what approaches will you use for the next one? For instance, what will you do differently and what will you do the same?
- What did you like about doing the case study? What didn't you like about it?
- Do you have any other responses or reflections on the assignment?

4 PRIVACY AND THE INTERNET

Case Scenario

The Setting

A suburban U.S. high school

The Characters

The school dean: Dean Schmidt
The journalism teacher: Mr. Gioni
Four students caught skipping school: Carla, Jose, Juno, and Marina
A student whose car was damaged: Devon

The Issues

A group of four senior students, Carla, Jose, Juno, and Marina, were caught skipping class and loitering in the parking lot of Hope School on a sunny day in late September. Only one of the students, Marina, was new to the school; the others had been there for some years, and none of the four had gotten in any serious trouble before. In the history of the school, skipping happened periodically with students, especially seniors; the dean knew that it occasionally happened at all high schools in the area. The punishment was a day of community service, and no chance to make up the work missed during the class skipped.

When the students were discovered around 11 a.m., they were sent to the dean, who admonished them, let them and their parents know of the punishment, and told them to avoid the behavior in the future. The students were sent back to their classes for the remainder of the class day.

After the school day ended, some students and a coach walking to a practice field discovered that a car had been badly vandalized in the parking lot. The tires had been slashed, and the paint had been visibly scratched with a key or other metal object in several places. That damage would obviously cost hundreds of dollars to fix. This was especially bad news for the student who had driven the car, who was borrowing it from her parents for the day and already had a job to save money for college. The cost of repairing the damage would be more than an entire semester's worth of college textbooks.

There was no explicit evidence to link the four students who were skipping class to the vandalism. It had not been captured in the parking lot video surveillance since the car had been mostly blocked by a concrete pillar and other vehicles. Many students were already gone for the day when it was discovered, including the four students caught skipping class. When asked about it via phone that evening, they denied committing vandalism or witnessing anything to do with it. Their parents said that the students were already being punished for skipping class and that they had to be taken at their word regarding the vandalism.

But two days later, Dean Schmidt was still concerned and curious about the coincidence in the timing. No other evidence had surfaced, and she didn't think it was fair that the student driver needed to pay for the damage. She was eager to see if there was an alternative in which the vandal(s) who committed the act would pay for the consequences of their actions.

The dean sought out the teachers of the four students who had been caught skipping class. Most of the teachers said that they knew the four students but didn't have a lot to say about them. One teacher, Mr. Gioni, a young faculty member who also ran the school yearbook, knew them a little better because he had all four students in journalism class together. The dean sought out Mr. Gioni after school for a private conversation and asked what he knew about the four students.

"Hmmm. Not that much," the teacher said. "They seem to be close friends. They haven't caused trouble in class that I know of. They keep to their group, at least in the few weeks since school started—they do group work together, and they don't talk to many other students. I know they use our yearbook social media site to communicate; they even set up a messaging group for themselves. I heard one of them say his phone is broken, so that may be why. That's about everything I know about them."

"Do you know what they message about?" Dean Schmidt quickly rejoined.

"No," said Mr. Gioni, looking surprised. "It's a private message group they created. I told them that I don't read their messages to one another so they can communicate freely on the site."

"But are you the site administrator?" the dean pressed.

"Well, yes," Mr. Gioni replied. "But I told them at the start of the year that unless anyone reports any bullying—which no one has—then I will not access student-to-student messages. I only read messages directed to me."

Dean Schmidt pressed on. "If you are the site administrator, then you have access to those messages. What if they include some detail that links the students to the car vandalism? We owe it to the student driver to find out. I don't think we have a choice. If the messages don't link the students to the car vandalism, then no harm done."

"I know you are concerned about the vandalism, and I understand that," said Mr. Gioni. "But I think that there *would* be harm done—a violation of privacy. I told them I don't read those messages. And I think we need to respect their privacy, like we do for all students, since there is no clear indication it was them."

"But they were caught skipping class in the parking lot. And they are using a school media site," the dean reasoned.

"Yes. But they were only caught for skipping class, and they are using the student-to-student chat feature on a school site that I told them I would not read unless there was bullying reported in the messages," responded Mr. Gioni. "We would be violating their privacy and suggesting that we do not abide by the respect for their privacy that we claimed we would, under the terms we said we would."

Dean Schmidt and Mr. Gioni have a difficult decision to make concerning the internet and user privacy, one that speaks to bigger issues today concerning the internet and privacy. On the one hand, many internet users value the free flow of information and communication. But many internet users also value the right to keep personal information and messages private.

Your Task

The dean and teacher agree that they need to make a decision that is clear and fair not only for this case but also for future questions regarding privacy and the internet that the school might confront. Because they cannot agree on a course of action, they seek a mediator to make the decision—you. How should they proceed?

Exploring the Case: Prewriting

Prewriting assignments are a useful way to explore case problems and issues as well as brainstorm and test out solutions. In addition, you can use them as a way to "think through writing" in order to explore your own opinions and ideas about the case. In turn, what you discover in your prewriting process can be used as a starting point for your paper or in class discussions.

Prewriting assignments will vary in length depending on the requirements of your instructor. Use the following prewriting activities to help you: (1) Case Analysis, (2) Exploration Questions, and (3) Interview Activities.

1. Case Analysis

The Stakeholders

Who are the stakeholders?
What is at stake for them?
What do they have to gain or lose?
How does the case appear to the different participants/stakeholders?

Come up with two questions you would like to ask each stakeholder.

The Issues

What are the main issues in the situation?
How would you rank the issues (from most to least important)?
What reasons can you give for your rankings?
How does the immediate problem or issue tie into larger social issues?
What conflicts in values or belief systems form part of the issue?

Come up with two questions that explore the issues you've identified in more depth.

Solutions and Their Consequences

What are the possible courses of action and solutions?
How would you rank them?
What are the advantages and disadvantages for each one?
Is your solution a short- or long-term solution?
What are the consequences of your solution for each of the stakeholders?

Come up with two questions that explore the consequences of your solutions.

2. Exploration Questions

What are the larger implications of violating the students' privacy based on a suspicion rather than solid evidence?
How should the school balance the rights of the accused students and the student whose car was vandalized?

How do you think the students will respond if the school administration violates their privacy?

What are the risks and possible consequences of (1) the dean reading the students' emails and (2) the students losing their privacy through an unsubstantiated suspicion?

What compromises can the mediator suggest that will satisfy the needs of all parties in the case?

How do you think the dean's attitudes toward privacy and her right to read the students' emails reflect wider attitudes on privacy and the internet?

3. Interview Activities

See the "Interview Your Audience" and "Interview Your Stakeholder" prompts in the Appendix. These two activities are designed to help you better understand the needs and goals of the case audience and stakeholders. This exercise of the imagination and empathy will help you step into the shoes of the audience or stakeholder so that you can identify with them, which will in turn help you to choose what arguments to make in your paper.

Arguing the Case: Writing Assignments

Paper Assignment 1

You are the head of the school judiciary council. You have been asked to mediate the question before the teacher and the dean regarding whether to access the internet messages of the four students caught skipping class in order to check for any evidence linking them to the vandalism. As part of your role, you will need to clarify both positions in a fair and clear way. Then, you will need to outline your take on how they should proceed and why those actions would be the best ones in this situation. In order to support your proposal, you will need to address the context of the wider issues involved in the case. This is the portion of the paper where you will need outside resources to provide you with evidence and other examples of similar cases. Imagine the paper as providing considerations not only for this case but for future questions regarding privacy and the internet that the school might confront.

You will need to consider the following stakeholders in your decision:

The journalism teacher
The school dean
The students caught skipping, whose messages would be accessed
The student whose car was damaged
The other teachers, students, and administrators

The audience is future students, teachers, and administrators who read the school's judiciary documents.

Paper Assignment 2

Choose a stakeholder and write your paper from their point of view. Be sure it is clear in your introduction which stakeholder you have chosen. Your goal is to persuade the mediator and the school administration to adopt your stakeholder's solution to the situation. You will need to argue for the actions you feel the school should take from the point of view of your stakeholder. As part of your argument, you need to take into account the needs of as many stakeholders as possible.

In order to support your argument, you will need to set it within the context of the wider issues involved in the case. This is the portion of the paper where you will need outside resources to provide you with evidence and other examples of similar cases.

You will need to consider the following stakeholders in your decision:

The journalism teacher
The school dean
The students caught skipping, whose messages would be accessed
The student whose car was damaged
The other teachers, students, and administrators

The audience is future students, teachers, and administrators who read the school's judiciary documents.

Alternative Assignments

1. Research the impact of social media on schools. As part of your research, you might consider legal issues or academic performance. Argue for the role, if any, you feel social media and the right to privacy on the internet should play in schools.
2. Research privacy, marketing strategies, social media, and teens. Based on your research, propose a social media protocol for schools.
3. Design an information campaign (posters, brochures, and/or activities) to educate students about their legal rights, internet privacy issues, and social media and internet safety. (This could be a service learning project.)

Reflecting on the Case: Looking Back

Reflection is an important part of the learning process. It gives you the chance to examine what you've learned, how you learned it, and how you can improve your learning strategies in the future. Here, you are being asked to reflect on what you have learned from doing this case study. Use the following questions to help you reflect on the case study process:

- What did you learn about the issues of the case?
- What did you learn about the process of constructing an argument and counterarguments for an issue?
- What did you learn about doing research, both how and why it is important to argumentation?
- Now that you have done this case study, what approaches will you use for the next one? For instance, what will you do differently and what will you do the same?
- What did you like about doing the case study? What didn't you like about it?
- Do you have any other responses or reflections on the assignment?

5 CLIMATE CHANGE AND COMMUNITIES AT RISK

Case Scenario 1: Alaska

"The land is going away."[1]

The Setting

Maggak village is located on a barrier island in the Chukchi Sea in rural Alaska. For many years, it was a good place to live, with access to the ocean and traditional hunting lands. There were beaches to play on and ample space for the drying racks for seal meat, and the houses sat on the bluffs above the sea. Now the houses tumble into the ocean, storms have taken the land where the drying racks stood, and the beach is gone. Now, big storms flood the island and erode the coastline.

The ice used to protect the island from the storms: The waves would batter the ice and the island would be safe. But no longer: The ice is gone, and the permafrost has melted. The big waves carve chunks out of the bluffs that were once frozen permafrost, and the houses tumble off the bluffs into the sea. The freeze comes later. The seasons come later, the winter is shorter, and the ice is thinner, making it dangerous for hunters to cross. Many have died.

Warming temperatures have contributed to the increasing severity of the storms. "Storms that affect Alaska are far, far bigger than hurricanes. Hurricanes are tiny compared to great storms that take up a

---

1. John D. Sutter, "Climate change threatens life in Shishmaref, Alaska," *CNN*, December 3, 2009, http://www.cnn.com/2009/TECH/science/12/03/shishmaref.alaska.climate.change/index.html

quarter of the Bering Sea."[2] In a single storm, the island can lose between 22 and 40 feet.

The landscape is changing in other ways as well. The freshwater ponds that used to be separated from the ocean by the ice now drain away into the seas, and their fresh water is gone.

Warming temperatures have created this domino effect on the Arctic environment. All of these changes to the landscape put the community at greater risk and threaten its long-term survival.

The People's Voices

"Now in December, it isn't safe to walk on the ice."
"I think the land is going to vanish one of these days."
"The waves would come and take a whole lot of the land."
"No room left. We need to move."
"We must have access to the ocean."
"In our culture, how we are raised, what we see every day, ties us to the land ... Here it's central, the connection with land, animals and family."

The Issues

Traditionally, the Inupiat people were nomadic and moved between summer and winter camps, following game (seal and caribou) and other types of food (berries and greens). This lifestyle allowed the community to be flexible and adapt to changes in the environment.

The villagers did not choose to abandon their nomadic lifestyle. They did not choose to settle in Maggak village. Rather, they were forced to settle permanently in the early 1900s, when the U.S. Bureau of Indian Affairs built a school on the island and forced Inupiat children to attend. The community resented the school. Teachers hit the children with rulers for speaking their Native language and forbade them to practice other aspects of Native culture.

Under continued pressure from white culture to assimilate, community members struggle to maintain their lifestyle, culture, and language. One aspect of their culture the community does not want to lose are subsistence lifestyles, practices spanning the past 400 years—across parents, grandparents, and great-grandparents. A subsistence lifestyle means generating just enough to feed families and to be self-sufficient as a community.

2. "No hurricanes in Alaska, but . . .," Alaska Science Forum, October 27, 2005, https://www.gi.alaska.edu/alaska-science-forum/no-hurricanes-alaska-0.

Subsistence practices are central to the survival of the people in the village since more than half of the adults in the village don't have a wage-paying job. The people depend on subsistence to provide for their families by hunting and fishing, and the location of the village has historically helped the community take advantage of both land and sea food resources. But now hunters have to go farther and farther to find game, and the thin ice makes it more dangerous.

Subsistence practices represent more than just meeting basic needs: They are essential to both the physical and cultural well-being of the community. Subsistence is integrated into all aspects of village life and represents the people's connection to the land, to the animals, to their culture, and to the past and the future. It represents a way of looking at the world that considers one's relationship with the land and with one's neighbors. For the village to give this up would mean giving up their identity, giving up who they are as individuals, and who they are as a people/culture. The community members feel strong ties to their cultural heritage.

Maggak village is one of 31 Native villages in rural Alaska threatened by climate change. The population is about 400 to 500 people. For the past 20 years, the village has suffered severe weather, storm surges, erosion, landslides, loss of land mass, higher temperatures, thinner ice, and shorter and earlier hunting seasons. The problems of erosion and flooding have created a domino effect in the community, adversely affecting other infrastructures such as sewage, trash disposal, the stability of fuel tanks, and the condition of the roads and airstrip.

Independently, the village people have tried to cope with effects of warming temperature on their island. As the land washes away, homes must be moved, or they will tumble into the sea. The villagers have moved some homes inland, and other homes have been moved to the other side of the island. The loss of houses and housing space has created overcrowding; sometimes as many as 12 people live in a three-bedroom house. In addition, many houses lack running water and sewer systems, creating serious health issues for the community.

Since the 1970s, various methods have been used to try to stabilize the shoreline. The Army Corps of Engineers has tried to create seawalls and other barriers using different materials, such as rocks, cement walls, sandbags, and even old trucks, but all of them have failed. Nothing seems to work: The warming sea is relentless and the storms are too powerful.

Your Task

As a member of the Maggak village, you have been tasked by the elders, the village council, and the Native Corporation to be an advocate for the village and find a solution for the community. How will you proceed? What are the questions you need to ask?

Case Scenario 2: The Pacific

"The sea is rising up."

The Setting

The Lilo islands are part of an atoll, a coral reef that encircles a lagoon. They are only three feet above sea level. Islanders use wooden canoes to travel between the islands within the atoll and open boats, called banana boats, to travel between their islands and the larger island nearest them—a three- to four-hour boat ride across open water.

Approaching from the sea, the Lilo islands look beautiful—a green disc in a field of blue. Closer, one can see white sand, green palms, and mangrove trees surrounded by turquoise water. Once on land, though, things look different. The beaches have been lost to the rising sea, and the uprooted palm trees have fallen headfirst into the lagoon. The mangrove trees, planted specifically to help stave off erosion, are being undermined by the relentless tides and rising water. The rock seawall has broken due to tides and storm surges. Over the last 20 years, Kala, the main island in the atoll, has lost 130 to 160 feet to erosion, an average of 6 feet per year.

The rising sea level has contributed to greater tide height, so now the tides are higher and go farther inland. The king tides have also become more frequent and higher. At three to six feet, they flood over the seawalls and have reached all the way across the islands, flooding homes and overrunning gardens and freshwater sources. These storm surges and king tides contaminate the island's freshwater supplies.

In the interior of Kala island is the village with its family homes, a church, a school, and a community center that boasts a satellite dish, a television set, and a two-way radio. Also in the interior are swampy ponds of flat, stagnant water created by the king tides. They have become a breeding ground for mosquitoes, and as a result many children are sick with malaria. The king tides have also inundated the community's garden plots and contaminated the soil with salt. Residents are no longer able to grow their crops of taro, bananas, cassava, yams, and greens.

Rising sea levels also threaten the coral reef, which supports a vast ecosystem that the community depends on. If the water gets too high, the reef will not receive enough sunlight to survive. In the lagoon, the community's main source of fish, the higher water temperature has caused the coral to bleach, which kills the coral and undermines the ecosystem on which fish depend to survive. Increasing levels of carbon dioxide in the water make the water more acidic, which causes additional damage to the coral reef, leaving it vulnerable to storm damage and erosion. All of these threats to the coral reef threaten the community's livelihood and a major part of their food supply.

The People's Voices

"Those times the sea wasn't as cruel as it is today."
"The water came from all directions. Houses were swept away."
"We can now paddle our canoes where we used to grow our gardens."
"We cannot stay here. The sea is rising up."
"It looks like in the future there will be no island."
"I would rather sink with the islands than leave."
"Our culture will have to live on in our memory."

The Issues

The Lilo islands have been inhabited for over 1,000 years, and its people represent a unique cultural and language group. Currently, the population is around 3,000 people. The islanders follow a subsistence lifestyle, growing and fishing only what they need to survive. Although the atoll is isolated and only accessible by boat, the Lilo islands are part of a larger nation made up of several island groups in the Pacific.

Life is very difficult on the islands. Because of the damage to their gardens by the king tides, for the past 10 years the islanders have not been able to grow food crops. People eat one or two meals of fish and coconuts a day if they are lucky. Because they are hungry and often ill, children are unable to pay attention in school. Although the government provides food aid, the supply boat with food supplies comes only twice a year. Aside from the short-term food aid, the national government has no long-term solution to help the people.

Your Task

As a member of the island community, you have been asked by the chiefs and the council of elders to find a solution for the island community. How will you proceed? What are the questions you need to ask?

Background Information on Climate Change

Climate change is a powerful force in our world today. Currently it is affecting communities all over the globe. Some of the visible effects of climate change are:

More frequent and more severe weather events (hurricanes, tornados, typhoons, cyclones)
Rising sea levels, erosion, flooding
Melting of the polar ice and permafrost
Desertification, resulting in the loss of crop and grazing land

Some Quick Facts[3]

- In 2008, 20 million people were displaced by rising sea levels, desertification, and flooding.
- In 2012, extreme weather drove 32 million people from their homes.
- In 2015, 39,200 people still remained displaced as a result of 2012's Hurricane Sandy.
- In 2015, 64,700 people still remained displaced from the Haiti earthquake in 2010.

Significant Storms to Hit the Bering Strait

- 1997, 2001, 2004, 2005: Powerful storms
- 2011: Bering Strait superstorm[4]
- 2014: Bering Strait cyclone, the most intense on record
- 2015: Monster Bering sea storm
- 2016: Severe storm

Who Is Most Affected by Climate Change?

Unfortunately, the communities most adversely affected by climate change are those least able to cope with its effects. These include:

- Poor communities
- Rural communities
- Native/indigenous communities
- Other minority communities
- Communities in developing nations

For these communities and developing countries, climate change is not something that can be relegated to "someday in the future"; it is a factor in their lives now. However, these communities and poor countries also do not have the resources to deal with environmental disasters or provide for displaced persons the way that wealthier countries can.

What happens to the people in these communities:

In the event of a sudden disaster?
In the event of a slow but steady destruction of their community's environment?

---

3. Internal Displacement Monitoring Centre, http://www.internal-displacement.org.

4. https://www.wunderground.com/blog/weatherhistorian/bering-sea-superstorm-bottoms-out-at-924-mb.html

Who Produces Greenhouse Gases?

Here is a breakdown of greenhouse gas production by country:[5]

Of the cumulative total of greenhouse gas emissions from 1990 to 2011, the United States has produced 15%, China 16%, the European Union 12%, and the Russian Federation 6% (2014 figures).

Ten countries produce 70% of the greenhouse gas emissions: China, the United States, the European Union, India, the Russian Federation, Indonesia, Brazil, Japan, Canada, and Mexico. In contrast, the lowest 100 emitter countries contribute less than 3% (2014 figures).

Per capita emissions (for each person) are as follows: Australia 24%, Canada 24%, United States 20%, Russian Federation 16%, New Zealand 17%, Ireland 12%, and Japan 8% (2011 figures).

What is the obligation of wealthier nations whose lifestyle produces most of the greenhouse gases to people in developing countries who will be/are being adversely affected by climate change?

Climate-Induced Migration

One of the long-term effects of climate change is, and will continue to be, the movement of people from areas that are no longer habitable to other areas. Displacement like this inevitably results in loss: loss of communities, family and friendship ties, culture, language/dialect, means of economic support, and lives.

Currently, most people displaced from their homes and communities by climate-induced factors are forced to move to another location in the same country. Sometimes they are temporarily displaced: They have to leave because of floods, severe storms, or other circumstances, but return later to rebuild. Governments are slow to respond to this impending crisis. For example, the U.S. government's main response is the Federal Emergency Management Agency (FEMA), which gives funds to communities and individuals only after a disaster has happened. There are currently no U.S. government agencies tasked with working with communities suffering from the long-term effects of climate change.

But some people may even be forced to leave their country if their land becomes uninhabitable. As climate change continues, storms, hurricanes, typhoons, and tornados are becoming more and more severe, glaciers are melting at unprecedented rates, sea levels are continuing to rise, and once-fertile land is becoming a desert. More and more people are being forced to seek refuge elsewhere.

---

5. World Resources Institute, "6 Graphs Explain the World's Top 10 Emitters," November 25, 2014, https://www.wri.org/blog/2014/11/6-graphs-explain-world-s-top-10-emitters.

People who have been displaced from their homes and traditional lands by climate change are called climate refugees, environmental migrants, climate exiles, environmental refugees, climate migrants, or climate-induced migrants. The lack of agreement over a name reflects several things, including the difficulty of pointing to climate change as a major contributor. Climate change is called a "threat multiplier": It makes a bad situation worse. Environmental stressors such as scarcity of resources like food and water can lead to political instability, which in term leads to out-migration.

Two prominent examples are:

- 2011: Food riots in Algeria and Tunisia contributed to the Arab Spring uprisings.
- 2006–2011: A severe multi-year drought affected Syria, contributing to massive agriculture failures, population displacements, and armed conflict.[6]

Moreover, climate-induced migrants do not fit the international legal definition of refugees (i.e., people who are fleeing persecution or who fear for their lives because of religion, race, nationality, being a member of a particular social group, or holding a particular political opinion). Because there is not an agreed-on international category for climate-induced migrants, there are no national or international agencies specifically set up to deal with this growing group of displaced persons. The creation of a new legal status would help climate migrants seek protection under the law and basic human rights such as food, water, shelter, job training, citizenship status, resettlement rights, and other types of assistance.

Exploring the Case: Prewriting

Prewriting assignments are a useful way to explore case problems and issues as well as brainstorm and test out solutions. In addition, you can use them as a way to "think through writing" in order to explore your own opinions and ideas about the case. In turn, what you discover in your prewriting process can be used as a starting point for your paper or in class discussions.

Prewriting assignments will vary in length depending on the requirements of your instructor. Use the following prewriting activities to help you: (1) Case Analysis, (2) Exploration Questions, and (3) Interview Activities.

---

6. Climate Institute, https://climate.org.

1. Case Analysis

The Stakeholders

Who are the stakeholders?
What is at stake for them?
What do they have to gain or lose?
How does the case appear to the different participants/stakeholders?

Come up with two questions you would like to ask each stakeholder.

The Issues

What are the main issues in the situation?
How would you rank the issues (from most to least important)?
What reasons can you give for your rankings?
How does the immediate problem or issue tie into larger social issues?
What conflicts in values or belief systems form part of the issue?

Come up with two questions that explore the issues you've identified in more depth.

Solutions and Their Consequences

What are the possible courses of action and solutions?
How would you rank them?
What are the advantages and disadvantages for each one?
Is your solution a short- or long-term solution?
What are the consequences of your solution for each of the stakeholders?

Come up with two questions that explore the consequences of your solutions.

2. Exploration Questions

What are the larger implications of climate change to developing world nations and indigenous peoples?
How should developed nations balance their lifestyle(s) and the health of the global environment?
How should the government respond to the situation faced by each community?
Discuss the risks and possible consequences of doing nothing.

What solutions could be found for each community?
What actions should individuals take in response to climate change?

3. Interview Activities

For the "Interview Your Audience" and "Interview Your Stakeholder" prompts, see the Appendix. These two activities are designed to help you better understand the needs and goals of the case audience and stakeholders. This exercise of imagination and of empathy will help you step into the shoes of the audience or stakeholder so that you can identify with them, which will in turn help you to choose what arguments to make in your paper.

Short Writing Assignment

Pick one of the following scenarios and write a short narrative. Imagine what the situation feels like for the person. Use your essay to tell the person's story. Your narrative could also be used as a springboard for class discussion.

1. **Hurricane:** You live in the Ninth Ward in New Orleans and have two small children. The levees have broken and there is widespread flooding. Public transit is no longer running and you don't own a car. There is no evacuation plan for your neighborhood. What do you do?
2. **Wildfire:** You live in the western United States in an area between a national forest and a town. A wildfire in your area has suddenly shifted direction, and you are forced to evacuate without any time to prepare. You don't know where all your family members are. The emergency shelter doesn't allow pets, so you can't stay there. What do you do?
3. **Drought:** You live in a rural community in a drought-stricken area in the United States. Your well has run dry and you have no water, but you can't afford to drill a new well. Because of the drought, you have lost your farm job. There is a six-month wait for county assistance. What do you do?
4. **External Displacement:** You are a lawyer working for the United Nations and serving on a taskforce preparing for the future needs of climate migrants. Come up with a set of criteria for international use defining who is a climate refugee/migrant. Your taskforce needs to develop a set of guidelines for helping these people. What areas of help will they need? What agencies will address these matters?

Arguing the Case: Writing Assignments

Paper Assignment 1

Pick one of the two scenarios to write about, either the community in Alaska or the community in the South Pacific. Come up with a relocation plan for that community. Write a formal report that argues for a specific plan of action to enable the community to relocate to a safer place.

To help you with your report, consider the following questions:

- What are the environmental, social, and historical factors that have contributed to the community's current situation?
- Why has the government been so slow to respond to the community's need to relocate?
- How can you build on work the community has already done?
- What can be done now that is different from what the community has already tried in the past?
- What plan can you come up with for funding sources for the relocation?
- What would be your new timeline and needed resources for relocation?

The audience is people in your community, government agency workers, politicians, and other affected communities.

Paper Assignment 2

Choose a stakeholder from either the community in Alaska or the community in the South Pacific and write your paper from their point of view. Be sure it is clear in your introduction which stakeholder you have chosen. Your goal is to persuade your audience that your chosen stakeholder's solution is the best one. As part of your argument, you need to consider the needs of as many stakeholders as possible.

In order to support your argument, you will need to address the context of the wider issues involved in the case. This is the portion of the paper where you will need outside resources to provide you with evidence and other examples of similar cases.

You will need to consider the following stakeholders in your decision:

Different stakeholders in the community
Elders in the community
Government officials
Stakeholders in the relocation area

The audience is people in your community, government agency workers, politicians, and other affected communities.

Alternative Assignments

1. Explore the local implications of climate change. What aspects of climate change are happening in your community? Make a proposal for the steps you believe your community should take to address climate change.
2. Visual argument: Design a poster that make an argument about climate change in general or one that makes an argument about the specific situation in your chosen community.
3. Design an information campaign for the general public or for public schools that informs people as well as offers steps ordinary people can take to address climate change in their daily lives. (This type of assignment could be adapted to service learning.)

Reflecting on the Case: Looking Back

Reflection is an important part of the learning process. It gives you the chance to examine what you've learned, how you learned it, and how you can improve your learning strategies in the future. Here, you are being asked to reflect on what you have learned from doing this case study. Use the following questions to help you reflect on the case study process:

- What did you learn about the issues of the case?
- What did you learn about the process of constructing an argument and counterarguments for an issue?
- What did you learn about doing research, both how and why it is important to argumentation?
- Now that you have done this case study, what approaches will you use for the next one? For instance, what will you do differently and what will you do the same?
- What did you like about doing the case study? What didn't you like about it?
- Do you have any other responses or reflections on the assignment?

6 CAMPUS SPEECH CODES

Case Scenario

The Setting

A small, private U.S. university, primarily serving undergraduate students. The student body reflects that of many universities today: Though a majority group exists, there are domestic and international students from many ethnicities, languages, and walks of life.

The Characters

Students
Professors
Parents of students
You, the president of the university
Other university administrators

The Issues

In recent months, two incidents debated as "hate speech" have occurred on campus. "Hate speech" is generally defined as verbal assaults and use of language or other expression to intimidate, often directed at groups or individuals designated by race, gender, ethnicity, or sexual orientation. In the case on this campus, one incident occurred outside of the LGBTQ Center. On a poster for an upcoming lecture on transgender identity in the 21st century, someone wrote "you will burn in hell." No one was identified in conjunction with the incident.

The other incident happened the next week, the day of the lecture. A group of students from a religious group on campus wore black T-shirts, on the front of which a rainbow flag appeared crossed out with a red "X," and on the back of which appeared a verse from the Bible calling for "sinners to repent." The group of students stood near the entrance to the hall where the lecture was to take place. Once the lecture was under way, the students left. When asked by a student journalist what the T-shirts meant, the students replied that their religion preached against homosexual and transgender lifestyles, and they wanted to "stand up for their beliefs." A picture of the students in their T-shirts, along with their responses to the questions, appeared in the campus newspaper the next day.

In response, some students expressed concern, describing that they felt threatened and less welcome on campus. Several felt that such incidents would make invited scholars feel less inclined to come to give lectures, thereby affecting the intellectual environment on campus. They suggested that the group of students did not have to attend the lecture, but neither did they need to draw attention to their opposition to it, especially given the poster vandalism the previous week.

Several students, faculty, and staff agreed with the students who said they felt threatened, and a group of members from the campus community petitioned the university president to implement a campus speech code. The campus speech code would identify the parameters of what is called "hate speech" on campus and would allow the university to forbid public expression of views deemed as hate speech. The rules would also enable students targeted by hate speech to report incidents to university personnel and would provide a protocol for handling these cases, following approaches such as that of Emory University in Atlanta, Georgia. The petitioning group argued that a campus speech code would allow the university to clearly identify what was discriminatory and inappropriate so that students would have a model for civility and would know what was expected.

Other students, faculty, and staff were not in favor of the campus speech code. They expressed concern that a campus speech code would stifle "free speech." "Free speech" is generally defined as the freedom of thought and expression, even when that expression includes discriminatory ideas. Those who opposed the campus speech codes suggested that although people disagreed with something—such as a T-shirt expressing that homosexuality was wrong—the right of freedom of speech protected such expression. They argued that threatening free speech would threaten freedom of expression, thereby stifling the expression of many different ideas, both those that people agreed with and those they disagreed with. They additionally argued that because society generally does not have speech codes, college campuses should not have them either, because college campuses should be an environment that prepares students for life after college.

Your Task

As the president of the university, you have been asked to make the final decision on whether the university should adopt a campus speech code. As you can see, some people in your campus community advocate campus speech codes that condemn certain uses of speech as a way to create a respectful, safe community for many different types of students. Others in your campus community view campus speech codes as an infringement on free speech and advocate alternative ways to ensure safe and civil campuses. You are not explicitly, legally obligated either way. The U.S. Supreme Court has not clearly ruled for or against campus speech codes vis-à-vis the First Amendment. Furthermore, as a private university, your university can have speech codes if it chooses regardless of the options available to state institutions. Now, the campus community awaits your statement as to what direction to take. What is the best way forward for the university? What case will you make?

You may find the following readings useful. They present a variety of perspectives and suggest a number of ways to create a respectful campus environment:

- Article by Deanna Garrett summarizing campus speech code cases: http://www.uvm.edu/~vtconn/?Page=v20/garrett.html
- AAUP statement on campus speech codes: www.aaup.org/report/freedom-expression-and-campus-speech-codes
- Article by Gerald Uleman on campus speech codes: http://www.scu.edu/ethics/publications/iie/v5n2/codes.html

Exploring the Case: Prewriting

Prewriting assignments are a useful way to explore case problems and issues as well as brainstorm and test out solutions. In addition, you can use them as a way to "think through writing" in order to explore your own opinions and ideas about the case. In turn, what you discover in your prewriting process can be used as a starting point for your paper or in class discussions.

Prewriting assignments will vary in length depending on the requirements of your instructor. Use the following prewriting activities to help you: (1) Case Analysis, (2) Exploration Questions, and (3) Interview Activities.

1. Case Analysis

The Stakeholders

Who are the stakeholders?
What is at stake for them?

What do they have to gain or lose?
How does the case appear to the different participants/stakeholders?

Come up with two questions you would like to ask each stakeholder.

The Issues

What are the main issues in the situation?
How would you rank the issues (from most to least important)?
What reasons can you give for your rankings?
How does the immediate problem or issue tie into larger social issues?
What conflicts in values or belief systems are part of the issue?

Come up with two questions that explore the issues you've identified in more depth.

Solutions and Their Consequences

What are the possible courses of action and solutions?
How would you rank them?
What are the advantages and disadvantages for each one?
Is your solution a short- or long-term solution?
What are the consequences of your solution for each of the stakeholders?

Come up with two questions that explore the consequences of your solutions.

2. Exploration Questions

What are the larger implications of banning or not banning certain types of speech?

How can you, as the university president, balance the rights of free speech with the rights of targeted groups not to feel threatened?

What other solutions could you consider besides a speech code that would provide groups with protection and recourse?

Discuss the risks and possible consequences to the school environment, both academic and cultural, if a speech code is implemented.

What compromises could you make in this situation that would satisfy both parties?

What parameters or restrictions should be included in a campus speech code? What definition of hate speech would be the most useful one? What mechanisms should be put into place for reporting hate speech? How should groups eligible for protections be determined?

3. Interview Activities

See the "Interview Your Audience" and "Interview Your Stakeholder" prompts in the Appendix. These two activities are designed to help you better understand the needs and goals of the case audience and stakeholders better. This exercise of the imagination and of empathy will help you step into the shoes of the audience or stakeholder so that you can identify with them, which will in turn help you to choose what arguments to make in your paper.

Arguing the Case: Writing Assignments

Paper Assignment 1

As the president of the university, you have been asked to make the final decision as to whether your university should implement a campus speech code. The code would identify the parameters of what is called "hate speech" on campus, allowing students targeted by hate speech to report incidents and allowing the university to forbid public expression of views deemed as "hate speech," such as by hanging a Nazi symbol in a dorm room window.

As part of your role, you will need to clarify the competing positions about campus speech codes in a fair and clear way. In other words, you will need to clarify the position in support of a campus speech code and the position opposed to a campus speech code. Then, you will need to outline your take on whether the university should adopt a speech code and why this is the best way forward for the university. In order to support your argument you will need to set it in the context of the wider issues involved in the case, both on and beyond the campus. To do so, you will need resources to provide you with evidence and other examples of similar cases (as a starting point, see the list of resources given in the "Your Task" section earlier in the chapter). Imagine the paper as providing considerations not only for this decision but for future questions or incidents related to freedom of expression and hate speech on campus.

You will need to consider the following stakeholders in your decision:

Students
Professors
Parents of students
Administrators

The audience is present and future students, instructors, staff, and administrators, as well as parents of students and local community members.

Paper Assignment 2

Choose a stakeholder and write your paper from their point of view. Be sure it is clear in your introduction which stakeholder you have chosen. Your goal is to argue from their point of view whether or not a campus speech code is the best solution to the current situation on campus. You will need to state the actions you feel the university president should take (your solution) and argue why those actions would be the best ones in this situation. As part of your argument, you need to take into account the needs of as many stakeholders as possible.

In order to support your argument, you will need to address the context of the wider issues involved in the case. This is the portion of the paper where you will need outside resources to provide you with evidence and other examples of similar cases (as a starting point, see the list of resources given in the "Your Task" section earlier in the chapter).

You will need to consider the following stakeholders in your decision:

Students
Professors
Parents of students
Administrators

The audience is present and future students, instructors, staff, and administrators, as well as parents of students and local community members.

Alternative Assignments

1. Write a campus speech code in which you determine the parameters for the code and define key terms such as "expression," "hate speech," and "debate."
2. Design a campus-wide tolerance campaign. This could include visual arguments in the form of posters as well as brochures and activities. Argue for how the campaign would improve the campus culture. (This type of assignment could be adapted to service learning.)
3. Research incidents of hate speech in your community or on your campus. Would a speech code have helped in your local context? Present an evidence-based case for the role of a speech code in those incidents and future incidents.

Reflecting on the Case: Looking Back

Reflection is an important part of the learning process. It gives you the chance to examine what you've learned, how you learned it, and how you can improve your learning strategies in the future. Here, you are being asked to reflect on what you have learned from doing this case study. Use the following questions to help you reflect on the case study process:

- What did you learn about the issues of the case?
- What did you learn about the process of constructing an argument and counterarguments for an issue?
- What did you learn about doing research, both how and why it is important to argumentation?
- Now that you have done this case study, what approaches will you use for the next one? For instance, what will you do differently and what will you do the same?
- What did you like about doing the case study? What didn't you like about it?
- Do you have any other responses or reflections on the assignment?

7 STUDENT LOAN DEBT

Case Scenario

The Setting

A small town that supports a number of small businesses and has a few major employers in largely manufacturing or agricultural jobs. There is one high school.

The Characters

You, a high school senior
Your family
The college
The lenders
The college recruiter

The Issues

You are a high school senior in a small town. It's an exciting time, but you also have a tough decision to make. Some of your friends are planning on going away to college, and you'd like to go to college too. If you went, you would be the first person in your family to go to college, and you want to make your family proud.

There is a small state school in a town a couple of hours away. It has a good program in the field you want to study, a field where there seem to be good opportunities. There are not many good job opportunities in your town for someone with only a high school degree, so a college education is something you think is important to your future.

But there's only one problem: How will you pay for it?

Your family owns a small business. Your mother, father, and brother work there. There is not a lot of extra money, but there has always been enough for the things the family needed. Your parents make too much money for you to qualify for most need-based scholarships but they don't make enough extra money to help you pay for college without some kind of financial help.

The college recruiter who visited your high school says getting financial assistance would be no problem: Student loans are easy to apply for and they are deferred until after graduation. However, you're not sure she is telling you the whole truth about student loans. You've heard some stories from friends and relatives.

For instance, your brother's friend Jason got a good job in his field right away making $45,000 a year, but he graduated from college with $30,000 in student loan debt in both federal and private loans. He has a monthly payment of $350 on his loans. He was doing all right until he had to have emergency surgery, and now he can only afford to pay either the hospital bill or the student loan payment.

Even worse, your cousin's best friend had to drop out of college, so she never finished her degree—but she still has $25,000 in student loans to pay off. Without a college degree, she's working at a minimum-wage job and just barely getting by. Every month it gets harder and harder to pay her $300-a-month loan payment. A couple of months ago she couldn't pay the loan payment because of an emergency, and now she and her fiancée have been turned down for the loan on the house they wanted to buy because of her bad credit rating.

However, your high school counselor says you are smart and there are many great opportunities beyond this small town. She thinks you should do whatever it takes to go to college. With a good job and a few loans, she thinks you should be all right. She knows of several students who have been able to pay off their loans and are now doing fine financially.

Your Task

The deadline for applications is coming up soon. What should you do? The following background information on student loan debt may be useful in helping you make a decision.[1]

---

1. Jason Delisle, *The Graduate Student Debt Review: The State of Graduate Student Borrowing* (Policy Brief, New American Education Policy Program), 2014, https://static.newamerica.org/attachments/750-the-graduate-student-debt-review/GradStudentDebtReview-Delisle-Final.pdf; The Institute for College Access and Success, *Student Debt and the Class of 2017* (13th Annual Report, 2017). https://ticas.org/sites/default/files/pub_files/classof2017.pdf; https://ticas.org/wp-content/uploads/legacy-files/pub_files/private_student_loans_facts_and_trends.pdf; The Institute for College Access and Success, *Students at the Greatest Risk of Loan Default, 2018,* https://ticas.org/sites/default/files/pub_files/students_at_the_greatest_risk_of_default.pdf; The Institute for College Access and Success. (2014). *Quick Facts About Student Debt,* https://ticas.org/sites/default/files/legacy/files/pub/Debt_Facts_and_Sources.pdf;

General Facts

- Total U.S. student loan debt is $1.56 trillion.
- 44.7 million Americans have student loan debt.
- 11.5% of student loans are 90 days or more delinquent or are in default.
- Average monthly student loan payment (among those not in deferment) is $393.
- Median monthly student loan payment (among those not in deferment) is $222.
- 65% of seniors graduating from public and nonprofit colleges in 2017 had student loan debt.
- Average debt at graduation from public and nonprofit colleges was $28,650 in 2017, a 1% increase from 2016.
- 66% of graduates from public colleges had loans (average debt of $25,550).
- 75% of graduates from private nonprofit colleges had loans (average debt of $32,300).
- 88% of graduates from for-profit colleges had loans (average debt of $39,950).
- About 15% of the student debt held by the graduating class of 2017 was private.
- 48% of borrowers who attended for-profit colleges default within 12 years, compared to 12% of public college attendees and 14% of nonprofit college attendees.

Private Student Loan Debt Statistics

- Private student loan debt volume hit $7.8 billion in 2014–15, up from $5.2 billion in 2010–11.
- More than half of undergraduates don't take full advantage of federal student loans, borrowing private loans before they've exhausted their available federal loans.
- In 2011–12, 48% of private loan borrowers attended schools that had tuition costs of $10,000 or less.

Federal Reserve Bank of New York Consumer Credit Panel/Equifax, *2018 Student Loan Update, 2014*, https://www.newyorkfed.org/medialibrary/interactives/householdcredit/data/xls/sl_update_2018.xlsx; Board of Governors of the Federal Reserve System, *Report on the Economic Well-Being of U.S. Households in 2016—May 2017*, https://www.federalreserve.gov/publications/2017-economic-well-being-of-us-households-in-2016-education-debt-loans.htm; Student Loan Hero, *A Look at the Shocking Student Debt Loan Statistics for 2020*, https://studentloanhero.com/student-loan-debt-statistics/.

- Nearly 1.4 million undergraduates borrowed private loans in 2011–12.
- About 15% of debt carried by seniors graduating in 2017 was in private loans (compared to 16% of the graduating class of 2016 with private loans) with an average burden of $18,550.
- Interest rates for private loans ran as high as 14.24% in September 2018.

Graduate Student Loan Debt

In 2012, about 40% of all student loan debt was used to finance graduate and professional degrees.

Combined undergraduate and graduate debt by degree:

- MBA = $42,000 (11% of graduate degrees)
- Master of Education = $50,879 (16%)
- Master of Science = $50,400 (18%)
- Master of Arts = $58,539 (8%)
- Law = $140,616 (4%)
- Medicine and health sciences = $161,772 (5%)
- Other master's degrees = $55,489 (15%)

Exploring the Case: Prewriting

Prewriting assignments are a useful way to explore case problems and issues as well as brainstorm and test out solutions. In addition, you can use them as a way to "think through writing" in order to explore your own opinions and ideas about the case. In turn, what you discover in your prewriting process can be used as a starting point for your paper or in class discussions.

Prewriting assignments will vary in length depending on the requirements of your instructor. Use the following prewriting activities to help you: (1) Case Analysis, (2) Exploration Questions, and (3) Interview Activities.

1. Case Analysis

The Stakeholders

Who are the stakeholders?
What is at stake for them?
What do they have to gain or lose?
How does the case appear to the different participants/stakeholders?

Come up with two questions you would like to ask each stakeholder.

The Issues

What are the main issues in the situation?
How would you rank the issues (from most to least important)?
What reasons can you give for your rankings?
How does the immediate problem or issue tie into larger social issues?
What conflicts in values or belief systems form part of the issue?

Come up with two questions that explore the issues you've identified in more depth.

Solutions and Their Consequences

What are the possible courses of action and solutions?
How would you rank them?
What are the advantages and disadvantages for each one?
Is your solution a short- or long-term solution?
What are the consequences of your solution for each of the stakeholders?

Come up with two questions that explore the consequences of your solutions

2. Exploration Questions

What are the larger implications of student loan debt for the student? For the education system? For the economy?
How can students and their families balance the possible advantages of higher education and the rising costs of education, both public and private?
Discuss how you think the government could respond to the student loan debt situation.
Discuss the risks and possible consequences of (a) the student taking on debt to get an education or (b) the student not going to college but remaining debt-free.
Are compromise solutions available for the student?
What are the responsibilities of the society to its young people to prepare them for a productive adult life? What are alternatives to student debt and the increasing costs of higher education? What are effects of student loan debt on students' future life decisions?

3. Interview Activities

See the "Interview Your Audience" and "Interview Your Stakeholder" prompts in the Appendix. These two activities are designed to help you better understand the needs and goals of the case audience and stakeholders. This an exercise of the imagination and of empathy will help you step into the shoes of the audience or stakeholder so that you can identify with them, which will in turn help you to choose what arguments to make in your paper.

Arguing the Case: Writing Assignments

Paper Assignment 1

Choose one of the stakeholders from the case study and write your paper from their point of view. Be sure it is clear in your introduction which stakeholder you have chosen. If you choose the student protagonist, be sure to argue from the student's point of view, not from yours. The paper should do two things. First, it should argue for a solution from that stakeholder's point of view: Should the protagonist go into debt for college or not? Second, it should argue for a longer-term solution to the issues of education costs, student loans, and long-term student debt.

In order to support your argument, you will need to set it in the context of the wider issues involved in the case, such as the economic impact of student loan debt. This is the portion of the paper where you will need outside resources to provide you with evidence and other examples of similar cases (as a start, see the information in the "Your Task" section earlier in the chapter).

You will need to consider the following stakeholders in your decision:

The student protagonist (you)
Your family
The college
The lenders
The college recruiter

The audience is other students, universities, government lenders, and private lenders.

Paper Assignment 2

Many people agree that the current student loan system needs reform. Come up with a recommendation or solution that will improve the current system. As part of your argument, come up with reasons why Congress should adopt your solution.

In order to support your argument, you will need outside resources to provide you with evidence and other examples of similar cases (as a start, see the information in the "Your Task" section earlier in the chapter).

You will need to consider the following stakeholders in your decision:

Students who currently have student loan debt
Students will need loans in the future
Their families
Colleges
Federal loan system
Private lenders

The audience is students, universities, government lenders, and private lenders.

Alternative Assignments

1. Research the student loan debt situation on your campus. How does it relate to the national situation? Interview students and administrators to get their views. What solution could you advocate for on your campus?
2. Design a campaign to educate students and prospective students on student loans. (This could be a service learning project.)
3. Research the situation in other countries. How do they handle the costs of higher education to students and student loans? Could the United States use other countries as a model to solve the student loan debt crisis here?

Reflecting on the Case: Looking Back

Reflection is an important part of the learning process. It gives you the chance to examine what you've learned, how you learned it, and how you can improve your learning strategies in the future. Here, you are being asked to reflect on what you have learned or come to understand from doing this case study. Use the following questions to help you reflect on the case study process:

- What did you learn about the issues of the case?
- What did you learn about the process of constructing an argument and counterarguments for an issue?
- What did you learn about doing research, both how and why it is important to argumentation?
- Now that you have done this case study, what approaches will you use for the next one? For instance, what will you do differently and what will you do the same?
- What did you like about doing the case study? What didn't you like about it?
- Do you have any other responses or reflections on the assignment?

8 SALMON VERSUS DAMS

Case Scenario

The Setting

A taskforce meeting somewhere in the Pacific Northwest. The task-force has been set up at the request of Federal Judge Blaine Fishman. He has called together representatives from different organizations like the Nez Perce tribe, the Army Corps of Engineers, farmers who ship goods down the river or use the dams for irrigation, the Bonneville Power Administration, and different conservation groups.

The Characters

The conservation groups
The farmers
The Native American tribes
The power company
The Army Corps of Engineers

The Issues

Federal Judge Blaine Fishman has issued a new ruling regarding the endangered salmon on the Columbia and Snake Rivers. Having reviewed the government's current plan for managing the Columbia River hydropower system, the judge has ruled that the government's plan for the managing and restoring the salmon runs on the Snake River violates both the Endangered Species Act and the National Environmental Policies Act. Further, Judge Fishman found that the management plan failed to consider the impacts of climate change on both fish populations and river habitat. Therefore, he has tasked the government with developing a new plan that is in compliance with the laws.

According to the judge's report, recent salmon numbers have suddenly dropped below 0.5%, raising concerns about their survival: "13 runs of Columbia and Snake river salmon remain endangered despite billions of dollars spent since 1991 to save them." In the 1970s, the wild Snake River fall Chinook populations reached about 30,000. Today the fish populations have declined by 90% and number far below their recovery target of 3,000. Because dams create major obstacles for fish migration, Judge Fishman has recommended that the government seriously reexamine the continued use of the four dams on the lower Snake River and, if necessary, should seriously consider removing or breaching one or more of them.

As part of a separate action, several Native American tribes, the states of Washington and Oregon, and several fish and conservation groups are discussing filing a lawsuit if the federal government does not come up with a plan that addresses the serious issues at stake here, including the role the dams play in the decline of the salmon populations. These groups have agreed to wait to file their lawsuit until the judge has examined the government's new plan.

A taskforce has been set up to study different aspects of the situation and make recommendations to the government. This taskforce comprises the different stakeholders who need to come up with a solution that will help the government not only avoid a lawsuit but more importantly better manage the restoration of the salmon. The taskforce members have asked representatives from all the stakeholders to present the case from their perspective so they can become informed on all aspects of the issue.

Your Task

As a stakeholder on the taskforce, you have been assigned to examine the possibility of breaching the dams on the Snake River. Together with the other stakeholders, you need to come up with a solution to recommend to the larger taskforce about the situation with the dams. What will you recommend? To breach the dam and restore the river habitat? To retain the dams and find another solution to the salmon decline?

We will provide some background information on the four Snake River dams[1] and then will present the positions of the stakeholders.

---

1. U.S. Army Corps of Engineers, *Snake River Dams Fact Sheet*, http://www.nwd.usace.army.mil/Missions/CivilWorks/LowerSnakeRiverdams.aspx.

IMAGE CS8.1. Lower Granite Dam on the Snake River
Source: U.S. Army Corps of Engineers

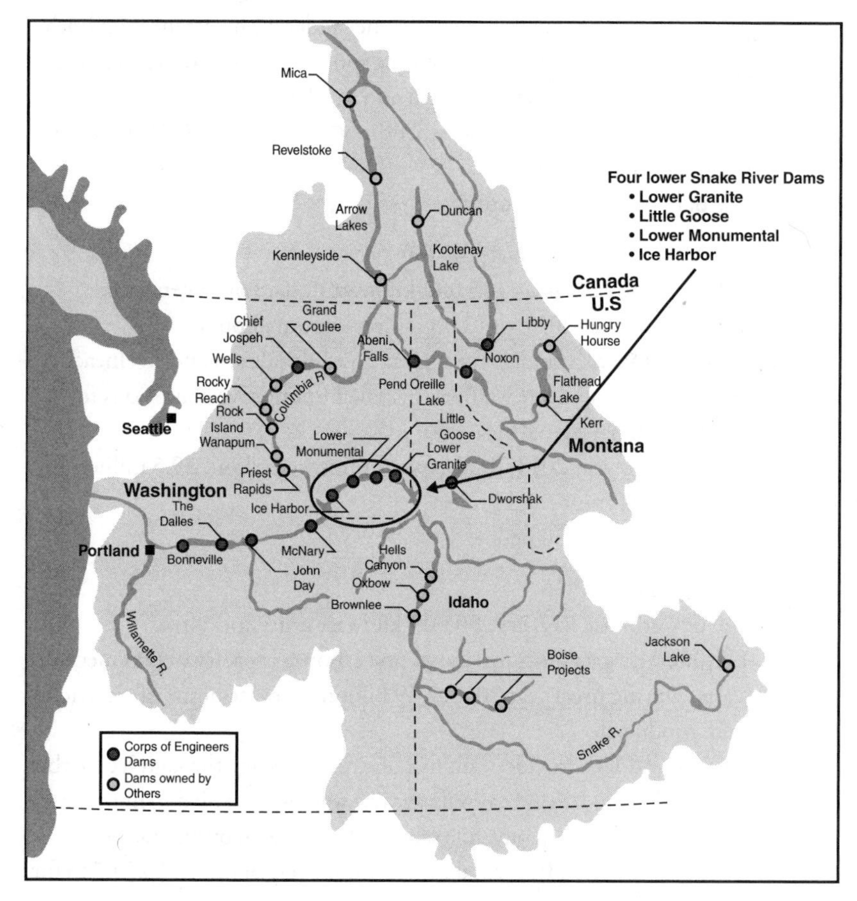

IMAGE CS8.2. Map of the four lower Snake River dams.
Source: Adapted from the US Army Corps of Engineers

Background Information

Lower Granite Dam (built 1965–84)

- The powerhouse has six 135,000-kilowatt units. Power generated during fiscal year 2011 was 3.17 billion kilowatt-hours.
- There is one fish ladder for passing migratory fish with entrances on both shores and a fish channel through the dam that connects to the south shore ladder. A spillway weir was installed in 2001, resulting in improved in-river passage conditions for juvenile salmonids via the spillway.
- Total expenditures during fiscal year 2011 were about $17.5 million.
- The dam employs 80 people.

Little Goose Dam (built 1963–70)

- The powerhouse has six 135,000-kilowatt units for a total powerhouse capacity of 810 megawatts. During fiscal year 2011, 2.9 billion kilowatt-hours of electricity were produced.
- Adult fish passage facilities include one ladder with entrances on both shores and a fish channel through the spillway, which connects to the powerhouse fish collection system and south shore ladder.
- During fiscal year 2011, total expenditures were about $7.8 million for the Little Goose Project.
- The dam employs 48 people.

Lower Monumental Dam (1961–69)

- The powerhouse has six 135,000-kilowatt units. Power generated during fiscal year 2011 was 3.38 billion kilowatt-hours.
- There are two fish ladders for migrating adult salmon and steelhead to use. In 2007, a spillway weir was installed to improve conditions for juvenile fish passage at the dam.
- During fiscal year 2011, total expenditures were about $9.5 million for the Lower Monumental Project.
- The dam employs 50 people.

Ice Harbor Dam (1956–61)

- The powerhouse has three 90,000-kilowatt units and three 111,000-kilowatt units for a total powerhouse capacity of 603 megawatts. During fiscal year 2011, 2.49 billion kilowatt-hours of electricity were produced.
- Two fish ladders provide adult fish upstream passage through Ice Harbor Lock and Dam. In 2005, a spillway weir was also installed to improve passage conditions for juvenile salmon downstream outmigration.
- During fiscal year 2011, total expenditures were about $11,274,746 for the Ice Harbor Project.
- The dam employs more than 80 people.

All the dams participate in the program to bypass the juvenile salmon and steelhead around the Corps' dams and reservoirs of the Snake and Columbia rivers. Transport began in the late 1960s. At Lower Granite, a total of 6,310,606 juvenile fish were collected in 2011, and 3,874,873 of those were transported.

Recreation activities and programs provided at the dam's reservoirs provide opportunities for family and friends to strengthen interaction, and for children to develop "personal skills, social values and self-esteem." They help to alleviate the lack of physical activity in the general public and increase water safety.

The money spent by visitors to the dam's recreation facilities provides a component of the economy of the communities near the lakes through shipping and hydroelectricity.

Stakeholder Positions

Army Corps of Engineers

You are a civilian engineer who works for the Army Corps of Engineers (ACOE). You represent the ACOE, which built the dams, as well as the Bureau of Land Reclamation, which operates them. The ACOE stands by the recommendation of the 2002 Feasibility Report, which advocated for creating better passageways for the adult and juvenile fish rather than breaching the dams.

The ACOE built the dams between 1956 and 1984. Overall, you have invested a great deal of money and time in terms of both the initial construction and design and their current upkeep. The dams currently generate hydroelectricity and provide irrigation, recreation, and navigation. The Corps feels the dams provide social, economic, and environmental benefits to the general public and that these benefits warrant their continued existence.

The ACOE did a seven-year feasibility study, the Lower Snake River Juvenile Salmon Migration Feasibility Study, between 1995 and 2002.[2] The study included the following:

Engineering work
Biological investigations (i.e., effects to salmon and steelhead, resident fish, and wildlife)
Effects on recreation, cultural resources, and water quality
Socioeconomic effects, including implementation costs, navigation, irrigation, and power

The study also included an environmental impact statement and public involvement as required by the National Environmental Policy Act process.

---

2. U.S. Army Corps of Engineers, *Lower Snake River Juvenile Salmon Migration Feasibility Study*, http://www.nww.usace.army.mil/Library/2002LSRStudy.aspx.

The final environmental impact statement, released in 2002, evaluated four alternatives to help lower Snake River fall Chinook get past the dams:

The existing condition
Maximum transport of juvenile salmon
System improvements that could be accomplished without a drawdown
Dam breaching

The study concluded that breaching the four dams would cost $911 million and by itself would not recover the fish, would take the longest time to benefit fish listed under the Endangered Species Act, and would be the most uncertain to implement of any of the alternatives. The study's preferred alternative was to make major improvements to fish passage systems at the dams.

Bonneville Power Administration

You represent the Bonneville Power Administration and the Northwest Pacific Waterway Association. The stance of these two groups is that the dams should remain because they serve an important economic purpose in the region. You feel that there are adequate plans in place for fish migration and these should be pursued more aggressively, perhaps with more funding and more manpower. For instance, a comprehensive management plan, the Biological Opinion ("Bi-Op"), which is supposed to manage the fish on both the Columbia and Snake rivers, was released by the National Oceanic and Atmospheric Administration (NOAA) fisheries in 2008 and has been supplemented in 2010 and 2014. The 2014 plan was invalidated by a federal judge. (The next one is due in 2021.)

These are some of the main reasons you oppose breaching or removing the dams[3]:

1. It would cost a lot of money. The estimated cost of breaching the dams is $1.3 billion to $2.6 billion.
2. The dams are an important source of hydroelectric power for the area. They produce $271 million in revenues and produce over 3,000 megawatts. Removing them would result in the loss of this power and an increase in electric rates for customers. According to the Pacific Northwest Waterways Association, it would cost $271 million to find alternative energy sources.
3. Breaching or removing the dams would increase carbon dioxide emissions by 2.0 million to 2.6 million metric tons every year.

---

3. https://www.bpa.gov/news/pubs/FactSheets/fs-201603-A-Northwest-energy-solution-Regional-power-benefits-of-the-lower-Snake-River-dams.pdf; Bonneville Power Administration, "Dam Breaching and the Lower Snake River Dams" (fact sheet), BPA.gov; Pacific Northwest Waterways Association, https://www.pnwa.net/.

4. Breaching or removing the dams would produce a loss of navigation on the river. Currently the locks on the dam serve barge traffic between Lewiston, Idaho, and Portland Oregon. If this barge traffic were to cease, it would mean loss of revenue for the barges and for the ports of Lewiston and Portland as well as the loss of a means of transportation for farmers, who depend on the barges to get their grain to market. The port of Lewiston shipped over 9 million tons of commercial cargo in 2012, most of it grain, timber, and pulses (different kinds of legumes).
5. Breaching or removing the dams would create a loss of irrigation water. The Ice Harbor Dam provides irrigation for 35,000 acres of farmland.
6. Breaching or removing the dams might cause a loss of jobs in the region.
7. If the dams were breached, modifications would be needed to compensate for changes in the water flow.

If the reservoirs were lowered, modifications to the reservoir infrastructure would be necessary. For instance:

Large quantities of rock would be necessary to stabilize the sections of railroad and highway embankments in order to protect them from erosion due to a faster-flowing river.
Modifications related to fish, wildlife, recreation, and cultural resources would be needed in each reservoir.
Lyons Ferry Hatchery would need extensive modifications so it could continue limited production during the process.
Recreation areas would be modified or, in some cases, closed.
A number of major agricultural and industrial modifications would be required by drawdown.
Modifications to existing water wells may be necessary to maintain current water yields, and modification would need to be made to the corporate irrigation system in use by the Ice Harbor Reservoir.

Farming and Riving Shipping

You represent the interests of the farming and the barge transportation groups. Your group is divided on the issue.[4]

---

4. Elaine Williams, "Corps OKs Dredging of Area Ports," November 19, 2014, http://portoflewiston.com/corps-oks-dredging-of-area-ports/; Molly Harbarger, "Container-terminal loss at Port of Portland felt deeply upriver," *The Oregonian*, April 12, 2015, http://www.oregonlive.com/business/index.ssf/2015/04/economic_pulse_remains_steady.html; Port of Lewiston, "Shipping Reports," http://portoflewiston.com/media-room/shipping-reports/; https://nowater-nolife.org/farming-dams/; DanSense, "Audit: Port of Lewiston Annual Operating Loss," https://damsense.org/port-lewiston-annual-operating/.

Some of the farmers favor breaching or removing the dams. Many of these farmers are no-till or dryland farmers. The government spends $800 million a year for the Snake River system on barging, dam repair, maintenance, and mitigation subsidies, which some farmers feel is too much. The primary benefit is shipping grain, but many of these farmers have shifted to moving their grain by rail. Rail is more cost effective for them, so they feel they are not getting benefits from the dams. With upgrades, the existing rail lines in the Northwest that run from Idaho to Portland could affordably and effectively replace the barge traffic and would provide a more cost-effective way to accommodate most of the grain currently moving down the lower Snake River.

Only 13 farms benefit from irrigation water from the Ice Harbor Dam. This water could be replaced by extending water intake pipes to a free-flowing lower Snake River. The farmers also believe the irrigation benefits of the Ice Harbor Dam are limited since the Snake River's flow varies by season. Its largest flow is in the spring, not summer or autumn when farmers need the water the most. Removing the lower Snake River dams would also help irrigators upriver, especially those in southern Idaho who, under an aggressive non-dam-removal plan, are required to let more water remain upriver to mitigate for the effects of the dams.

Removing dams could restore the river habitat, offer more and varied recreation, and improve the economics of the area. Many farmers feel restricted by limited access to the rivers, including being warned or threatened after boating on or fishing in the water. These actions also create negative feelings toward the ACOE. These farmers feel that there's been much misinformation about the dams, and they want transparency and accurate information about the dams from the government and the ACOE. They want to be included in any decision-making process over the fate of the dams.

Other farmers, however, are against breaching the dams, especially those in the Ice Harbor area. These farmers benefit from the irrigation water from the dam. They would be hurt economically if they no longer had access to the water for irrigation. These farmers also support the use of barges for transportation on the river and the generation of hydropower.

The river barge shipping industry is one of the main beneficiaries of the four dams. Many in the shipping industry would like to see the dams remain since they and the industry have benefited from the waterway for many years. However, in the last few years, the industry has suffered an economic downturn and many of the customers have turned to other shipping alternatives. Some in the industry claim that this is just a periodic dip in the economy and believe the industry will rebound, while other in the barging industry want to work on ways for the industry to recover. Both groups feel the dams are vital.

In 2013, Lewiston experienced a historic low, shipping out only 3,240 containers. The last time the number was that low was in 2011, when the ACOE closed the locks for three months to do major maintenance work. This downturn continued in 2014, when container traffic in Lewiston was down 31%. This decrease in container volume was largely due to management/labor issues at the Portland port.

In April 2015, container shipping from Lewiston to Portland was on indefinite hold when a major shipping company pulled out of Portland over labor disputes. Many customers needed alternative ways to get goods to market. However, the grain shipments from the Lewis Clark Terminal at the port of Lewiston continue. Container shipments between Lewiston and Portland remain suspended. In 2017, the port of Lewiston reported an operating loss of $134,000, although it did bring in income from sales and property development. The only cargo shipments were those of peas and lentils.

The ACOE has classified the lower Snake River as a "negligible waterway." Barge traffic is currently moving less than 300 million tons, which would have to triple to qualify as even a "low-use waterway."

The shipping channel at Lewiston must be constantly dredged due to the silt and sediment buildup trapped behind the Lower Granite Dam. It costs between $1 million and $5 million annually to maintain the shipping channel—on top of the cost of dredging. In 2015, American Construction Co. of Tacoma was awarded the contract for the $6.74 million project to dredge the shipping channel at Lewiston.

Orca Whale Preservation

You represent the Southern Resident Killer Whale Chinook Salmon Initiative, an organization formed recently by San Juan islanders in Washington State and the Center for Whale Research. These organizations are dedicated to preserving the orcas or killer whales in the Puget Sound. In 2005, the southern resident orca population was declared endangered.[5] The number of whales dropped to 75, a level not seen since 1985, according to a census by the Center for Whale Research. The pod hasn't had a live birth since 2015. The most recent birth occurred in 2018; the calf survived for 30 minutes but the mother carried the dead body for 10 days.

5.. Southern Resident Killer Whale Chinook Salmon Initiative, https://srkwcsi.org/; Susan Casey, "The Orca, Her Dead Calf, and Us," *New York Times*, August 4, 2018, https://www.nytimes.com/2018/08/04/opinion/sunday/the-orca-her-dead-calf-and-us.html; Lynda V. Mapes, "Hunger: The Decline of Salmon Adds to the Struggle of Puget Sound's Orcas," *Seattle Times*, February 24, 2019, https://www.seattletimes.com/seattle-news/environment/hunger-the-decline-of-salmon-adds-to-the-struggle-of-puget-sounds-orcas/; Center for Whale Research, https://www.whaleresearch.com/.

The National Marine Fisheries Service lists lack of food as one of the major threats to orca survival. When the whales don't get enough to eat, they metabolize their fat stores, which compromises their immune system and reproductive capacity. One of the main food sources for the orca whales are Chinook salmon, which come from the Snake and Columbia rivers. The whales need to consume 18 to 25 adult salmon a day to meet their basic nutritional and energy needs. According to the NOAA's Southern Resident Killer Whale recovery plan, the greatest change in the whales' food availability has been the decline of the salmon population on the Columbia River to 8% of what they were before the dams were built.

Your group believes that the orcas are declining due to starvation. This is because the number of salmon is declining due to the dams. Your group advocates that the dams be breached to save both the salmon and the orca whales from extinction. According to Save Our Wild Salmon, removing the four lower Snake River dams would open over 15 million acres of prime salmon habitat. Studies show that tighter regulation of the commercial fishing industry would not make up for the loss of the salmon the whales need. Treaty obligations to First Nation Tribes in Canada and Native American tribes on the U.S. side of the Columbia River Basin are another main component of why the coalition is pushing for dam removal.

Salmon Protection

Wild salmon are a keystone species, an indicator of an ecosystem's overall health. Salmon and steelhead form an key component of the food chains of at least 150 other species, including humans. Currently many salmon runs on the West Coast are endangered or threatened. A combination of factors have contributed to their steep decline in numbers, including overfishing, habitat loss, hydropower and dams, hatchery fish, ocean conditions, and climate change.[6]

The following Snake River salmon and steelhead runs are listed under the Endangered Species Acts. The goals for recovery of the wild fish returns (not hatchery fish) must be met before the fish can be delisted.

Sockeye salmon were listed in 1991. Historical runs numbered 100,000-plus. The recovery goal is 2,500 wild adult fish per year for eight consecutive years.

6. Idaho Department of Fish and Game, https://idfg.idaho.gov/; Fredericks, Jim, Idaho Department of Fish and Game. *Idaho Salmon and Steelhead Overview of Management, Status and Factors Affecting Abundance*, 2019; NOAA Fisheries, Federal Columbia River Power System (FCRPS) Final Supplemental Biological Opinion, January, 2014, https://www.fisheries.noaa.gov/resource/document/consultation-remand-operation-federal-columbia-river-power-system; Oregon, Joseph, Nez Perce Tribe, Department of Fisheries Resources Management, *Emigration of Juvenile Chinook Salmon and Steelhead from the Imnaha River*, 2017; NOAA Fisheries' Northwest Fisheries Science Center, https://www.fisheries.noaa.gov/about/northwest-fisheries-science-center.

Table CS5.1. Sockeye Salmon Recent Adult Returns

Year	Wild	Hatchery
1990	0	NA
2001	26	NA
2011	150	1,118
2012	55	189
2015	78	192
2015	455	1,063
2017	445*	
2018	297*	

*Both wild and hatchery fish.

Snake River Chinook were listed in 1992. Historical runs numbered 2 million. The recovery goal is 80,000 wild adult fish per year for eight consecutive years.

Table CS5.2. Chinook Salmon Recent Adult Returns

Year	Wild	Hatchery
1990	9,524	15,066
2001	45,481	140,653
2011	22,522	69,245
2012	20,522	59,028
2015	14,254	50,214
2015	29,879	63,275
2016	24,840	91,442
2018	11,339	56,257

Snake River steelhead were listed in 1997. Historical numbers were 1 million. The recovery goal is 90,000 adult fish per year for eight consecutive years.

Table CS5.3. Steelhead Recent Adult Returns

Year	Wild	Hatchery
1990	24,979	100,569
2001	20,575	96,727
2011	44,859	165,457
2012	40,151	140,169
2015	26,175	85,009
2015	25,795	82,117

According to the Federal Columbia River Power System report in 2004, 50% to 80% of young salmon are killed by the dams during their migration downstream to the ocean, while 15% are killed by the dams during their migration upstream. The survival rate was even lower in 2017, when only 17% of the young fish made it past the dams, according to the NOAA.

Another figure scientists measure is the smolt-to-adult return (SAR) rate. Young salmon stay an average of two to four years in the ocean before they return to spawn. Restoring the salmon runs requires a minimum of a 2% to 6% return rate; however, in 2012, the average SAR rate for Chinook salmon was only 1.12% to 1.29%.

The dams have a measurable impact on the decline of salmon. Despite many different interventions, such as fish ladders, weirs, spillways, and trucking smolts around the dams, the fish numbers have not returned anywhere close to historical numbers, nor have they come close to the recovery targets.

Native American Tribes

As a member of the Nez Perce tribe, you represent the tribes in the Columbia Basin region. You argue that the dams should be breached or removed since the social, cultural, and economic survival of your people is at stake.[7] The tribes feel that the federal government should act to restore the Snake River salmon and steelhead runs because of treaty rights and past treaty violations. Data from the tribe's Department of Fisheries Resources and Management show that the federal government's Bi-Op is not working; more aggressive measures are needed to save the salmon. In 2011 and in 2016, the courts declared the Bi-Op plan illegal. So far, the government has not come up with another option the courts will accept.

The data that Nez Perce scientists have gathered shows that removing the dams on the lower Snake River is the best way to restore numbers and harvestable stocks. If no alternative plan is proposed, the tribes will go forward with their lawsuit. The compensation they are asking is between $6 billion and $12 billion, which is higher than the cost of removing the dams ($400 million).

As a member of the tribe, a great deal of your culture and many of your religious beliefs and customs center around the fish resources of the area. For you, fishing is not just an economic issue but an integral part of your way of life.

---

7. https://nezperce.org/government/fisheries-resources-management/department-of-fisheries-resource-management/; see the Columbia River Inter-Tribal Fish Commission's *Executive Summary: Tribal Circumstances and the Impacts of the Lower Snake River Project on the Nez Perce, Yakama, Umatilla, Warm Springs and Shoshone Bannock Tribes,* for 1999 and 2014, https://www.critfc.org/.

The destruction and the subsequent extinction of the salmon and the other fish in the area will lead to the destruction of the tribes.

> *The sacred salmon runs are in decline. It is the moral duty, therefore, of the Indian people of the Columbia to see them restored. We have to take care of them so that they can take care of us. Entwined together inextricably, no less now than ever before, are the fates of both the salmon and the Indian people. The quest for salmon recovery is about restoring what is sacred to its sacred place.*—Ted Strong, Yakama[8]

In 1855, the Nez Perce, Yakima, Warm Springs, and Umatilla tribes signed a treaty with the federal government that guaranteed them the "right of taking fish" at their usual and accustomed fishing sites. The tribes believed that they would be able to maintain their exclusive fishing rights in the area. However, the fishing resources, rights, and allocations granted to the tribes by the 1855 treaty have been systematically eroded over time as non-Indian property owners seized land and the dams were constructed. Commercial fisherman usurped so much of the fish harvest that the U.S. Supreme Court had to rule, in 1979, that the tribes were entitled to half of the Columbia Basin salmon harvest.[9]

As the number of salmon continued to decline, tribal fisherman were often attacked by non-Indian fisherman who blamed the tribes for the lack of fish. However, you feel that the biggest threat to the salmon is not non-Indian fisherman but rather the changes made to the rivers. The rivers have been heavily dammed for hydroelectricity, waste disposal, transportation, and irrigation projects, which have altered the river's flow and temperature, causing fish numbers to decline dramatically. Overall, salmon numbers had dropped from as many as 16 million during the time of European settlement to around 1 million in 2013. The tribes have had to cut their harvest by 80% to 90% since 1985 because they feel they can harvest only when there are sufficient fish to sustain the healthy fish population.

The tribes have a strong legal argument that treaty fishing rights prohibit actions that reduce fish harvests to levels below those necessary for the tribes to make a "moderate living." According to the tribes, the only solution that meets treaty and trust responsibilities and environmental criteria is to breach the dams and restore the river.

---

8. "The Plan: Wy-Kan-Ush-Mi Wa-Kish-Wit," Columbia River Inter-Tribal Fish Commission, accessed August 1, 2020, https://www.critfc.org/fish-and-watersheds/fish-and-habitat-restoration/the-plan-wy-kan-ush-mi-wa-kish-wit/

9. *Washington v. Washington State Commercial Passenger Fishing Vessel Ass'n.*, 443 U.S. 658 (1979).

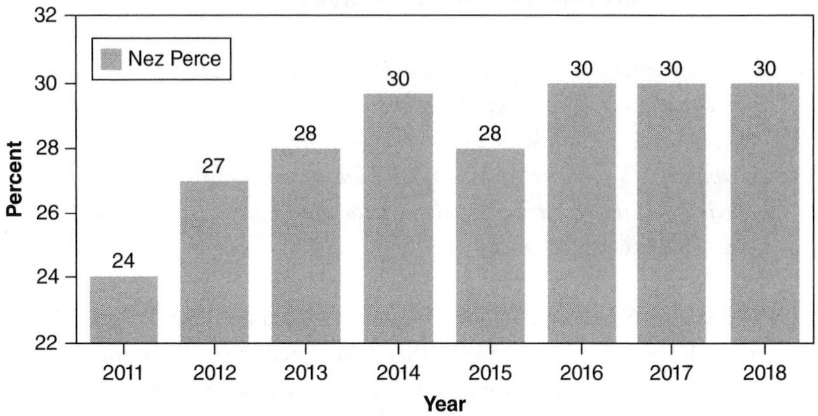

FIGURE CS8.1. Poverty Rate of American Indians.
Source: Indicators Idaho

Conservation Groups and Scientists

As a fisheries biologist, you represent a number of conservation groups and scientists who have been trying to get the dams removed for a number of years. These groups include American Rivers, Save Our Salmon, Idaho Rivers United, and Friends of the Clearwater. Your group argues that the status quo is not working.[10] Fish ladders, weirs, spills, and transportation of juvenile fish over and around the dams have not increased the fish runs. The number of endangered fish remains stagnant; in fact, many argue that the fish are as close to extinction now as when they were first put on the endangered species list 20 years ago. No fish species is close to its recovery target, a benchmark that must be met for eight consecutive years before a species can be removed from the list.

Before the completion of the lower Snake River dams, wild Snake River fall Chinook populations were about 30,000. Now, the numbers have plummeted by more than 90%. Wild Snake River spring/summer Chinook have had some

10.. Save Our Wild Salmon, "Who Supports Lower Snake River Dam Removal?", http://www.wildsalmon.org/facts-and-information/who-supports-lower-snake-river-dam-removal.html; Save Our Wild Salmon, "Why Remove the 4 Lower Snake River Dams," http://www.wildsalmon.org/facts-and-information/why-remove-the-4-lower-snake-river-dams.html; J. Waddell, "Comments to the U.S. Army Corps of Engineers Waterway Users Advisory Board at Their Meeting of August 14, 2014 in Walla Walla, Washington;" https://www.americanrivers.org/; Nic Lane, *Dam Removal: Issues, Considerations, and Controversies. CRS Report for Congress* (Washington, DC: Library of Congress, 2006); National Marine Fisheries Service, Northwest Region, "Proposed ESA Recovery Plan for Snake River Spring/Summer Chinook Salmon and Snake River Steelhead;" http://www.friendsoftheclearwater.org/.

growth but have never reached their recovery targets since the dams were completed in 1975. Since the completion of the dams:

- Wild Snake River steelhead have not reached their intended recovery target of 90,000 fish.
- In 2007, only four sockeyes reached their spawning grounds (in the mid-1950s, 4,300 sockeyes returned to Redfish Lake)
- The 28 listed spring/summer Chinook salmon populations are rated at high risk of extinction, with a low probability of persistence over 100 years.
- Return rates for adult fish have only rarely exceeded the 2% survival minimum. Minimum sustainable return rates for population restoration are 2% to 6%. From 1994 to 2004, they ranged from 0.35% to, once, 2.5%.
- Juvenile and adult salmon and steelhead are killed by colliding with the dam structures, from getting sucked into the turbines, and due to disorientation and pressure changes. This leaves them vulnerable to predators and disease.
- Pacific lamprey numbers have declined by an estimated 95%. They are likely to soon be listed as threatened or endangered.
- Multiple plans have been ruled illegal for relying on uncertain or unspecified habitat restoration projects. They have failed to adequately mitigate the salmon's largest source of human-caused mortality—the Columbia and Snake river dams and reservoirs.

The dams also have an impact on water quality and greenhouse gases:

- Dams produce methane, a greenhouse gas created by the rotting and growing organic matter that collects behind them. This contributes to global warming.
- In 2001, the federal district court ruled that the federal government's operation of four dams on the lower Snake River violates the Clean Water Act.
- Warmer water temperatures in the reservoir slow down and stress the fish, contributing to delayed mortality figures, meaning the fish appear fine in the reservoir, but actually die later.

Over the past 11 years, the dams have produced only 33% of their designated capacity. Overall, they generate only about 4% of the power produced in the Pacific Northwest. This power could be replaced by other renewable energy sources, such as wind and solar. In the past few years, wind energy has increasingly accounted for power generation in the Pacific Northwest: In 2012, wind energy production totaled 2,007 megawatts, while the dams produced only 1,039 megawatts. The Idaho Public Utilities Commission recently approved 13 solar power projects in southern Idaho with a total capacity of approximately 400 Megawatts.

The cost of maintaining the aging dams needs to be justified with a real return to the taxpayers, the tribes, and the residents of Washington, Oregon, and Idaho. The turbines have exceeded their expected life span of 25+ years and the ACOE budgeted $321 million for turbine rehabilitation. Currently, it is costing $91 million to rehabilitate the first 3 turbines, and 21 more turbines will need repair. Projected costs for turbine repair for all the dams total $776 million to $1 billion. The cost of operating the dams approaches $300 million per year. The maintenance and operating costs of the lower Snake River waterway are well over $10 million per year. These costs are paid for by the American taxpayer.

Initially the cost of breaching all four dams would be around $400 million, and the project would take four to seven years. The overall benefits for breaching on an annual average basis range from $130 million to 400 million. The American people could receive least $130 million in economic benefits if the dams were breached.

We know that dam removal and fish/river restoration has been very successful on other river systems, such as the following:

Edward Dam, Kennebec River, Maine (1999): More than 2 million alewives returned to the Kennebec, the largest migration of its kind on the Eastern Seaboard.

Penobscot River Restoration Project, Maine (2013 and 2014): The removal of two dams significantly improved access to critical spawning and juvenile rearing habitat for Atlantic salmon and 10 other species of migratory fish.

Elwha and Gilnes Canyon Dam, Elwha River, Washington (2011–14): Salmon have returned to the river; the reservoir bed has been replanted and sediment once trapped behind the dams is rebuilding beaches at the Elwha's outlet to the sea.

Conduit River Dam, California (2014): White salmon started returning to the river even before all of the concrete had been removed from the dam. Habitat has been replanted in the reservoir area and river recreation has returned.

In conclusion, you want to emphasize that your group is not calling for the removal of **all** the dams on the Columbia River; rather, dam removal should be evaluated on a case-by-case basis. Certain dams, like the four under discussion, have outlived their usefulness and a much greater return both environmentally and economically can be gained by their removal. Your group feels that scientific evidence showing that breaching the dams is necessary to the restoration of the salmon fish runs has long been in place. Even NOAA in its report states that dams on the Columbia and Snake rivers represent the primary threat to the viability of Snake River spring/summer Chinook salmon and steelhead. Only the political will has been lacking to do what needs to be done for the fish, the environment, and the communities involved. You hope that this committee's recommendation will be able to persuade the federal government before it is too late.

Exploring the Case: Prewriting

Prewriting assignments are a useful way to explore case problems and issues as well as brainstorm and test out solutions. In addition, you can use them as a way to "think through writing" in order to explore your own opinions and ideas about the case. In turn, what you discover in your prewriting process can be used as a starting point for your paper or in class discussions.

Prewriting assignments will vary in length depending on the requirements of your instructor. Use the following prewriting activities to help you: (1) Case Analysis, (2) Exploration Questions, and (3) Interview Activities.

1. Case Analysis

The Stakeholders

Who are the stakeholders?
What is at stake for them?
What do they have to gain or lose?
How does the case appear to the different participants/stakeholders?

Come up with two questions you would like to ask each stakeholder.

The Issues

What are the main issues in the situation?
How would you rank the issues (from most to least important)?
What reasons can you give for your rankings?
How does the immediate problem or issue tie into larger social issues?
What conflicts in values or belief systems form part of the issue?

Come up with two questions that explore the issues you've identified in more depth.

Solutions and Their Consequences

What are the possible courses of action and solutions?
How would you rank them?
What are the advantages and disadvantages for each one?
Is your solution a short- or long-term solution?
What are the consequences of your solution for each of the stakeholders?

Come up with two questions that explore the consequences of your solutions.

2. Exploration Questions

What potential benefits would arise from breaching the dams?
What potential economic gains would result from breaching the dams?
What potential benefits would arise from retaining the dams?
What potential economic gains would result from retaining the dams?
What are some alternative solutions in the case besides the two choices? How feasible are these alternatives?
How should the government balance the environmental needs of the river and its wildlife, including the salmon, with the population demands on the river?
What role does climate change play in deciding a potential solution?

3. Interview Activities

For the "Interview Your Audience" and "Interview Your Stakeholder" prompts, see the Appendix. These two activities are designed to help you better understand the needs and goals of the case audience and stakeholders. This exercise of the imagination and of empathy will help you step into the shoes of the audience or stakeholder so that you can identify with them, which will in turn help you to choose what arguments to make in your paper.

Arguing the Case: Writing Assignments

Paper Assignment 1

Choose a stakeholder and write a research paper that argues their position on dam removal to the taskforce. Be sure it is clear in your introduction which stakeholder you have chosen. The purpose of your paper is to assist the task-force members in writing their recommendation to the government agencies in charge of the salmon restoration. The paper should include solutions to the various issues involved in restoring the salmon runs by either removing the dams or keeping them. As part of your decision-making progress, consider the following:

- Are your stakeholder's gains short term or long term?
- If they are short term, how quickly will these gains be realized?
- If they are long term, how long can the gains be expected to endure?

In order to support your argument, you will need to set it in the context of the wider issues involved in the case. This is the portion of the paper where you will need outside resources to provide you with evidence and other examples of similar cases.

You will need to consider the following stakeholders in your decision:

The conservation groups
The farmers
The Native American tribes
The power company
The ACOE

The audience is the federal judge, the other members of the taskforce, the government agencies in charge of the Endangered Species Act, and the communities that will be affected by the decision.

Alternative Assignments

1. Research successful dam removal and river restoration cases. Argue their relevance to the situation in this case.
2. Research the impact of dams, dam removal, or river restoration in your area.
3. Design an information campaign for the public schools on the impact of dams, both positive and negative. (This could be a service learning project.)

Reflecting on the Case: Looking Back

Reflection is an important part of the learning process. It gives you the chance to examine what you've learned, how you learned it, and how you can improve your learning strategies in the future. Here, you are being asked to reflect on what you have learned from doing this case study. Use the following questions to help you reflect on the case study process:

- What did you learn about the issues of the case?
- What did you learn about process of constructing an argument and counterarguments for an issue?

- What did you learn about doing research, both how and why it is important to argumentation?
- Now that you have done this case study, what approaches will you use for the next one? For instance, what will you do differently and what will you do the same?
- What did you like about doing the case study? What didn't you like about it?
- Do you have any other responses or reflections on the assignment?

APPENDIX

Common Assignments

The following assignments provided in this appendix can be used with all the cases:

- Writing Goals Checklist
- Interview Your Stakeholder
- Interview Your Audience
- Self-Assessment Paper Checklist

Writing Goals Checklist

Rhetorical Goals

1. Purpose
   The central goals for this task are __________________
   The purpose or goal that matters most to me is ____________
   To fulfill my purpose, I need to do _____________
2. Audience
   My audience(s) is/are __________________
   My audience will need to know ________________
   My audience already knows ___________________
   My audience cares about _____________________
3. My perspective as a writer is _________________
   I am writing from this perspective: ________________
   This perspective influences my writing because ____________________
   This perspective matters because ______________________

Practical Writing Goals

Due dates I need to be aware of: ___________________________
Overall steps to fulfill the requirements of the assignment: ____________

Research
I need to know more about ________________
Aspects of the case I will need to research: _________________

Drafting
I will generate ideas for this assignment in the following ways: _______
Some options for organizing my ideas and writing include ___________
I will need ____ drafts by _________________ (date).

Interview Your Stakeholder

This exercise is designed to give you more insight into your stakeholders and their perspective. Exploring the points of view of the different stakeholders will help you practice learning and writing from a point of view different than your own.

This assignment is not asking you to actually go out and interview someone; rather, it asks you to critically think about the stakeholders and what they need. In other words, it is designed to get you into the minds of relevant stakeholders. The more familiar you are with your stakeholders' needs and concerns, the better you will be able to present their point of view to your audience. Acknowledging the perspective of a specific stakeholder is also one way you can construct your ethos or authority.

For this exercise, use an assigned stakeholder or pick the stakeholder you wish to use in your paper. The steps are as follows:

1. Begin with brainstorming. Who is a stakeholder of interest for your paper? Who will be affected by this?
2. Write a brief biography for your stakeholder. Be creative. Consider things like your stakeholder's age, gender, professional training, occupation, and interests relevant to the case. Provide useful information rather than stereotypical and irrelevant details.
3. Answer the following questions about your stakeholder. Be as detailed as possible.
   - How will my stakeholder be affected by the issue/problem/solution?
   - What influence does my stakeholder have in the situation?
   - What emotional investment does my stakeholder have in the issue/problem/solution?
   - What motivates my stakeholder in this situation?
   - What does my stakeholder want?
   - What does my stakeholder value?
   - What is most important to my stakeholder?
   - What things might influences my stakeholder's opinions, actions, etc.?

- What are my stakeholder's expectations for a specific outcome?
- How will my stakeholder react to the problem/issue/solution?
- What actions can my stakeholder take in this situation to get their desired outcome?

4. Put it all together. Discuss how you will use the biography you wrote and the answers to the preceding questions to help you write your paper.

Interview Your Audience

This exercise is designed to help you understand your audience better. Use these tasks and questions to help you build a picture in your mind of the audience for your paper. Use them to build a picture of an imagined person, someone you can relate to. Step into their shoes in order to understand them better. As with the Interview Your Stakeholder exercise, this assignment is not asking you to go out and interview someone (unless your instructor indicates you should). Instead, it asks you to do critical thinking about who your audience is and what they need.

This exercise is designed to get you into the heads of your audience. The more familiar you are with your audience's needs, the better you will be able to get them to listen to your argument and persuade them to consider your point of view.

The steps are as follows:

1. Begin by brainstorming. Who is the audience for your paper? Usually there is more than one audience for any type of writing task. Check the assignment sheet to see who is listed as the audience for the current assignment. For this exercise, pick one.
2. Write a brief biography for your audience member. Be creative. Consider things like age, gender, professional training, occupation, and interests relevant to the case. Provide useful information rather than stereotypical and irrelevant details.
3. Keeping in mind who your audience is, answer the following questions. Be as detailed in your answers as you can.
   - What does my audience believe about the topic/issue?
   - What attitudes does my audience have about the topic/issue?
   - What does my audience value?
   - What is most important to my audience?
   - What does my audience need?
   - What does my audience want to achieve in this situation?
   - What does my audience already know/understand about the topic/problem/issue?
   - What do I want my audience to know/understand or do?
   - What aspects of the topic/issue will my audience likely not care about?

- What types of evidence would work best to convince my audience?
- What are the best ways for me to connect to my audience?

4. Put it all together. Discuss how you will use the biography you wrote and the answers to the preceding questions to help you write your paper.

Self-Assessment for Writing Assignments

This assignment and self-reflection are designed to help you improve your writing by becoming more aware of your prewriting process. Specifically, this form is designed to help you evaluate your own preparation for this paper and allow you to adjust your approach to writing papers in the future. Remember, it is designed to help you improve. Being brutally honest with yourself here is a useful and important part of self-examination.

Reflection

1. How much total time did you spend writing the paper? _____
2. What % of your time was spent on each of these activities:
    1. Finding sources ___
    2. Finding different types of sources ___
    3. Reading ___
    4. Reading and taking notes ___
    5. Looking up words ___
    6. Discussing ideas with others ___
    7. Re-reading ___
    8. Thinking ___
    9. Brainstorming or conceptualizing ___
    10. Coming up with reasons for my claims ___
    11. Developing an argument map ___
    12. Sharing ideas with others ___
    13. Preparing ___
    14. Researching ___
    15. Drafting ___
    16. Revising ___
    17. Editing ___

Comparison

1. How did you feel about the first draft of the paper:
   Good ___
   Needs a little work ___
   Needs a lots of work ___
   Rough ___

2. After you got feedback on the paper, did the feedback confirm your sense of the paper? ____ What surprised you? How can you anticipate this in the future?
3. What aspects of the paper (main ideas, organization, evidence, etc.) do/did you need to focus on in your revision?
4. How much did you change? What aspects of the writing process did you focus on?
5. Do you feel your revision was an improvement over your first draft?

Prewriting

How did you meet your rhetorical goals for purpose, audience, and writer identity?

How did you meet your practical writing goals?

In what ways can you improve on using rhetorical goals to order to make your writing better?

If you were assigned the audience/stakeholder interviews, how did they help your critical thinking process?

If you were assigned the audience/stakeholder interviews, describe the ways you were able to use your answers to the interview questions in drafting your paper (be detailed in your answer):

Thinking about the paper

As part of the paper draft

Coming up with reasons for arguments

Coming up with reasons for counterarguments

Other (please describe)

Adjustment

1. What aspects of the prewriting and writing process worked the best for you in writing this paper (preparation, research, reading, drafting, etc.)?
2. Which didn't work as well?
3. Name at least three things you will do differently in preparing to write the next paper. Be specific. Think about which aspects of the writing process you need to practice or concentrate more on.

INDEX

References to figures and tables are indicated by "f" and "t" following the page numbers.